MANAGING TO SURVIVE

Managerial practice in not-for-profit organisations

Alun C. Jackson and Frances Donovan

OPEN UNIVERSITY PRESS

Buckingham • Philadelphia

Open University Press
Celtic Court
22 Ballmoor
Buckingham
MK18 1XW

email: enquiries@openup.co.uk
world wide web: http://www.openup.co.uk

and
325 Chestnut Street
Philadelphia, PA19106, USA

First published 1999
First published in Australia by Allen & Unwin

A catalogue record of this book is available from the British Library

ISBN 0 335 20353 1 (pbk)

Library of Congress Cataloging-in-Publication Data applied for

Set in 10/11.5 pt Garamond by DOCUPRO, Sydney
Printed by South Wind Production(s) Pte Ltd, Singapore

Professor Alun C. Jackson, co-author with Frances Donovan of *Managing Human Service Organisations*, holds the Chair of Social Work at the University of Melbourne. Past academic experience includes appointments at Bristol Polytechnic (now University of the West of England) and Monash University. A former student of Frances Donovan at the University of Melbourne, he has emerged as a leading academic in the field of human service administration with particular expertise in program design and evaluation, and a commitment to practice research. In addition to his academic work, he has practised in the UK in local authority social work and in Australia in Aboriginal Affairs. His human service design and evaluation research and practice has involved close collaboration with policy makers, managers and front line workers in fields as diverse as AIDS prevention and treatment, child abuse and neglect, disability, Vietnam veterans and ethnic services. He has served as a Board member and Chair of a number of not-for-profit organisations in the UK and Australia. He is currently directing a large research and evaluation program on the social impacts of problem gambling, and is Director of Social Work Research at the Royal Children's Hospital.

Frances Donovan AM has been recognised for her services to social work education and social welfare administration by being awarded membership of the Order of Australia. She has also been recognised as a prominent and senior member of two professions through being made an Honorary Life Member of both the Australian Association of Social Workers and the Australian Human Resources Institute. She is currently a Senior Academic Associate of the School of Social Work at the University of Melbourne. Her previous academic appointments were at the University of Western Australia and the University of Melbourne and as Foundation Head of the School of Social Work at Phillip Institute of Technology (now part of RMIT University). Her wide experience covers training and practice in secondary school teaching and in personnel/human resource management in private industry in both Australia and the UK. Many years of practice have included management in small and large health and human service organisations, including a period as Director of the Social Work Service of the Victorian Branch of the Australian Red Cross Society. She currently works as a management consultant with her own agency and has worked in joint consultancies for some years with her co-author, Alun Jackson. She also brings to this book extensive experience as a trainer of volunteers, a service volunteer and as a member and Chair of the Boards of a variety of not-for-profit organisations.

CONTENTS

v

ACKNOWLEDGEMENTS

It is always difficult to identify all those who have contributed to the process of writing a book. So many of the positive influences are subtle and not so obvious, such as the encouragement and sharing of ideas that arise out of every day contacts. Working in the human services area, and in the not-for-profit field, means contact with a wide group of interesting, committed and often challenging people.

A special group of friends and colleagues provided stimulus and the benefit of their current and wide experience in the not-for-profit field that is the focus of our book. This group included Val Conboy, Ian Hardisty, Josie Prioletti and Melanie Sheldon all management practitioners or consultants working with not-for-profit agencies, and Jerome Winston of RMIT University and Bruce Lagay of Melbourne University, who were of assistance because of their special knowledge and interest in particular areas of our book. In acknowledging their contribution we need to stress that they of course cannot be held responsible for any faults in the final result.

Our thanks go to Allen & Unwin also for the encouragement we received from the outset, and for the assistance and expertise that helped us in the various hurdles to be overcome in the long process of writing a book. The indexer is often overlooked, but in a book aimed at practitioners the index plays a particularly important role and Elizabeth Wood Ellem was as usual very professional and co-operative.

Finally, each of the authors would like to acknowledge the contribution of their co-author. When two authors are working on a book together, not merely contributing separate chapters, a great deal of co-operation is necessary. The writing of this book, and the other publications that we have shared, has involved working together closely for many years. We have also shared a number of management consultancies and have found the collaborations stimulating and enjoyable and never marred by conflict. This may be due to the fact that both authors have a respect for the contribution of the other. Also, there are few differences of approach and no major differences in basic philosophies, although there are naturally some factors influenced by gender differences and the generation gap. All these influences have, we hope, contributed to the book.

vii

INTRODUCTION

Whether they are welfare, health or educational organisations, arts companies or sporting groups, not-for-profit organisations are facing unfamiliar challenges. The reasons are many and we mention a large number of them throughout this book. Whatever the causes, there is a great deal to be learned from the experiences of organisations that may appear to be different, but in fact have many similarities.

In many ways the stimulus to write this book arose out of our first book, *Managing Human Service Organisations*.[1] In completing that book there were so many areas that could be considered only briefly, such as the role of Boards and committees of management, and so many practice examples that we could not give. One reviewer recognised this and hoped that we would: 'soon write a follow-up'.[2] We have followed that advice, although it has not been as soon as we would have liked.

The title *Managing to Survive* can be interpreted in a number of ways.[3] We have been closely involved in practice with organisations that are struggling to survive. They are being faced, willingly or otherwise, with the need to come to terms with aspects of management that were not their concern in the past, and with financial constraints that are a recent development. The agencies that are our target are often small, under-resourced and under-skilled. Many are looking for help in this new and bewildering world of 'managerialism', 'economic rationalism' and 'privatisation', which are accompanied by accountability demands, allied to performance and outcome measurement.

We hope that this book will not only answer some of the survival questions but will also be relevant to attempts to improve practice and provide a better service. As will become evident, our basic position is that good management has a major contribution to make to the quality of an agency's practice, and that the quality of this management and practice must underpin any attempt at survival. As the title is rather general, we have found it necessary to add a subtitle 'Managerial practice in not-for-profit organisations' to clarify both our target audience and the main purpose behind our writing. Within the group identified as 'not-for-profit' we are giving particular attention to small agencies, with some emphasis on what could be called 'human services'. These categories are explained later in this Introduction. Much of the management literature assumes that organisations are relatively large and there is little recognition of some special issues related to 'smallness'. This is particularly important for the human services, as the majority of the agencies are not large. This is explored further in chapter 1.

In addition, our material could refer to small, devolved units of larger government agencies. The reasons for believing that our material is relevant to such devolved units are as follows.

• There is a trend towards devolving responsibility to local or regional levels which means that many staff have responsibilities for which they are ill-prepared, such as management of devolved service delivery, often involving the management of tendering processes, and other areas such as budgeting and planning.

• The devolved units of the larger government agencies interact with the small voluntary agency because both are often most active at the local level.

• There is a trend towards privatisation and contracting which has meant that government and non-government agencies interact to a greater extent than in the past. This interaction means that both types of organisation need to know more about how the other functions.

• There are similarities in the management processes that concern the two groups, that is, the devolved units of government agencies and the small local agency.

The question of who will read and benefit from a book is always of importance to authors no matter how much they enjoy the writing process itself. Within the types of organisations we have mentioned, we have in mind the following:

- members of Boards/management committees of not-for-profit organisations
- practitioners in the above organisations
- practitioners in devolved units of government organisations.

In addition, students in Human Services and related courses, such as Public Administration, are included in our target.

The level of students depends on the particular institution. Our prime target group is not necessarily those studying at managerial level. All students who are going to work in, or have contact with, not-for-profit agencies should understand the managerial processes involved. A brief comment about the educational consequences of the broadening of all students' understanding is made in the final chapter, Conclusion.

As well as the above specific groups we consider that all levels of government agencies, that is all levels of public administration, should be concerned with the management of not-for-profit agencies that receive government funds. This is due particularly to the recent trend towards the contracting out of services and to the funding of such agencies. The funding organisations need to know how the agencies to which they allot funds are spending that money and this involves a wide range of skills and the question of standards and monitoring.

Positive feedback from practitioners and students about our first book has encouraged our belief that the combination of theory and practice was what our readers wanted. In this book there has been some change, with more emphasis on practice, although elements of the combination do exist. We have also included endnotes on theoretical aspects which some readers may wish to pursue.

Our decisions about balance have involved questions concerning the type of service and, because of our particular experience, we have given more emphasis to those traditionally classified as 'human services', such as child care, disability, community health and residential services. In addition to these we have included a range of small not-for-profit agencies which provide services of many different kinds, for example, educational and leisure activities.

The focus will be on how organisations *manage* their activities rather than on the services themselves, but we believe there is a direct link between managerial effectiveness and service delivery. This is the crux of the book. We believe that the *quality of the management influences the quality of the service* given to the users of the service. Commitment and understanding are very important but they are not enough without the competencies related to the managerial aspects that we consider in this book.

This emphasis on management and the use of the word itself causes discomfort in some people, but it will become clear in the following chapters that our perception of 'management' should not be equated with 'managerialism'. We believe that there are processes that must take place whatever the terms used—administration or management, facilitation or leadership. For some agencies, even the word 'service' has negative connotations—an issue we consider in chapter 1.

Terms such as 'human services', 'service user/client/consumer', or 'administration/management' are used differently in different English-speaking countries. In the Australian, British and American literature most relevant to our book there are different uses of many basic terms. Our definitions of those terms are therefore listed below, along with the term we have chosen to use where a choice of terms exists.

Client/consumer/recipient/service user
Recent usage replaces 'client' with 'consumer' but even the latter term now has its critics.[4] Some practitioners and writers have tended to use 'recipient', that is, the person who is receiving the particular service. We prefer the term 'service user' as the one being most descriptive of the nature of the relationship of the person to the organisation.

Service provider/service deliverer
The more favoured term is 'service provider', although the actual product is usually referred to as 'service delivery'. There is some resistance to the word 'service' itself, particularly in some self-help or advocacy groups, because they see it as allied to the 'bureaucracy'. There is also the criticism that the word is dehumanising, or implies dependency on the part of the service user. While recognising these criticisms, we have decided to use the generally accepted term.

Human services
This is a particularly difficult area to clarify although there is a generally accepted understanding about the application of the category. We define a human service organisation as one in which 'the prime product is a service that is designed to optimise the welfare of the client'. This leaves open the question of 'welfare',

which may be defined with various degrees of specificity or broadness.[5]

Organisation/agency/association

An 'organisation' is often a generic term for a group of people who come together in order to achieve certain goals and objectives. Agencies may be seen as a particular type of organisation, or the words may be used interchangeably. We tend to use 'organisation' as a generic term as well as using it as a more specific term for larger bureaucratic or governmental organisations. 'Agency' is generally used for the smaller body. Associations are seen as less formal types of organisations.

Voluntary/non-governmental

Agencies can be difficult to classify and the terms 'voluntary' and 'non-governmental' are usually interchangeable. It means that they are organisations that do not have any formal organisational link with the government and are governed by a Board that is independent of the government and consists of volunteers. The agency does not necessarily consist entirely or even predominantly of volunteers in delivering a service. The voluntarism of some agencies has become blurred, with government nominees on their Boards and high levels of government funding.

Volunteering/volunteers

There are many simple uses of the word volunteer, but when it is applied to people working in not-for-profit organisations or projects it usually refers to those who participate in the volunteering process 'for no financial payment, and of their own free will'. Modifications and additions to this definition are discussed further in chapter 1.

Governmental/statutory

These words are sometimes used interchangeably but this is confusing as 'statutory' is also interpreted as meaning 'by statute'. Government departments may be classified as those that have a formal accountability to the government, usually through a minister. To confuse the issue, some government organisations or semi-government agencies have Boards with varying degrees of responsibility or accountability. Because of this ambiguity we do not use the word 'statutory' as an organisational classification.

Not-for-profit/non-profit organisations

These have sometimes been equated, in the human services area, with 'voluntary' or non-government. However, as some non-government human service agencies do operate to make a profit, such as private hospitals or residential accommodation for the elderly, we are using the term 'not-for-profit'. We include those organisations that are classified as 'not-for-profit' in the sense that there are no shareholders but they are still expected to 'make a profit' in the sense of an operational surplus, at least in some sections of their operations.

Ex officio
This phrase means 'by virtue of an official position'. It is used, for example, for those members of Boards who are there because of their particular position, such as the chief executive.

Accountability/responsibility
These words are also often used interchangeably but there is an advantage in distinguishing between them. Accountability can be seen as a direct relationship (sometimes financial) to another group, organisation or person. The two parties accept the degree of accountability and the processes that go along with it. Responsibility is a general relationship to a more vague constituency, sometimes, for example, to such concepts as 'the community', with no recognisable reporting or accountability procedures.

Board/committee of management/council
The UK literature tends to use 'management committee' for voluntary agencies while in the US the preferred term is 'Boards'. We will use the latter as this is becoming more common in Australia. 'Council' is used for some organisations, usually those that are a federation or association of smaller units, although there are also historic reasons for its use by particular organisations, for example, municipal councils.

Management/administration
These are sometimes differentiated and there are differences primarily in the American and British literature on human service management. We use them interchangeably. In general terms they refer to the process involved in enabling the organisation to achieve its goals as efficiently and effectively as possible. The process is discussed throughout this book.

Governance
This is contrasted with 'management' and refers to the core functions of Boards, namely policy making and monitoring, establishing the organisation's goals and strategic direction, ensuring

xiii

organisational survival and ensuring that organisational values are reflected in policy and practice.[6]

Manager

In simple terms managers may be defined as 'persons whose major role is to carry out a management task involving other people for whose work they are responsible'. There are complications in this definition as the word 'manager' has been extended in practice. It is often used so broadly that practically everyone is a manager. For example, people working alone but 'managing' technology may use the term. For the purposes of this book we prefer to keep to a more restricted interpretation. Terms such as 'leader' and 'facilitator' describe particular ways of carrying out the management task.

Monitoring/evaluation

Monitoring generally refers to a process where specified aspects of practice, either administrative practice or client-centred practice, are routinely recorded and analysed using a range of methods to identify, for example, trends in program operation. Evaluation refers to a process in which effectiveness, including cost effectiveness, is measured against some standard, where the standards may differ for different stakeholders/interest groups, and where such standards may be determined as part of the evaluation process.

Effectiveness/efficiency

Effectiveness has two aspects. It involves meeting the purpose of a program or service and meeting the needs of the service user. Hopefully they will be the same. Efficiency is the relationship, often expressed as an actual or implied ratio, between the effectiveness and the degree of effort (in the broadest sense) utilised to achieve the level of effectiveness.

A final issue that we need to address is the importance of confidentiality in the use of practice examples. When it is management that is being considered, rather than the process of working with service users, extra difficulties are encountered. It is frequently possible to disguise service users' situations with a name change but details of organisations are less easily disguised. As a consequence we have not used case studies but have illustrated our points with smaller vignettes. We have often changed details and only identified an agency or organisation where the material is already public. Readers sometimes say 'I didn't know you had had contact with our agency' when in fact we had not. We regard this as a compliment as it shows how the situations we describe are common and relevant to many organisations.

The first chapter covers general managerial issues and clarifies our approach. The following chapters cover major areas of practice, starting with the early processes of recruitment and selection, induction and orientation, training and development, and leading to ways of maximising the effectiveness of the service. The later chapters are slightly more technical in that we cover financial management, office management and, finally, management information and program effectiveness.

The details of service delivery cannot be covered in the space we have available. The challenge to the reader is to apply general managerial principles to their particular service. We are continually surprised at how much managerial knowledge can be transferred and it is because of our faith in this process of transference that we have written this book.

NOTES

1. Donovan, F. and Jackson, A.C. (1991) *Managing Human Service Organisations*, Prentice Hall, Sydney.
2. Anonymous review in *Management Review*, October, 1991, p. 20.
3. 'Managing to Survive' was used as the title of the AASW State Conference in Perth, Western Australia, in 1991 at which one of the authors, Frances Donovan, gave the keynote address, 'Managing to Do the Job Better'. The title is used with the permission of the conference organisers.
4. See, for example, the discussion in de Carvalho, D. (1996) *Competitive Care: Understanding the Implications of National Competition Policy and the COAG Agenda for the Community Services Sector,* Discussion Paper No. 11, Australian Social Welfare Commission, Canberra, relating to the concept of citizenship as a better conceptualisation of the service user.
5. See also chapter 1, 'Introduction to human service management' in Donovan, F. and Jackson, A.C. *Managing Human Service Organisations* (1991) for a discussion of the complexities of definition of some of these terms.
6. For a very detailed discussion of the concept of governance see Kilmister, T. (1993) *Boards at Work: a New Perspective on Not-For-Profit Boards,* NFP Press, Wellington.

1

GENERAL MANAGEMENT ISSUES

• General political and economic environment • Management and leadership • Organisational and community relationships • Inter-relationship of Board and staff roles • Volunteers/volunteering • Impact of smallness on management practice • What can be done?
• Conclusion

A local newspaper reported on a situation concerning pre-school centres under the headline: 'Pre-schools lash out over unfair checklist'. The article described the events and included discussions with some staff and committee members.

It was reported that the department providing funds for the centres had sent out a checklist to be completed, which dealt with the agencies' performance. This Pre-school Quality Assessment Checklist required the formation of a sub-committee of the pre-school's committee, which would use the checklist to report on 'the pre-school program and environment, interaction between teachers, children and parents, health and safety, administration and responsibilities and training'. A number of centres were objecting on the grounds that it was 'an insult to teachers' and that 'parents lacked the knowledge of pre-school teaching as a profession which was necessary to complete the list'. It was also said that 'parents on committees of management were volunteers who were already struggling to handle the increased duties since the State Government made cuts'. One president commented that they were 'now responsible for administering the payroll, tax, WorkCover, superannuation for pre-school staff, formulating and implementing policy, setting fees and fundraising'.

One of the people interviewed stated that the relevant department used to employ children's services officers who 'did the kind of evaluation set out in the list . . . they are asking us to do a job that they should be doing and have done in the past themselves'. The department's reply was interesting. The minister said that completion of the checklist was not compulsory but that 'pre-schools were required to undertake some kind of service evaluation as a prerequisite for funding'. The letter included the comment that 'a quality improvement process should be viewed as part of pre-school planning and evaluation rather than an additional task'.[1]

The above situation illustrates many of the issues that we will be discussing in this book, for example:

- the changing role of committees of management
- the link being made between funding and accountability
- the significance of evaluation and program planning
- the roles of staff and the committee/Board
- the devolution of many formerly government roles onto the non-government sector.

In this chapter we present a number of general factors affecting the way small human service/not-for-profit organisations need to be managed to ensure their survival. These factors include a range of both external and organisationally based influences that have significant effects on the way the organisations operate. It is important to consider these important aspects briefly in the first chapter as they provide an overview of the issues and the questions that arise throughout the book. Later chapters will provide more detailed discussions of specific topics and some of the day-to-day management practices.

We have identified six major factors for general discussion in this chapter:

- the general political and economic environment, including attitudes towards management
- relationship between management and leadership
- organisational and community relationships
- interrelationship of Board and staff roles
- volunteers/volunteering
- impact of 'smallness' on management practice.

2

GENERAL POLITICAL AND ECONOMIC ENVIRONMENT

Since the development of the welfare state the acceleration of change has reached a pace that has caused bewilderment and, in some cases, a degree of panic. This has had major organisational consequences.[2]

Change and its consequences

Three phases of welfare organisation can be identified. There are differences between countries but in general terms these can be applied to Australia and the United Kingdom:

1. the traditional welfare state
2. the 'two worlds' of welfare
3. the 'mixed' organisation of welfare, or the growth of welfare by contract.[3]

The traditional welfare state phase resulted in the expectation that most welfare services were to be provided by the state and such voluntary 'agencies' that existed were small, personal, not funded by the state and rarely used paid or professional staff.

The 'two worlds' phase was characterised by the growth in number and size of voluntary agencies and their assumption of some characteristics of government bureaucracies. The consequences included the following.

- The non-government agencies began to develop some of the management hierarchies and accountabilities that were a feature of the government bureaucracies.
- The large non-government agencies usually retained committees, voting and elections, and the community participation patterns created some confusion around issues such as organisational governance.
- These expanding agencies became increasingly dependent on the financial assistance of governments.

The 'mixed organisation' of welfare/human services phase has resulted in a number of features, as follows.

- Increased funding of voluntary agencies has generated a parallel development of what is now often called the 'contract culture', with governments contracting out services to voluntary agencies. This contracting has seen the encouragement of

3

markets or quasi-markets with the attempt to introduce a plurality of providers.

- A further blurring has occurred of the distinction between the 'two worlds', with governments seeing themselves more and more as 'enablers' and purchasers of services rather than service providers and with many of the traditional government services being at least partially 'privatised'.
- Problems have arisen in deciding 'who monitors whom'. In the case of the bureaucracy the responsibility for monitoring lay with the organisation itself. Later, professionals and their official bodies took over much of the responsibility for standards. The dilemma now facing the agencies and the government is who monitors standards and how can it be done. (This issue is considered further in chapter 5.)

One feature that has been constant is the lack of planning and, in many cases, the lack of awareness of the significance of the changes or what Billis (1993) has called 'the slide into unplanned change'. When the context and the changes that are taking place are better understood it is possible in practice to adjust to them and sometimes to modify them.

So far we have mentioned changes that have taken place in the welfare or human service area. We turn now to some of the changes in the broader environment that are also significant. One of these major changes is the increasing influence of politics and economics and the influence of 'economic rationalism'.

Economic rationalism

The meaning of this term is being hotly debated at the present time. The main criticism from those who believe it has had a negative effect is that it gives absolute priority to the economic aspects and takes little or no account of the possible negative social effects of any particular action. The economic argument is that ultimately the benefit will overcome the negative effects, after a period of time and by what has been called a 'trickle down' process.[4] 'If you only wait long enough it will work out' seems to be the philosophy, with the assumption that the advantages are 'worth' the current pain to some groups and that there is no demonstrably effective alternative.

The problem of the emphasis on economic factors is that a fundamental mind set influences all decisions. When it is difficult to find a concrete way of proving the benefits or otherwise of any particular action, agencies find themselves trying to identify an 'economic' argument for their activities.

> Members of one agency were told by senior staff and the Board to find 'economic' arguments for every expenditure, even though they did not have the concrete evidence to back up their claims and they knew of no way that the assumptions could be proved. One argument was that their counselling and financial assistance program would keep children from being taken into care. They were told by management that value-based justifications for a service must never be expressed, because values were subjective and not acceptable. It must never be said that it ought to be part of the service because it was part of a planned social policy or because there was a community obligation to care in a particular way for a special group. These were regarded as 'soft' reasons and therefore suspect. This strategy appeared to work in the short term until the agency was asked to 'prove' that its statements and claims were correct.

The irony is that the 'proof' of the economic assumptions is often equally doubtful, although the economic rationalist approach to services tends to focus on simple relationships that appear easier to 'prove'. Economic rationalists may say that they are concerned with quality but in practice the complexities of quality are often ignored. An example is the simple counting of service users rather than measuring the quality of the service. The amount of income received by the agency is related to the number of clients seen rather than to the complexities of the relationships and the outcome of the service. 'We are helping x numbers' is the claim, with no real indication of what 'helping' means, whether it is successful and what 'success' means. One of the consequences of this oversimplification is that the search for the causes of problems and the most appropriate ways of intervening are given scant attention by service funders. Agencies can be trapped into this way of thinking as well, and can distort their practices to fit the expectations of the funding body.

The emphasis on economic rationalism described above generates an oversimplification that causes distortion throughout many aspects of practice in the human services area, not only in service delivery.

The members of a group of small agencies, funded by government to provide specialised counselling services in urban and rural localities, adopted very different practices in recording client attendances. Some of the agencies gave their service users a new identification number each time the person reappeared at the agency rather than allocating one unique identifier to each service user. Other agencies only recorded each 'case' once, no matter how often they appeared. One of the consequences was that, when attempts were made to aggregate information about the service users of the agencies, the information was unreliable as a source of planning. It was only when the funding body wanted the information to see if the services were located in appropriate places according to demand that they discovered the discrepancies in recording procedures. Their earlier acceptance of the poor management practices was based on their over-reliance on 'hard data' and oversimplified recording.

Privatisation and competitive tendering

Privatisation, while not unknown in the past as part of a mixed economy of welfare, is currently proceeding at a pace that will be unfamiliar and uncomfortable to many people in the community services. The extent of privatisation and its corollaries, such as competitive tendering, is having a major effect on the way in which not-for-profit agencies function. These effects are mentioned throughout this book, one noticeable example being the friction and conflict that has increased in inter-agency relationships.

Privatisation raises the general issue of the transfer of public services, that is, what people believe should be provided by government and what may be provided by the private sector. The problem with privatisation, for many people, is that it is seen to do away with notions of citizen rights by placing services into the marketplace to be purchased, with all the inequities that differing abilities to pay bring.

An additional issue is that there may be little agreement on what services are appropriate to be privatised. There are those who object, for example, to prisons or child protection services being privatised but have no objections to aged care nursing homes or some health services being privately run. For others, their objection to privatisation hinges on the fear that quality of service will suffer at the expense of making a profit, and they do not believe that the corporate or business sector is necessarily more effective or efficient than the public sector.[5]

Competitive tendering is in some senses a 'logical' outgrowth of privatisation, with governments wishing to test publicly funded services by making them compete in an open market. The test is whether they can deliver their services for a 'competitive' price. An obvious objection to this process is that, if judgements about awarding government contracts are made primarily on the grounds of cost containment, then service quality may suffer. In addition to these concerns about the distorting of quality, many people in the community services object to the tendering process itself. (Practical questions and processes related to tendering are discussed further in chapter 6 on financial management.)

The privatisation trend is particularly significant as it is a major philosophical change. It has special significance in those countries where government responsibility for community services has been a long tradition.[6] The changes are too recent for a final analysis but they are especially important in the delivery of local human services.

Managerialism

It is with some trepidation that we have used the word 'manage' in our title, even though it has a double meaning in that title. The trends mentioned earlier have brought about an approach which is viewed negatively by many in the non-government sector and which is classified negatively as 'managerialism'. One writer, Charles Handy, has said that he would not use the word 'management' and describes the negatives of the 'managerial' approach and its language:

> The implicit model of the organisation is an engineering one . . . The organisation can be 'designed'. People are 'human resources'. There are 'plans' and 'control systems', 'outputs' and 'inputs'.[7]

We use some of the 'managerial' language for convenience but this does not mean that we approve of the values underpinning many of the 'managerial' developments. We obviously accept that organisations exist and that they need to be made to work, or 'managed'. Our areas of concern are how this is done, according to what principles and how it can be done as effectively as possible.

The influence of 'business' and the concept that management is a generic quality, no matter what is 'managed', is another aspect of 'managerialism' which has caused concern to the non-government sector. In practice this has meant that management positions may be held by people who have no experience of the particular service, or even of the sector as a whole. One commentator on this, an accountant, recognised the problem of different values and stated that 'voluntary organisations have different control problems in that they are antithetical to the management control strategies commonly used in business organisations'.[8] The issue is whether one believes that voluntary organisations should learn to be more like 'businesses' or whether business can learn from voluntary organisations.

Values

There are many values inherent in the human service area that are significant in their influence on what is perceived to be good management. Values that influence the management role include individualisation, self-determination and confidentiality. To many practitioners there appears to be an inherent conflict between management and service delivery, because they are seen to be based on different sets of values.

Funding bodies traditionally have not been so concerned with philosophies or values but there have been indications that some government departments have had certain expectations, even where they are not spelled out. One example of differences in emphasis is the importance of generalisation in management on the one hand and individualisation in service delivery on the other. How these two emphases can be balanced and accommodated is a constant theme in this book. It is necessary to distinguish whether the difficulty of reconciling this potential conflict is due to 'managerialism' or to poor management. One attempt to specify a number of value stances which should inform human service management suggests the following:

- full acceptance of accountability
- participatory approach to management
- concern to get things done, not just to formulate policies
- concern to achieve good internal and external communications
- commitment to organisational effectiveness
- personal code of conduct for managers based on integrity and rigorous intellectual standards
- acceptance of personal responsibility.[9]

We would suggest that a manager who is committed to effective

8

human service practice could be expected to possess these particular values.

Negative attitudes to management

Partly because of the influence of values, but also because of the long history of rejection of managerial requirements in the human services, a number of negative attitudes have developed. These include:

- criticism of management of a particular type, that is, hierarchical, non-consultative or non-human relations oriented
- the view that management of services may be motivated by a commitment to 'technology' and organisation rather than to the service user
- tension in organisations, such as self-help groups, between the values and practices of service users who are members of Boards/committees and 'professionals' who are employees.

In small organisations there is often a feeling that management is what happens in larger organisations. Smaller organisations are seen more as 'family', where formal rules are not needed, and there can be resistance to any 'organisational' identity. This may result in the use of language that avoids such words as 'agency', 'program', 'client', or 'service delivery' and never uses 'managing' to describe organisational processes.

MANAGEMENT AND LEADERSHIP

Relationship between management and leadership

The relationship between leadership and management is a complex one and has generated a wealth of different writings and disagreements, often quite heated. A hierarchy exists for some people, with leadership being on a much higher plane than management, instead of both roles having importance.

- For some, management and leadership are quite distinct—leadership is about goal setting, values and the 'big picture', while management is about implementing.
- For others the terms are interchangeable or closely interrelated. Leadership has been identified as forming a set of qualities that are an integral part of being a 'good' manager.

In our view, the most useful way to think of management and leadership is that they are distinct from each other only at their extreme ends. In other words, a small number of activities may be 'purely' leadership or 'purely' management but most activities are both. Increasingly, notions of leadership have moved away from images of inspiring or charismatic individuals with certain personal qualities towards a general acceptance that leadership can be learned.

In small organisations, it is clear that anyone designated a 'manager' must have some leadership qualities and anyone designated a 'leader' must have some managerial qualities, as in many cases the 'manager' and the 'leader' will be the same person. This is one of the special problems of the small organisation, as finding the one person with a balance of the required qualities is not easy. The result is that organisations will often concentrate on finding someone with personal, vaguely defined 'leadership' qualities and ignore the importance of managerial competence to at least a basic level.

Distinctions become even more complex when the role of the manager, for example, the chief executive, is considered in conjunction with the chairperson of the Board. There may be oversimplified views as to their respective roles. The latter may be seen as a 'leader' in the sense of policy making and the chief executive may be seen as merely an implementor.

The definitions in the Introduction included the term 'governance' as it is particularly relevant to any discussion of management and leadership. It has special significance in its application to the Boards of not-for-profit organisations. The Board's role is not to manage but to lead through governance. This is often difficult, and the use of the term 'committee of management' causes confusion unless there is a clear explanation of the interpretation of 'management'. For this reason we have used the term 'Board' throughout, although some small and more informal agencies may think that it is too grandiose.

Different patterns and styles of leadership and management will also be influenced by the history and circumstances of the organisation. These influences include:

- whether the organisation is in a developmental, maintenance or declining phase
- the significance of a crisis situation
- the extent of change, its rapidity and intensity

- the extent to which the leader is seen to be in place for a short or long term.

Gender issues in management and leadership

The importance of gender aspects will be evident in many of the general issues in this book and in many of the practical details. We consider that there is a management style that is generally accepted as being a female style, although there are varied views about why and by how much it is different. Differences are often expressed in practical ways, for example, in speaking of a more 'caring' female approach. Sometimes the male approach is said to be 'instrumental' and the female 'expressive', or the male is described as being 'outcome oriented' and the female 'process oriented'.

A number of general issues need to be mentioned if it is accepted that there are different management styles.

- Are these differences an advantage or disadvantage both for the organisation and the managers themselves?[10]
- What are the particular circumstances that illustrate the differences?

These questions are of special importance in this book because we are paying close attention to smallness. The growing numbers of females who prefer to work in small business is evidence of some compatibility between the small organisation and female roles. The fact that there are more females in the practice level of not-for-profit organisations and fewer in the managerial level warrants some closer study. There are in practice a number of areas where gender is significant and these will be discussed later.

Planning

Planning is generally recognised as one of the core management functions. It is suggested that wherever management practice occurs, in whatever organisation, there is a tendency for the same sorts of functions to be performed. These functions are usually described as planning, organising, staffing, leading and control-ling.[11] Planning, in particular, involves a number of processes:

- establishing policy, goals and standards—in small human ser-vice organisations, in particular, managers will work with the Board to develop these
- developing rules and procedures, that is, a framework for implementing the policies and goals

- developing plans, particularly plans relating to the design and operation of programs which are ways of achieving the organisation's goals
- forecasting new developments and directions for the organisation by closely monitoring developments outside the organisation that may affect the organisation, such as changes in legislation, changes in funding arrangements, moves by funding bodies or larger human service organisations to contract out, and devolution.
- evaluating the effectiveness of the planning process.

Another way of looking at some of the core requirements of a manager is through identifying those activities that a manager carries out competently. A useful definition of competency, which allows us to begin this task, is 'the ability to perform effectively in a given context, the capacity to transfer knowledge and skills to new tasks and situations, and the inclination or motivation to energise these abilities and capacities'.[12]

Interestingly, a competency-based approach to management and leadership tends not to treat planning as a separate function, seeing it instead as part of a cluster of activities around problem solving and decision making. In addition, it is a very important element of strategic and change management.

In various sections of this book, planning will be seen to be involved in program development, appropriate staffing, financial issues and, most importantly, in dealing with change.

Managing change

We are all familiar with the expression, 'the only constant is change'. This is a truism when applied to many organisations today. We have already noted that a feature of human service management practice is the need to deal with the rapidity of change. It is also obvious that, generally, the less effectively people deal with change, the less control they have over the process. The social and community services sector is replete with examples of how practice becomes distorted and less controllable through:

- changes having to be made with not enough information about either their purpose or content or about how to implement them
- changes having to be made too quickly
- too many changes having to be made to the core operations of the organisation

- change being seen as something that is imposed on the organisation from outside, thereby heightening resistance.

Numerous examples could be given of the consequences when such negative change processes take place. Sometimes unexpected changes are forced on an organisation and there is no way that the agency could have been prepared. However, there are many occasions when the signs have been ignored (as in the vignette at the beginning of chapter 6). Boards and management sometimes make the situation worse by overhasty reactions, panicking and forcing change too quickly.

All managers, but particularly human service managers, have to be competent in managing change. More than this, there is a requirement that they be able to anticipate, to be proactive rather than reactive in bringing about change. The word 'proactive' has become popular and it is sometimes used to distinguish between 'managers' and 'leaders' with leaders seen to be proactive. In many ways it is how managers handle change that will determine the survival or otherwise of their organisation.

Part of competence in change management is the ability to recognise that some changes are beneficial, some are less obviously so, and some are inappropriate for a variety of reasons. A threat to the range of programs that an organisation offers may not necessarily be bad in the long term if it helps the organisation to focus and do more of what it does best. Similarly, expansion is not always a good thing, if it takes the organisation into peripheral areas that stretch its capacity to cope and dilute its core business.

There are different views about the justification for drastic and rapid change as opposed to incremental change. It is recognised that rapid change brings more discomfort and, often, severe distress, but this is justified in terms of long-term goals. The argument is that the only way to alter entrenched attitudes and behaviour is to eliminate rather than modify them. New patterns can then be substituted. In the human services field this approach is often regarded as not only undesirable but also unethical. It is considered to be inconsistent with human services values. Managers wishing to bring about rapid change have to decide where they stand in relation to change strategies in general and rapid change in particular.

Increasingly, attention is being given to such aspects of change management as how 'transitions' are handled. This view suggests that we need to focus not so much on the content of the change as on the types of adjustments that people need to make in order to cope with the transition. Much of what might seem to be resistance to change is actually more to do with the difficulties that people are having in making the transitional adjustments and identifying with the changes. To work with change effectively, managers need a wide range of people management skills, recognising that it is not only organisations that change but also the people in them.

ORGANISATIONAL AND COMMUNITY RELATIONSHIPS

The complexity of interorganisational relationships often surprises new members of a small agency. They see what appears to be a simple service to help the particular group that is their target. The agency is small and therefore they think it is uncomplicated by any 'bureaucratic' aspects. The reality is that the agency is part of a network of services and there is inevitable interaction with other members of that network. Some of the interactions are cooperative but, unfortunately, some are competitive and conflictive. There is also interaction with the funding body or bodies. Some of these issues and their practical consequences are discussed further in later chapters.

One of the points which will crop up continually in this book is the importance of knowing what one is doing (analysis) and, after that analytic process, thinking as clearly as possible about what has to be done (planning). It is suggested that there should be a regular process of interorganisational analysis. Most agencies keep some records of their contact with other agencies and scattered throughout the filing systems there is valuable information about interrelationships with other agencies. Unfortunately staff and Board members also keep a great deal in their heads, and new members must find out, in a haphazard way, the information that would help them in their interaction with the rest of the network. How often one hears, 'If only I'd known, I would have done this/not done that'.

Development of organisational agency maps

Generally, maps are ways of graphically illustrating and describing the agency's place in the service network and aspects of its operation. Intra- and interorganisational maps can be similar in style with variations in content. The historical developments outlined earlier mean that the boundaries are blurred and intra- and interorganisational factors are intertwined.

The content of a planning or organisational map could include the following (particular types of maps are examined in more detail later, for example, communication charts in chapter 5):

* the organisations and community groups with which the particular agency relates
* the nature of this interaction, such as whether it is positive or negative, with conflict indicated (confidentiality issues relating to storage of information will need to be considered here)
* the organisational level where interaction with the different organisations occurs, significant gatekeepers and indications of whether the levels themselves are relevant and appropriate
* funding patterns and levels.

The style of 'maps' may vary from narrative descriptions through to charts, spreadsheets and graphs. The form or style of representation obviously should match the purpose for which the map is being prepared. Complex information can be presented in diagrammatic form, for example, with arrows representing flows of service users, the thickness of the lines representing strength of relationships, and unbroken lines or dotted lines used to represent permanent or transitory strategic relationships. A further development that assists in planning could be to use the maps to represent:

* the official situation (manifest)
* reality as seen by the planners (extant)
* perception of reality as seen by various groups (assumed)
* the goal or future expectations (requisite).

Use of the interorganisational agency map

There are many ways in which the agency map(s) can be used and it is important that they are dynamic and easily updated. There are many practical advantages in the process of preparing the maps, including the following:

* The formation of the maps is a collaborative effort and the process itself helps increase awareness. It is preferable to commence with a practical and relatively simple exercise, such as communication mapping, and then add fuller, more complex maps as required.

- Using the mapping process allows different groups to interrelate in a way that increases mutual understanding, and different perceptions can be revealed that were not previously suspected. The realisation of such differences can bring about noticeable improvements in relationships: 'I had no idea that they thought this way'.
- Structural anomalies are often revealed. In one analysis it became evident that *senior* staff of the small voluntary agency were interacting with *junior* members of a large bureaucracy, that is, with persons who had little decision-making authority. This created frustration and breakdowns in communication.
- Analysis can reveal similarities and differences in service delivery that are hidden within the overall target group. As an example, two agencies dealing officially with homelessness were in fact very different because one dealt predominantly with elderly people and the other mainly with youth.
- Other more subtle differences can be revealed, such as differences in philosophies and ideologies. This becomes most significant in emotive areas, such as child protection or adoption.

Interorganisational maps can show a wide variety of relationships with various sections of the community. One particular group, which is often not sufficiently identified, is the 'constituency' of some of the Board members.

Constituencies and networks

A constituency can be defined as a group to which the organisation or individual believes it is accountable. It is importanat that the relationship be clarified. For example, is it a general responsibility or are there laid down patterns of accountability? Though the word usually refers to outside groups, there may be a situation where a Board member has an inside constituency, for example, as a staff representative or delegate whose constituency is the staff group. The word 'stakeholders' is sometimes used for members of the constituency, but it is a broader term that refers to those who have an interest or 'stake' in the organisation without there necessarily being any formal or informal accountability. The use of the word stakeholders is sometimes extended further to refer to any group or person who may be affected by the organisation.
Self-help and advocacy organisations must be clear when defining their constituency and working out how that account-

ability can be monitored. Such groups sometimes say that their responsibility is to 'the community' or to a particular 'community' group. This responsibility may be only vaguely defined, with questionable boundaries, and there is a danger that the organisation ends up being accountable to no-one. In such a situation, certain personalities or powerful interests may take over the organisation. There is also the risk that lack of clarity about responsibility will lead to warring factions. Both outcomes can seriously disrupt the provision of services. This is particularly noticeable in organisations where the service delivery is characterised by strong emotional involvement, such as those agencies involving children.

The concept of networking has for many years been of particular importance in not-for-profit organisations. A network could include funding sources, service providers and service users. One consequence of the changed political climate and the increase in tendering (discussed in chapter 6) has often been the weakening of the supportive networks that were previously of such value. Competition has often replaced cooperation. In addition, networking can suffer because of the increased volume of work being undertaken in agencies. The emphasis is on delivering services and not necessarily building the interorganisational infrastructure which agencies would like to have for optimum functioning.

Public relations and public image

Management of the public image of the organisation is one aspect of interorganisational relations that may be particularly foreign to some human service managers. Public image affects the way that the organisation is viewed by its constituents and by members of the organisation's network. There are a number of aspects of the public image of an organisation for which managers are responsible. In addition to the more direct methods of promotional material, such as brochures, pamphlets and newsletters, there are less obvious aspects that are important in influencing an agency's image. These include the need for monitoring the way that staff relate to service users. The direct practice worker plays an extremely important role in interpreting and conveying agency policy and practice to actual and potential service users. To do this effectively, workers need to believe in the product or service that they are delivering, or they may discourage people from using the service. Similarly, reception staff convey a strong message to service users, as does the condition of the physical surroundings where people receive the service.

The quality of the relationships that the organisation has with others in its service network will depend on the degree to which it is able to satisfy other organisations' expectations about what it can deliver. If the agency finds itself repeatedly performing short of expectations, then the manager will need to determine if this is a fault with the expectations of others or of the agency itself. Other organisations may simply be mistaken or working from outdated information, or the agency may actually be failing to perform, including failing to inform others of changes.

Managers have a major responsibility, shared with the Board, for contributing to the overall identity of their organisation. The identity of the agency is made up of a number of factors such as:

- the target group or service user
- people in the organisation
- constitution
- goals
- service given
- philosophy, or ethos, as distinct from the service or function
- name
- buildings or physical setting
- history of the organisation.

The public image is a product of the mix of these factors, as they are seen by the community.

INTERRELATIONSHIP OF BOARD AND STAFF ROLES

In addition to questions involving the outside community, there are a number of internal aspects that are of general significance. One of the most important is the interrelationship of Board and staff members and roles are a major factor in that interrelationship.

Importance of role clarity

Clarification of the roles of the Board and the staff requires constant attention, particularly as the emphasis on 'teamwork' in small organisations sometimes leads to confusion and diffusion of roles. When problems arise from lack of clarity of the various roles, often the more superficial problems are tackled and the basic role issues are not addressed.[13]

Implementation problems in carrying out roles

Some of the more significant problems arising from a failure to clarify roles are outlined below. The first three items refer to clarification of the roles of the Board and staff. The final item relates to the Board alone.

Board involvement in day-to-day functions

Board involvement in day-to-day functions is probably one of the most common dysfunctions and one that not only causes severe friction but can be extremely time-consuming, thus creating inefficiencies in the delivery of services. Some examples occur when Board members:

- take part in decisions about individual situations rather than restricting themselves to their role of policy formation and generalised decision making
- see themselves in a hierarchical role that they believe allows them to advise or control individual staff, rather than doing this through appropriate channels. This includes the situation where a Board member does not observe the usual reporting arrangements and demands extra information from individual staff. This can be experienced by that staff member as undue pressure and can interfere with planning and priorities.
- state a preference for a particular person when services are being allocated. It is often difficult for Board members to explain to service users, or people outside the agency, that such individual action is inappropriate unless the request for special preference raises general questions of policy that need to be addressed.

Under-utilisation of Board expertise

Under-utilisation of Board members, which is often allied to the lack of time that Board members are willing or able to give, can have negative results. Sometimes Board members are appointed for their technical competence and 'free advice', but it is not realised that such people may want to restrict their contribution to matters that relate only to their particular area of expertise.

Such a member may be of more value on an expert subcommittee, or retained as a volunteer adviser.

Negative consequences of under-utilisation include:

- uninformed policy decisions, with a general lowering of standards and negative effects on service delivery
- inappropriate development of the power of one or two members of staff
- money wasted on programs that are the personal favourites of dominant members of Boards, rather than being spent on clearly planned programs that are concerned with community needs and balanced with available resources
- money poured into programs that are just 'window dressing', rather than ensuring that financial decisions are based on the more time-consuming but valuable processes of analysis, planning and priority setting.

Under-utilisation and exclusion of staff

In small units in particular, it is inappropriate to assume that the Board manages and the staff implement. It is essential and valuable for staff to make recommendations based on their practical knowledge. The practice of some Boards of only allowing the presentation of 'facts' or options without recommendations is not utilising the full experience of staff and gives them the impression that their views are not valued. If staff do make recommendations they must be able to accept that their recommendations will not always be adopted—the Board still has the right to decide. If reasons are given and there is a general atmosphere of trust and cooperation, such differences should not have negative consequences.

Staff dominance of Board

Staff dominance can be a danger where there are insufficient Board members with expertise related to the service delivery, or with available time to give to Board activities. A few hours of meeting time once a month is not sufficient to generate informed decisions. In order to fulfil their role, Board members need to participate in projects, subcommittees and special purpose meetings. The question of the powers of executive directors and the lack of responsibility on the part of Boards has received some prominence in recent years in private and public industry. There is still a tendency to see the powerful managing director as representing a 'business' model, although this particular model is now being discredited in some business circles. There has been a growing recognition that it is the role of the Board as a whole that is important, and too important to leave to one powerful person.

Differing perceptions of Board/staff relationships

The relationship of staff to the Board is a key factor (if not *the* factor) in the successful functioning of an agency, but difficulties in this area are often 'swept under the carpet'. Consultants are often called in to help agencies with difficulties that the Board interprets in a wide variety of ways, such as the need to improve management techniques, or to develop training programs, or to evaluate the service delivery or any number of specific 'problems'. The one area that is hardly ever mentioned by Boards, or treated as a side issue, is that of the relationship between Board and staff. In addition, there is often a wide divergence between the perceptions of Board and staff.

In one organisation the Board thought that it had a good relationship with staff, and that the few problems that it was prepared to acknowledge were due to a few 'difficult' staff members. In contrast, the staff felt that they had major problems with the Board. Staff acknowledged that there were areas of harmony but considered that these were due to only a few Board members. The staff made conscious efforts to focus on the positives wherever possible and considered that this effort on their part was the reason that the Board had not recognised the problems in staff/Board relationships. The reality surfaced when a particular crisis revealed the deep divisions. These divisions, not only the crisis, had to be addressed. The issue was not what the 'truth' of the matter was but the perceptions of the two groups, and how this affected the day-to-day functioning, communication and service delivery of the agency.

A consultant was called in to help with the problem, and the Board was shocked to hear how the staff regarded the situation. After their first defensive and negative reaction, it was possible to work with the two groups to devise a program to overcome some of the difficulties. An atmosphere of trust is not built up overnight, but the acceptance of the findings by most of the Board was the first step. This particular organisational intervention also illustrated the importance of ongoing processes and implementation strategies. One-off reviews are not the best way of tackling problems in Board/staff relationships.

Developing effective Board/staff relationships

If the Board and staff see each other as adversaries, then a serious problem needs to be addressed. It is not too idealistic to expect the Board to see itself as a support to staff, not solely as a controlling and managing body. Because the two groups are officially seen as having common goals, or at least expected to have them, it does not happen automatically that they will work in harmony. In one organisation where cooperative and supportive relationships were eventually achieved by a conscious and planned process, the difference in the service delivery was noticeable, and was commented on by service users. In addition the rewards and enjoyment for the Board and staff were very high.

One of the responsibilities of the Board is to strengthen and support the staff role. If this is carried out successfully, Board/staff relationships will improve. The Board will then provide:

- a sounding board from the wider community against which staff can assess their own functioning in the light of the general framework provided by the Board
- support and encouragement to staff, including a conscious policy of recognition of achievement
- funding and financial security for staff and programs.

It is sometimes forgotten that the latter point is a major responsibility for the Board. The question of finance and budgeting is often neglected by Boards because of their lack of expertise in this area. All the good intentions in the world are of no value if there is no clear program or its future is so precarious that attention cannot be given by staff to their major role of providing the service.

Dysfunctions such as work overload and work underload are allied to lack of clarification of role. If staff roles are not clear then it is easy for the staff to be overworked in terms of the volume of work or of having to perform tasks that are beyond their capacity. Similarly it is possible to be underworked if the role is not clear and staff are expected to accomplish too little, or to perform work that is unchallenging.

VOLUNTEERS/VOLUNTEERING

A characteristic of not-for-profit organisations is the role of volunteers, both as Board members and service deliverers. In particular, Board and Committee members are usually volunteers. Throughout the following chapters there will be references to specific tasks carried out by volunteers, but in our discussion of Boards no general distinction is made between volunteers and those members who are ex officio, that is staff members and members nominated by other organisations. The grey area of 'their own free will' becomes relevant in ex officio appointments, particularly if such appointees' contributions are carried out within paid working time.

> The assumption that Boards are basically made up of volunteers was challenged by the Executive Officer of one small not-for-profit agency. The Board consisted almost entirely of members nominated by Government departments, and it was obvious that their participation was generally not 'by choice'. They were also constantly changing. This pattern had a very negative effect on the functioning of the Board and the Executive Officer felt that the only real 'volunteers' were the two 'consumer' members. They, in turn, saw themselves as isolated from the other members.

Service volunteers are discussed specifically in a number of chapters, especially where we consider there may be significant differences between the processes used for managing staff and volunteers. We also consider that many managerial principles and practices apply to both staff and volunteers and this is illustrated in a developing literature covering volunteering.[14]

Definition and principles of volunteering

The requirement that there be 'no financial payment' (definitions p. xi), is often expanded upon. Volunteering Victoria, for example, adds that volunteering, must be:

- of benefit to the community and the volunteer
- undertaken of the volunteer's own free will and without coercion.

In addition, there is a requirement that volunteering should be based on certain principles. These are quite detailed and reinforce the definition by stating, for example, that 'volunteering is always a matter of choice'. Reference will be made to a number of these principles in the discussion following.[15]

The significance and benefits of volunteering

Not-for-profit organisations have traditionally used the services of a wide variety of volunteers, including Board and committee members, service volunteers and many different types of consultants and advisers. All make significant contributions to the agencies in which they are involved and to the community as a whole.

Though there is general agreement that volunteering is a 'good thing', there is historically a wide divergence in the use of volunteers between countries and communities. It is difficult to get accurate figures, but there is a popular belief that the number of volunteers is declining because the 'middle class ladies' who used to be considered the largest group of volunteers are no longer as significant. In Australia the volunteer rate has been given as one in five persons over 15 years, with a relatively even breakdown between males and females.[16]

Just as there is some confusion about who volunteers are, there are differences in perceptions about the ultimate benefits of volunteering. There has been a history of *noblesse oblige*, or doing good to the poor, mixed up with altruism and idealism. This concept has now been expanded to include the benefits the volunteer receives. And the recipient may not necessarily be a specific individual or a group, for example where conservation groups aim their benefit at the environment.

The question of benefit to the volunteer has sometimes been treated with suspicion by members of the community who consider that such a benefit takes away from the 'altruism' they see as the core of volunteering.[17]

At a meeting in a small agency to discuss some aspects of volunteering there was positive discussion about co-operation and achieving shared goals. However, during the process some staff members present expressed doubts about some volunteers' motivation, and about what demands could be made, the level of reliability and so on. At first the inferences were covert and then one member stated 'many of the volunteers only contribute to satisfy their own needs, not to help others and make a contribution'. This brought a response from some of the volunteers present, who retaliated with a corresponding negative statement about staff motivation, 'staff only work for the money, that's their main concern'.

There was surprise at the evidence of negative feelings that had never been so clearly expressed before and which obviously needed attention. The group process enabled them to be expressed and acknowledged. A follow-up program was

devised to deal with this and other issues associated with the use of volunteers.

There is now more acceptance that volunteering can be of benefit to the volunteer in a wide variety of ways, for example, in increasing social awareness, in increasing feelings of self-worth and in providing training and development. Financial benefit is still a difficult aspect and the Volunteering Victoria Principles exclude all payment, even an honorarium. Some organisations regard this as too narrow. The line is even more blurred where such benefits as free services or travel allowances are allotted to volunteers.

Another of the principles outlined by Volunteering Victoria is that 'volunteering is an activity performed in the not-for-profit sector only'. This includes the large army of volunteers who work for not-for-profit Government agencies. With increasing privatisation and the blurring of the roles of Government and nonGovernment organisations, there are situations where volunteers may find themselves in a changed environment that creates new problems. They may have to decide whether they can continue to contribute to organisations such as private prisons, residential services for the elderly and so on, that now 'make a profit'. Another new development has been the growth in the pattern of seeing voluntary work as a useful option for people seeking work. This new development needs to be watched very carefully, particularly for its effect on paid staff.[18]

Inter-relationship of staff and volunteer roles

It is important that staff and volunteers are not seen as rivals, or as pursuing different ends. Though the needs of both groups must be taken into account, the ultimate goal of all those working for the organisation should be to function in the way that *best serves the stated goals and aims of the organisation*. However, that shared goal does not eliminate the fact that the two groups have quite different roles. This is recognised in two of Volunteering Victoria's principles; that is, 'volunteering is not a substitute for paid work' and 'volunteers do not replace paid workers nor constitute a threat to the job security of paid workers'.

These last two principles illustrate that it is important that volunteers are not seen as a cheaper alternative to using paid staff. It is sometimes evident that agencies have not sufficiently understood that volunteers are not there to save money, but should be used to benefit the community, the organisation and the volunteers themselves. In addition, agencies often fail to accept that the employment of volunteers requires additional expenditure of time and money on recruitment, selection and training. These aspects are developed further in the following chapters.

It has to be recognised that sometimes there are negative aspects of the relationship that need to be acknowledged. These can be caused by:

• lack of understanding and knowledge on the part of each group about the other's contribution to the organisation.
• a perception by some volunteers that their contribution is not appreciated sufficiently.
• a perception by some volunteers that their contribution is superior to that of staff because it is unpaid and therefore more altruistic.
• a perception by some staff that volunteers are less well trained and less reliable because of other commitments.

These issues should be seen as relevant to the total human resource/personnel pattern of the organisation. Volunteers should receive the same attention that is given to paid staff, including in the areas of standards and accountability. This is considered further in chapter 4.[19]

The way that volunteers are used will depend to some extent on the size of the organisation. Some small agencies may have extensive service delivery programs, a large pool of volunteers, but a small number of paid staff. This places a strain on the available staff and often means the need to use outside staff, with the extra complexities that result. In contrast, some not-for-profit agencies, though voluntary, may not have any service volunteers, although they will have a voluntary Board and Committees. The recruitment, selection and training requirements of these two types of agency will be very different although they may both be classified as small not-for-profit organisations.

IMPACT OF 'SMALLNESS' ON MANAGEMENT PRACTICE

It is sometimes stated that the principles of management and their implementation are the same, whether the organisation is small or large. We suggest that, although there are aspects common to all sizes of organisation, there are also consequences of size difference that can be positive or negative. There are therefore advantages in identifying the positive and negative features of size and structure. One is the recognition that there are differences that are significant, and another is that it enables the positives to be developed in order to outweigh the negatives.

Smaller organisations are influenced by size and structure in a number of ways. One is that the range of tasks requiring extensive knowledge and skills has to be carried out by a small number of people. This means that one person often has to carry out multiple roles, such as both service provider and manager.

Many of the effects of size vary according to whether we are looking at the staff or Board role. One particularly significant feature is that staff can more easily overcome the problems of smallness by networking and professional development. In the case of Board members, who may have commitments to their own job situations, there are problems because of the time involved in networking, development and training.

We have made the assumption that there are both positives and negatives associated with the size of organisations and that they can be utilised. This assumption is in contrast to a tendency in certain circles to regard large organisations in a consistently negative light, as reflected by the slogan 'small is beautiful'. The negative view of large organisations is related to the view that management belongs to large organisations and that management techniques are not applicable to, or even suitable for, small organisations. If management itself is regarded negatively then a lack of ability to use management techniques may be regarded positively.

There is a general belief that small organisations are often more favourably regarded by women as places of work. This could be for a number of reasons, such as their more personalised approach compared with the larger bureaucratic organisation characterised as 'male'. These beliefs need to be critically examined and their consequences analysed.

The chart in figure 1.1 summarises the management issues related to size and the resulting positives and negatives. The six points used as a basis are discussed briefly in this section, and developed further in the following chapters.

Wide range of tasks requiring extensive knowledge and skills

Even when the organisation is a small, single-purpose agency, the complexity of human services means that a wide range of tasks has to be completed. For example, a small number of staff, even one person, may be required to deal with individual problems,

Figure 1.1 Management issues related to size of organisation

Management issue	Positives	Negatives
Wide range of tasks requiring extensive knowledge and skills	• Interesting and stimulating work • Sharing of knowledge and skills	• Overload • Lack of specialist backup • Lack of consultancy/mentor support
Significance of interpersonal relations	• Warmth and support • Ease of communication	• Greater stress/strain • Confusion of boundaries
Decision making	• Flatter profile resulting in fewer levels to negotiate • Clarity of decision effects • Potential for consensus decision making	• Decisions are sometimes emotionally based and inappropriate due to the strength of interpersonal relationships • Such decision making can generate high levels of conflict
Multiple roles: service deliverer and manager	• More empathy with service user problems • More informed decision making due to increased understanding of practice • Closer contacts and participatory patterns with clients	• Role conflict and stress due to the above-mentioned individualising/generalising patterns • Overload due to the difficulty of containing the limits of two very different roles • Multiple accountabilities
Communication	• Less formality • Increased visibility and participation	• Inappropriate expectation that communication occurs naturally in small organisation • More personal barriers to communication
Supervision, training and Board and staff development	• An in-group or 'family' atmosphere which is conducive to non-stressful learning • Learning and practice can be more clearly related	• Lack of clear structures and patterns • Lack of assessment of what learning has actually taken place

community education, community networking and social action. This will be illustrated in the job descriptions of senior personnel of small organisations. Also, small programs with few staff and a large volunteer base can require the manager to work in direct service provision, advocacy, training program design and delivery and program evaluation, and to have high-level skills in negotiating with government departments.

Significance of interpersonal relations

The importance of interpersonal relations is often seen as a major characteristic of the small unit and ability in this area is highly rated (and often underrated in larger organisations). In the human services field, skills in interpersonal relationships are highly valued and generally perceived to be part of the required training. However, these skills do not always assist in overcoming the dangers of excessive personalising of organisational relationships that may arise due to the interpersonal emphasis and the particular training of human service personnel. The consequences of excessive personalising can be seen in many of the managerial activities considered in later chapters.

Decision making

There is a tendency for people to join small organisations in the belief that they will have more opportunity to influence decision making and policy formation than in a larger organisation. Such influence, however, may not always be as appropriate or as positive as expected. This can result in a high degree of conflict and increased stress and strain. It may also mean that decisions are seen not as part of a necessary organisational process but as 'personal' decisions. It is not uncommon to see examples of resistance to the formalising of decision making, with the consequence that the organisation lacks consistency in its decisions.

Multiple roles: service provider and manager

The wide range of tasks noted above is due to the need for people in small organisations to perform multiple roles. One particular characteristic of small organisations is the combination of service delivery and management roles. Of all the problems related to overlap and diversity of roles the individualisation/generalisation dilemma causes the most difficulty. This occurs when the service provider dealing with the individual problems has to make the generalised decisions of a manager. The problem is accentuated by the fact that many managers, even if not carrying out both roles simultaneously, will be influenced by their previous roles in direct practice or service delivery.

Communication

Because an organisation is small it is often assumed that problems of communication are minimal—'everyone knows everyone'. In practice the reliance on personal and verbal communication can have severely negative consequences. When verbal communication alone is accepted as the norm, distortion can be created and a lack of continuity, particularly when there are staff and Board changes. When people work in close proximity there can be resistance to putting communications in writing, which can then mean that distortions and misunderstandings may not be identified.

There are also long-term effects in that policy and processes may not be recorded or may be seen as over-formalisation in a small organisation and longer term planning therefore is handicapped. Whether the organisation consists of one employee or a large number, the same statutory and community obligations remain and need to be recorded and communicated. (Some of these communication issues are taken up again in chapter 5.)

Supervision, training, and Board and staff development

Smallness allows the possibility of effective training and development and there is often a climate of mutual help and encouragement. This type of learning is valuable in the human services where it is supportive and close to adult learning models. There is still a need to formalise training programs and to formalise the appraisal and evaluation of staff performance. Because of the personalised nature of the organisational relationships it is often very difficult for the employers (Board) to ensure that standards are appropriate. One of the problems is that Boards themselves often need training but there is a lack of suitable training programs and a reluctance among Board members to undertake the training.

WHAT CAN BE DONE?

There are many practical examples in the following chapters of ways in which the problems can be overcome. However, there are also some general managerial practices which are important no matter what the specific issue may be, and can be applied to many different situations. These managerial patterns, their interrelationship and their importance to practice are in effect a basic theme of this book. They include:

- constant awareness, with a self-critical approach
- careful and skilful recording at a number of levels
- ongoing performance monitoring at all levels
- planning and analysis linked to continuing policy reviews.

The words 'continuing' and 'constant' have been used because it is essential that the management practices are consistent throughout the organisation and not just a once-off or crisis pattern.

We have stated that we are giving special attention to small agencies because they are common in the not-for-profit sector. The difficulty is that such agencies may see many problems and issues, such as those discussed throughout this book, as not relevant to them. This is an unfortunate assumption and has proved fatal to many a small agency. Many personnel have joined small agencies precisely because they want to avoid 'all that paper and the bureaucracy' and regard 'management' as a dirty word. This makes it hard for them to adjust to the demands that are made when they find themselves in managerial type positions.

CONCLUSION

This chapter has introduced the general issues, with special attention to Boards and the question of smallness. We have not defined 'smallness' as it is not possible to be precise and there will be grey areas. The general concept can be understood in practical terms (see figure 1.1). Some of these issues will be developed in the following chapters as they relate to practice. As the emphasis is on practical managerial questions it has not been possible to consider many theoretical, philosophical and ethical aspects which underpin so many of the day-to-day problems. This book is about survival, and practice problems are of vital importance to so many small agencies in their attempts to remain viable.

NOTES

1. Yu, Jane 'Pre-schools Lash Out Over Unfair Checklist', *Diamond Valley News*, 17 September 1997.
2. For a detailed discussion of these changes, see Beilharz, P., Considine, M., and Watts, R. (1992) *Arguing About the Welfare State*, Allen & Unwin, Sydney. Chapters 6 and 7 in particular examine the implications of these changes for the management of human service organisations.
3. This framework is derived from Billis, D. (1993) *Sliding Into Change: The Future of the Voluntary Sector in the Mixed Organisation of Welfare*, Working Paper 14, Centre for Voluntary Organisations, London.
4. For a critique of economic rationalism and its management expression, 'managerialism', see Considine, M. (1988a) 'The Corporate Management Framework as Administrative Science: A Critique', *Australian Journal of Public Administration*, Vol. XLVIII, No. 1, 4–18; Considine, M. (1988b) 'The Costs of Increased Control: Corporate Management and Australian Community Organisations', *Australian Social Work*, 41, 3. For a counter-response, see Paterson, J. (1988) 'A Managerialist Strikes Back', *Journal of Public Administration*, Vol. XLVII, No. 4. For a very useful collection of papers relating to managerialism, as both doctrine and practice, written by both supporters and opponents, see Considine, M. and Painter, M. (1997) *Managerialism: The Great Debate*, Melbourne University Press, Melbourne.
5. See Alford, J. and O'Neill, D. (eds) (1994) *The Contract State: Public Management and the Kennett Government*, Centre for Applied Social Research, Deakin University, Geelong; de Carvalho, D. (1996) *Competitive Care: Understanding the Implications of National Competition Policy and the COAG Agenda for the Community Services Sector*, Discussion Paper No. 11, Australian Social Welfare Commission, Canberra.; Kramer, R.M. (1994) 'Voluntary Agencies and the Contract Culture: "Dream or Nightmare?"', *Social Service Review*, March.
6. There is a wealth of literature about the history of the changes but we have found two sources of particular value and we use their material in the comments following. Those sources are the *Working Papers* of the UK Centre for Voluntary Organisations and the books of Charles Handy, particularly *Understanding Voluntary Organisations* (Penguin, London, 1988). Because of the influence of British patterns on the Australian development we have used these sources more than those of the United States or other English-speaking countries.
7. Handy, C. (1988) *Understanding Voluntary Organisations*, Penguin, London, p. 20.
8. Booth, P. (1996) 'Understanding Management Control and Accounting in Voluntary Organisations', *Third Sector Review*, Vol. 2, p. 35.
9. Open University (1987) *Better Management 3: A Third and Final*

Report for the Management Education Syllabus and Open Learning Project Group, The Open University, Milton Keynes.

10. See, for example, Zanetic, S. and Jeffrey, C. 'Understanding the Other Half of the Workforce', *HR Monthly*, May 1997; see also the classic article by Gould, M. (1979) 'When Women Create an Organisation: the Ideological Imperatives of Feminism', in D. Dunkerley and G. Salaman (eds) *The International Yearbook of Organisational Studies*, RKP, London; Weeks, W. (1994) *Women Working Together*, Longman Cheshire, Melbourne. For a very different perspective on the gendered nature of management, see D. Collinson and J. Hearn (1996) (eds) *Men as Managers, Managers as Men*, Sage, London.

11. See, for example, our discussion of management roles and tasks in chapter 1 'Introduction to Human Service Management', and chapter 11, 'Implications' in Donovan, F. and Jackson, A.C. (1991) *Managing Human Service Organisations*, Prentice Hall, Sydney.

12. Definition given in Hunt, J. and Wallace, J. (1997) 'A Competency-based Approach to Assessing Managerial Performance in the Australian Context', *Asia Pacific Journal of Human Resources*, 35, 2, p. 59. For further discussion on managerial competency see Boyatsis, R. (1982) *The Competent Manager*, Wiley & Sons, New York; Sandwith, P. (1993), 'A Hierarchy of Management Training Requirements: The Competency Domain Model', *Public Personnel Management*, 22, 1, 43–62; Wallace, J. and Hunt, J. (1996) 'An Analysis of Managerial Competencies Across Hierarchical Levels and Industry Sectors', *Journal of the Australian and New Zealand Academy of Management*, 2, 1, 36–47).

13. A particularly useful analysis is developed by Margaret Harris in *Exploring the Role of Voluntary Management Committees: A New Approach*, Working Paper 10 November 1991, Centre for Voluntary Organisation, London School of Economic and Political Science. She uses a process called Total Activities Analysis (TAA) which analyses the committee role in its inter-relationship with other roles in the agency.

14. This is illustrated by the material issued by Volunteering Australia and its State branches. *The Australian Journal on Volunteering* is a valuable source of practice information and general literature. We have used the material prepared by Volunteering Victoria in the discussion of the definition and principles of volunteering. See also McSweeney, P. and Alexander, D. (1996) *Managing Volunteers Effectively*, Arena, Aldershot 1996.

15. See Volunteering Victoria Inc. Information Sheet 'Definition and Principles of Formal Volunteering', Policy Document 1997.

16. *Voluntary Work Australia*, Australian Bureau of Statistics, June 1995 441.0.

17. The confusion about motivation, and its effect on the inter-relationship between volunteers and staff has been the subject of discussion for some time. See for example the chapter 'Inter-personal relationships, with special emphasis on staff/volunteer, professional/nonprofessional

relationships' in Donovan, F. (1977) *Voluntary Organisations*, PIT Press, Melbourne.

18. This development is discussed in Cordingley, S. (1997) 'Unemployment and Volunteering', *Australian Journal of Volunteering*, vol. 2, 1, Feb. 4–8.

19. See *Standards for Involving Volunteers in Not for Profit Organisations*, Volunteering Victoria, Melbourne, 1997. Especially relevant is Standard 8, 'Recognition, Support, Supervision and Monitoring'.

2

GETTING THE RIGHT PEOPLE

A mother raising a child with a disability found that the resources available were inadequate for the child's needs. After months of writing letters, talking to politicians and government agencies, she decided to do something herself. She enlisted the help of other parents who had experienced the same problem and they decided to join together to have greater strength and influence, and also to provide mutual support.

By chance a property became available and the group added the role of 'service provider' to its existing role as a support or influence group. After a short period, money became a major issue, not merely due to maintaining a building but because the project could no longer rely so much on volunteer members. When the question of appointing paid staff arose, two opposing views developed in the group. Some were in favour of applying for government money while others resisted this idea.

Another problem was that people who wanted the 'hands-on' experience had found themselves struggling with the unfamiliar territory of meetings, dealing with budgets, submissions, reporting and records. They suddenly realised that as employers of staff they were faced with difficult decisions. Two members of the committee had friends whom they were sure would be suitable as staff. They could not understand the argument of another member who insisted that all jobs should be advertised. The members of the group were unable to resolve their different views and the original initiator of the project was hurt and disillusioned by the friction. The final result was disbanding of the group, legal action between the members and financial problems related to the disposal of assets.

As the account above illustrates, people in small organisations may be too ready to rely on personal feelings and hope that good intentions will overcome all difficulties. Smallness is often seen as a refuge from the large bureaucracies and from the necessity to follow plans and observe the basics of good management. Yet getting the right people into an organisation and ensuring that they are able to produce their best once there, does not happen by accident.

This chapter outlines some common problems in recruiting people and presents some ideas for dealing with these problems. In addition, we address a number of issues relating to selection and the management of the early stages of someone's involvement with the organisation, particularly relating to their induction and recruitment. First, we will look at some frequently asked questions about recruitment in not-for-profit organisations. These brief answers are elaborated throughout the chapter.

Isn't recruitment a specialist area that should be done by 'human resource' experts?
Large organisations have the luxury of specialist staff to undertake recruitment and staff development. One of the challenges of effectively managing a small organisation is that many of the areas of management that are thought of as 'specialist' have to be done by people without any formal training in those areas.

Does it make sense to talk about a 'recruitment strategy' when you're lucky to get anyone applying for some of these jobs, given the low rates of pay and often difficult conditions of work?
In spite of the difficulties raised in this question, we owe it to the service users to get the best people and attention must be paid to the quality of people working in the organisations. This not only holds true for service delivery staff but for members of the Board and service volunteers as well.

Even if we recruit good staff we still have a lot of trouble getting volunteers for the Board and to deliver services. How can their recruitment be made easier?
Volunteers are a core feature of most not-for-profit organisations. Though it is not easy, there are ways of motivating good people to join the organisation in these roles.

Isn't it good to recruit former service users whenever you can to staff and Board positions?
This issue is complex. The experience of being a service user and having gone through some of the problems with which the agency deals is one type of experience that people may bring to the job. It may or may not be the most important one, but the task of the organisation is to work this out before it starts recruiting.

Aren't recruitment and selection the job of the director?
While the director of the organisation will have day-to-day oversight of the staff, they are employed by the Board and accountable, through the director, to the Board. This role of 'employer', with all the knowledge it demands of issues such as awards and conditions, occupational health and safety require-ments, is one of the most difficult for many Board members to accept.

Aren't recruitment and selection the same thing?
They are not the same but closely related and it is important to make sure that the interrelationship is carefully monitored. It is important to understand what has motivated people to apply to join the organisation. Inconsistencies between what people thought they were joining the agency to do and what they end up doing are a blueprint for future dissatisfaction and poor morale. The complaint is often heard: 'That's not what I expected to do, it wasn't made clear'. Once the person is selected and is doing the job, it is often hard to tell if the complaint is justified.

Although there are common requirements for Board, staff and service volunteers regarding basic values and commitment to the organisation, there are some major differences in the processes of recruitment and selection of the different groups. To make these differences clear they will be considered separately in this section.

BOARD MEMBER RECRUITMENT AND SELECTION

In the case of Board members oversupply is rare, and there are sometimes so many problems with recruitment that there is in effect *no* selection of members.

How often does a small organisation have the luxury of an election? As the AGM approaches most community-based organisations are racking their brains for suitable people to approach to be Board members. Often the people 'selected' through this process have only a tenuous connection with the agency or service. Therefore members may not be chosen on the basis of their understanding and sympathy with the service given, the soundness of their policy platform, or competence, but on less relevant personal grounds. There are alternatives. Even small organisations are capable of producing a strategy that is an ongoing process, not just something that is put into place at Board election time.

Recruitment and selection of Board members should follow a logical sequence. Such a sequence is outlined below, although it is recognised that this sequence may be difficult to achieve fully.

1. Draw up a profile of what is required in Board members.
2. Develop a recruitment and selection strategy based on the profile, varying the particular techniques of recruitment according to the primary qualities being sought in the Board members. All members need not be the same in their background experience and other qualities and therefore a 'menu' of recruitment targets and strategies should be developed.
3. Recognise that most potential Board members who will fill the profile given below are busy, and it will be necessary to 'sell' the benefits of Board membership to them. In many cases this 'selling' is simply an appeal to a person's sense of community service. This sort of appeal is more likely to be successful if it is made at a time when the person has a change in work arrangements and is actually more available.
4. Use clear election processes based on the formal constitution. It is surprising how many agencies do not follow their own constitutions, perhaps regarding them as unnecessary 'red tape'—until a crisis occurs.

Profile of the Board

Some important features of the Board are listed below, such as size, knowledge and skills required, attitudes and values, and personal qualities, followed by a number of points to consider about the profile.

Size
- Minimum of 9, maximum of 15, depending on size and complexity of the organisation

Knowledge and skills
- Knowledge of service delivery
- Experience of service delivery
- Financial expertise
- Managerial expertise
- Networking knowledge and experience
- Fundraising ability
- Skills in committee procedures
- Interpersonal skills, particularly in communication and conflict management

Attitudes and values
- Commitment to the values of the particular service delivery, including goals, aims and philosophies
- Agreement with accepted human service values, such as self-determination and confidentiality

Personal qualities
- Integrity and honesty
- Stability and continuity
- Reliability
- Creativity and far-sightedness
- Altruism
- Compassion

Size

It is preferable to keep Boards small and form subcommittees, for example, for finance, policy, staffing and recruitment, rather than have an unwieldy and overloaded Board. The suggested minimum of nine allows for a spread of expertise and avoids the risk of domination by a very small number but we stress that the following points refer to the Board *as a whole.*

Balance of skills, knowledge and attitudes

It is the Board overall that needs to incorporate a balance of the required skills, knowledge and attitudes, rather than require that each individual member has all the attributes listed. In drawing up its profile the agency needs to decide what its own priorities are and the way these might vary at times, such as when the need arises for fundraising skills at times of economic stringency.

There is a widespread belief that, before election, potential Board members ought to know a great deal about the service, including characteristics of the service recipients and often about the 'technology' of agency practice. We do not agree that all this knowledge is necessary to become a member of the Board. Much of the knowledge required by the Board members can be learned after they have joined the organisation, particularly if there is an induction and orientation program followed by further development and education.

In contrast, basic and more general qualities and attitudes are not so readily acquired. Organisations need to be flexible in their requirements but a lack of agreement about basic values can lead to conflict and dysfunction and it may be difficult to maintain the organisation. Child protection services, for example, will not operate effectively if all members do not follow the basic value of the primacy of the welfare of the child.

When we go beyond the basic requirements more variety is possible and the question of balance arises. One way of characterising the need to achieve a balance among members of a Board is to speak of the 'three Ws'—workers, wisdom and wealth creation.

- 'Workers' does not refer to staff members but to those volunteer members who have the time and enthusiasm to contribute beyond their attendance at Board meetings. They are often the office bearers.
- The contribution of 'wisdom' includes knowledge and experience and therefore refers to service users in the Board member role, as well as those who have background knowledge of the particular area.
- The 'wealth-creating' group has been an essential of United States not-for-profit organisations and has become more significant in United Kingdom and Australian organisations in recent years, for example, in relation to fundraising. This group includes those who know how to obtain funds and involves submission preparation and networking, as well as the more traditional fundraising activities (see chapter 6 where fundraising is discussed further).

Personal qualities

The personal qualities listed earlier may seem idealistic but in the human services it is important that all Board members possess these personal qualities, as well as the attitudes and values, at least to some degree. The other qualities under 'knowledge and skills' can be spread throughout the Board. However, as we comment later in our discussion of selection methods, the actual assessment of these personal qualities is difficult.

Service user participation

Service user participation on the Board can sometimes be contentious because of the particular abilities needed of a Board member. The issue is whether special consideration should be given to service users in their role as Board members. Some organisations in the intellectual disability area set aside special time for service user members, or allocate a particular person to work with them in order to develop their capacity to carry out their Board role. This can be seen both negatively and positively, as some may regard the special attention as either patronising and/or discriminatory. There is also the danger that such assistance can have a distorting effect. The views expressed may be stated to be those of the service user, but may have been unduly influenced by the 'assistance' given. One group commented to the authors that many of their Board members could do with such help, not only service user members. In one agency the more experienced members were expected to carry out a mentoring role, but some of the Board said that they did not want the new members to be over-influenced and wanted them to bring 'fresh ideas'.

The issue of special attention to some members highlights all the issues about general selection and training of Board members raised in this chapter. The practical question of the amount of training and time required has to be considered for *all* members. Some organisations may consider that the principle of service user participation increases the time involved but is so important that any negative aspects are outweighed by the positive benefits of participation, both to the service users themselves and to the organisation.

Another view is that service user experience in itself should *not* outweigh other required skills and knowledge. These skills and knowledge may be considered as a normal requirement for Board membership, and the issue is whether, in the case of service

41

users, the requirement should be varied. Our view is that organisations that believe that service users will require special assistance must decide how fundamental the participation of service users is to their operation. There is also the need to take account of the requirement in some funding arrangements that service users should participate in certain activities. If the importance of the principle of service user participation is accepted, then selection can take into account the resources that will be committed to the required support and training.

A final consideration is that, even with special assistance for service users, some organisations may decide that some users may not, on balance, be accepted as members of the Board. If this decision is made it need not necessarily apply to all branches of the Board structure. Subcommittees, task forces, action groups and reference groups, could benefit particularly from the users' participation.

Staff participation

An issue confronting many Boards is staff participation. Staff membership may be ex officio, with or without voting rights, or as elected or nominated representatives or delegates. There are different issues that need to be addressed depending on the type of participation of staff, particularly in relation to the representative or delegate function. Although a seemingly technical distinction, experience has shown that it has fundamental practical consequences if it is not clarified.

Senior staff members of the Board, typically, would be the director, with the addition of departmental or section heads if the organisation is big enough. Some organisations regard it as inappropriate that employees have voting rights in what is technically the employing body. However, there are precedents for this situation, for example, in private industry, in tertiary educational institutions, and in some human service organisations themselves.

The argument *for* staff having voting rights includes the following points.

- Having voting and non-voting members of a Board creates two classes of membership, with non-voting members seen as inferior in status.
- Certain groups, such as staff or service users, who are affected by the decisions of the Board, should be able to influence

those decisions by means of voting. An advisory role is not seen as sufficiently influential.

The argument *against* staff having voting rights includes the following points.

- There are problems of accountability and maintenance of standards because staff have difficulty in distancing themselves enough from their practice to carry out a policy and planning role.
- As the Board is the employing body, staff who are members of the Board are technically in the position of being both employer and employee and this can create a conflict of interest.

In spite of the difficulties, few organisations in the human service area would not allow some staff to participate as members of the Board, with or without voting rights. Some members of the Board who have not had contact with the culture of human service delivery may, in anger or bewilderment, say, 'I don't understand what the issue is; we run this organisation, not the staff'.

Our view is that the director should be ex officio with voting rights, and that there should be an elected staff representative (or representatives, depending on size), also with voting rights. This staff member should be capable of recognising and handling any conflicts of interest that may arise. Service delivery professionals who see the value of service user participation, self-determination and the importance of communication in their day-to-day work with service users expect the same principles to be applied in their relations with the Board.

Staff can add to the value of service user participation at Board level because of their close contact with service users. This contact often enables the worker to give support and interpret the service users' contribution to decision making. It is to be hoped that staff would not be seen as opposed to the interests of service users but, if such a situation exists, its exposure at committee level is important. In addition, staff participation should be maximised by the use of joint Board/staff standing subcommittees and special purpose working groups.

There is another important advantage of staff participation on Boards. If staff have the opportunity to participate in discussion of reports that they have submitted to the Board, the decision-making process is enhanced by their first-hand explanation and clarification. Frustration and poor morale are often created when staff see their reports and recommendations rejected, if they feel that the Board has not understood the material. This situation is exacerbated when the Board gives no explanation for its decision.

Development of the Board recruitment and selection strategy

Whether there are elections or not, the recruitment strategy influences the choice of those nominated to become members of the Board. Because there are rarely large numbers over and above those to be elected, the people nominated need to be matched as closely as possible to the agency profile. Sometimes members of organisations are so overwhelmed by the day-to-day struggle to find and hold people willing to be responsible for its operation that they lose sight of the strategic importance of recruitment.

Sometimes it might seem the only option for survival is to recruit friends, 'friends of friends' and like-minded people. This can produce a narrow base that those outside the charmed circle may regard with suspicion and may see the process as 'stacking'. A different group may see the process as an example of organisational change, where the 'taking over' of an organisation by a group wishing to change its direction is seen as legitimate. This raises a number of philosophical, ethical and organisational issues which are often ignored but which, at some stage, have to be addressed. One of these issues is the question of legitimacy. As an example, a group was discussing the action of some community groups and their efforts to become the power influence in a particular organisation. The success of the strategy was hailed as a triumph for the community. When a different group managed to gain influence, though it was also a part of the 'community', this was regarded as a disaster. Questions about values and their relationship to the accepted goals of the organisation must be addressed.

The 'friends of friends' and stacking dangers can be seen in the small agency where recruitment is often left to the senior staff member or coordinator. The result may be that the Board has difficulty in carrying out its employer role, in monitoring and assessing the work of the staff member. The Board may become dependent on the particular staff member, consciously or unconsciously, and this will have a negative influence on the maintenance of the standard of service delivery.

The recruitment and selection strategy should not only set out the required profile but also designate those who will carry out the functions. To do this the agency may:

- develop a file of the appropriate background material to be given to potential members
- identify the targets to be approached for potential members such as:
  — various formal and informal networks
  — groups, e.g. community associations, professional groups
  — public relations outlets and the media
  — personal contacts
- identify the important aspects to be stressed, for example:
  — the particular service, what the agency does
  — philosophy/values of the service
  — expectations, what the Board members will be doing
  — the amount of commitment required
  — benefits/rewards of membership
- allocate tasks by the Board to:
  — Board members
  — special task groups or committees
  — staff
  — service users
  — other interested members, for example, from the general membership.

Apart from these general guidelines, recruitment techniques depend on the particular organisation and the potential pool of Board members. The essential feature is that the strategy and the techniques associated with that strategy should be planned and carefully checked to ensure that the profile is used as a guide. Care needs to be taken that anxiety about filling positions does not lead to taking 'just anyone' on to the Board. If, after careful planning and active effort on behalf of staff and Board members, it is not possible to fill the required positions in accordance with the principles and profile above, then the agency must examine its viability. Lack of success in recruitment and selection should be a signal to examine the strategy adopted and ask some hard questions about the organisation itself.

The organisation could ask itself a number of questions in response to the query, '*Why didn't we get the people we wanted on the Board?*'.

- Did we target the wrong group, that is, people who were

unlikely to be suited and/or were too far removed from the organisation?

- Was care taken to make sure that the people being targeted actually *wanted* Board membership rather than a service delivery role?
- Did the strategy stress the positive features of the agency and Board participation?
- Were diverse and informed tactics being used to reach the target audience, such as networking, media publicity, newsletters and other publications?
- Were there attempts to cooperate with other organisations to avoid overlapping recruitment, such as in timing?
- Were current Board members finding the role rewarding enough to encourage others to become members?
- Was the question of competence considered, as well as the other qualities needed in a Board member?

Subcommittees and task forces

In addition to the Board itself, there are other groups that are part of the Board complex, such as permanent subcommittees, ad hoc committees and task forces, set up for special purposes. The total recruitment and selection strategy needs to include these groups, as they are in a sense part of the Board structure.

Very often people who would not necessarily be suitable for Board membership can be included in these groups. The advantages of these groups are as follows.

- The agency is able to recruit people who do not want to take part in *general* Board activities but have a particular expertise to offer.
- This expertise can enable the Board to make more informed decisions.
- Special task forces can explore issues in greater depth than could be done in Board meetings and this will streamline Board activities.
- Extra groups can spread participation into a much wider group than that covered by the Board alone. As well as the benefit of increased input, the extended groups can be of importance in increasing links with the community.

Fears have been expressed that the groups may create divisions, or may become unelected power groups acting against the stated organisational goals. It is important that all subcommittees

46

are seen as part of the Board structure and the recruitment and selection of such groups should be as carefully planned as for Board membership itself.

There should also be clear lines of communication between Board and committees. If possible, the chairpersons or conveners of the groups should be Board members so that the links between the Boards and committees are close. The Board should be kept in touch with what is happening, with a clear and carefully planned reporting process. If the process is too detailed, the Board agendas can be overloaded.

STAFF RECRUITMENT AND SELECTION

When staff recruitment and selection are being considered it is necessary to take account of the overall staffing expectations, whether they are based on short-term or long-term predictions and plans.

Staff profile/establishment

Profile and establishment are terms that are often used interchangeably but their meanings are different in some organisations. A staff profile gives an indication of the staffing situation at a particular time and in some organisations the profile changes quite frequently. An 'establishment' usually means a fixed pattern of staffing with levels and number of positions set and with conditions laid down about changes to that establishment, which may indicate the number of people doing certain functions, or with certain 'ranks', titles and salaries. The public service often uses the term establishment to mean a staff situation that has been relatively fixed, for example, some armed services have two different establishments, one for peacetime and one for wartime. The use of a fixed establishment is now changing in many organisations.

The risks in the 'take what you can get' philosophy noted earlier may apply to staff as well as Board members, with a recruitment strategy of 'throwing the net widely'. Such a process may haul in people who would be clearly identified as unsuitable if care were taken, and this would save a lot of wasted time. The degree of 'spreading the net' will vary with different jobs and also different economic situations.

As was apparent from our discussion of recruitment and selection of Board members, often the major problem with Boards is trying to achieve any sort of profile rather than specifying what it should be. In the case of staff recruitment, even in small organisations, the drawing up of a staff profile is more complicated. This is due to the need to be more specific in job requirements, particularly because they will involve a number of industrial issues not relevant in the case of Board members. Budgetary matters and financial resources are also more relevant for staff than Board appointments.

The appointment of staff must fit into the strategic plan of the organisation. It is important to recognise the interrelationship of the aims of the organisation and the strategic plan and therefore the staff profile. If the aim is to develop a research element, or to change the target group, or to alter the type of service delivery, the staff profile will change accordingly.

An organisation was changing in its service delivery from a psychiatric hospital to a long-term geriatric hospital. The type of staff required for these services was quite different in terms of qualifications, training and career expectations. This was not addressed sufficiently in both the planning and the subsequent implementation processes and the result was dissatisfied staff and expensive redundancies. The negative consequences lasted for some time, as recruiting difficulties continued because of the poor reputation that the organisation now had as an employer.

Many organisations develop their structure around the profile, which results in establishments that have varying degrees of flexibility. Small organisations often resist having any establishment or profile at all on the grounds that the result would be a rigid structure which they believe would be harmful to their organisation because their smallness requires complete flexibility. On the surface, this appears to be a sensible decision. However, it must be carefully monitored that the service delivery, and the structure based on that delivery, is not distorted or constantly changing because of fluctuating staff patterns, which are not in accord with agency priorities.

A small community agency, which attempted to maintain a balance between individually oriented practice and community development, found itself in a difficult situation. The senior position had a number of administrative duties in addition to the community development role. When it became vacant, one applicant for the position had individually oriented practice skills and, because the organisation was anxious to appoint this particular person, the job was redesigned to fit that individual. The distortion of agency practice and subsequent problems persisted for some time even after the appointee had left. In other words the organisation was misguided in building its structure/profile around personalities.

So often, organisations develop through the enthusiasm of particular people who may then identify the organisation as 'theirs'. The transition from the influence of that particular person, which may become necessary because of changes, can be a gradual process and therefore can be absorbed by the organisation. However, very often the strong identification of the founding person(s) and the structure built around them mean that the change can only be traumatic and sudden. This may even lead to the demise of the organisation, or a feeling of disloyalty to the original founders. One way of tackling some of these issues before they become difficult is to appoint people to contracts, thus avoiding, to some extent, the building of expectations that these jobs are for life.

Guidelines for staff recruitment and selection

The criteria on which the recruitment is based should be well thought out before the total process is undertaken. The techniques used to produce the criteria include analysis of organisational goals as well as specific job analyses.

There should be an awareness of the danger of overemphasising personality and values when choosing people, which can result in an underemphasis on competence. In non-government organisations there can be some philosophical resistance to accepting competence and skill as being equally as valuable as such personality traits as loyalty and kindness.

There should be clear staff job descriptions, particularly relating to seniority, accountability and responsibility. 'We're a team, and we don't make distinctions' is used by some as an excuse for vagueness and ambiguity.

The pros and cons of recruiting service users as staff should be worked through. This is a fundamental issue of recruitment and selection in non-government human service organisations. The employment of service users does not exist to the same extent in government agencies.

Induction/orientation programs should be used as a form of selection. This is more often possible with volunteers rather than staff, as staff probationary periods usually follow rather than being part of a selection process. The probationary period is, however, now seen as more than a token exercise and this issue should be examined.

Industrial issues should be considered adequately. The smallness of the organisation cannot be an excuse for not doing this, and Boards need to have a full understanding of their role as employers.

Staff recruitment and selection strategies

The recruitment process is designed to ensure that the organisation has the best possible pool of applicants from which to fill a position, using conscious recruitment techniques. There are a number of important matters to be considered, depending on whether staff are recruited from within the organisation or from outside.

Internal recruitment

Service volunteers are sometimes recruited as paid workers. One advantage of this is that such people are committed to the organisation and have knowledge of it. There is a danger, however, that insufficient attention is paid by those hiring the staff to the differences in the roles of a paid worker and volunteer. One example of this is the non-recognition of differences in time commitments and accountability. In addition, there may be a reluctance to submit people who are known to the organisation as volunteers to the same selection process as other candidates, which may result in the best applicant not being chosen. It may be considered that volunteers resent the normal selection process. Another closely related resentment has sometimes been expressed by volunteers who feel that their past contribution has been undervalued. In one agency this meant that a number of its best volunteers were lost when they were not successful in their applications for a staff position. They felt rejected 'after all the years I have given to this organisation' and left the agency.

Another source of internal recruitment is when a Board member becomes a paid worker. The issues noted in relation to 'service' volunteers in the last section also apply to Board volunteers. An additional difficulty for the Board members is that they have had a policy and planning role with certain decision-making powers, which are not related to a staff role. Past linkages, personal contacts and roles may interfere with their new staff role, and may handicap relationships with other staff. As an example, an agency appointed a past president as a coordinator without any examination of the different qualities required and without recognising that the appointment aroused a strong suspicion of unfair influence.

Promotion of existing staff can also occur. This issue is faced by large organisations continually, but can also affect small organisations. There are advantages in existing staff members moving into a new position as they already have knowledge of the service and organisation. This can bring with it a number of problems, however. There is a danger that the organisation stays 'safe' by never having to expose itself to new ideas and ways of doing things—a dimension that outside appointees may bring. Also, existing staff may carry over 'baggage' from their previous role, such as difficult relationships with some other staff members, and this may hamper their acceptance in the new role.

External recruitment

Advertising is a key method of external recruitment. The advertisement has to match the job description. Other material such as organisational information should be linked to the job advertisement so that candidates have enough information to make a judgement as to whether to continue with the application. The layout and the choice of medium for advertising should also be related to the type of candidates sought.

Networking and 'headhunting' are external recruitment processes that share many of the features, both positive and negative, of the internal recruitment noted above. It is often difficult for candidates who have been approached through the networking process to understand that their appointment is not a foregone conclusion, and that they are still subject to the selection process. In the case of 'headhunting', the emphasis is sometimes different, as it is often intended that the person being 'headhunted' will be assured of that position. It is a form of recruiting much favoured in the higher echelons of business but has a number of dangers, including the development of 'old boy' (and to a lesser extent 'old girl') exclusiveness.

51

Recruitment of staff from students on field placement often occurs in human service organisations and is a useful way of filling junior positions.

Recruitment of clients or service users can be seen as falling within either the 'internal' or 'external' categories. It has both advantages and disadvantages. The positives include some knowledge of the organisation, and of service delivery. Negatives include the significant adjustment needed to a different organisational role, as well as the dangers of overidentification with one particular group.

Selection processes

There are three important components of the selection process:

1. the job application and other written material supplied by the applicant
2. use of referees
3. interviews and tests, if given.

Job application

Applicants should be encouraged to contact the agency and receive background material before applying, that is, not simply to respond to the advertisement. Applicants will then understand more about the agency and the role and their applications will be more appropriate and relevant. Such material, if carefully prepared in accordance with the required profile, can also enable the interview process to be streamlined and focused.

Use of referees

It is generally accepted by human resource practitioners that written references are of little value. Opinions vary on whether the referees of all people to be interviewed should be contacted before interview, or whether referees are only contacted at the point of drawing up a shortlist from which a choice will be made. The procedure depends on the time and resources available.[1]

The time element is influenced by how much value is placed on contact with referees. The use of referees is an under-valued part of the selection process, but this is often because referees are not used properly. The value of referees is maximised if certain procedures are carried out.

- The most experienced and competent member of the selection panel should be chosen to contact the referees. If possible this contact should be through interview in person rather than by phone, particularly when the job is an important one. However, it may not be possible to carry out face-to-face interviews for all referee contacts, because of the time involved.

- To maintain consistency it is an advantage if the same person can do the contacting for all candidates. If it is not possible to have the same person, there should be close contact between the team involved, including the use of common questions.
- The person doing the contacting of referees should follow a structure that is carefully planned and *approved by the selection committee*, but used flexibly.
- The person checking referees needs to be very familiar with the job profile and requirements of the job and sufficiently experienced to be able to judge the validity of the referees' comments and assess their honesty and the quality of their judgement.
- It should be made clear to applicants that it is more valuable if their referees have knowledge or experience of the applicant's potential related to the particular job, rather than simply offer a generalised 'character' testimonial.

There are some practical problems associated with the use of referees. These problems can often be overcome but if they cannot in a particular situation, then this may limit the use of this method. Some of these problems are as follows.

- Applicants may not wish certain people who would be obvious referees, such as a current employer, to know that they are applying for the particular job.
- Referees may not be as forthcoming as hoped about an applicant's faults. This may be out of loyalty, or even because they want to get rid of them. Direct questions about the applicant's limitations and current performance are therefore critical, even though they may be of limited value with the person who wants to be rid of an employee at any cost. Skilful questioning, especially in a face-to-face interview can reveal the latter situation.
- Referees may regard their comments as confidential and may therefore object if they are passed on to the applicant. This question must be clarified with the referee at the initial contact.
- It should generally be understood that any comments from

other sources, which in effect means the source is acting as a referee, should be accepted only with the applicant's consent.

This last point is one of the most difficult to put into practice. Requests for information about an applicant are sometimes made in social situations where many people know one another. In the business field people do not seem to follow the same ethical principle that is observed by many human service agencies—that information is not given, or accepted, without the applicant's permission. The requirement of the applicant's permission takes on an extra dimension where there is a possibility of danger to the service user if an incompetent, unstable or even criminal person is employed. There is a dilemma if a person not specifically nominated as a referee decides that there is an ethical responsibility to reveal certain negative information to an employer, for the sake of the potential service users. The question arises whether such action should only be taken in dangerous situations, for example, where the wellbeing of children is concerned.[2]

If the above suggestions for the use of referees are followed, the referees' comments can be one of the most powerful tools in job selection; they can be the next best process to trying the person out on the job.

Interviews

There is a tendency in human service organisations to over-rely on interviews in selection, because of workers' perceptions that they are 'experts' in interviewing—a perception gained from their own direct practice. There are different interview skills required in job selection, but the interview can still be useful if carefully planned. There are a number of features of the job interview to be considered.

- The interview can be used to clarify and explore further the written material provided by the candidate.
- It is important that the interview is structured in accordance with the job description and job profile.
- Techniques can be used to overcome the dangers of subjectivity, including the structuring mentioned above, but also to develop self-awareness on the part of interviewers about their own subjectivity. This awareness includes their own biases and prejudices. For these reasons, the selection committee should meet once or twice before the interviews commence in order to identify and resolve these issues.

- The committee should participate in sorting out and shortlisting applications. The sorting process will help clarify the 'official' job criteria and bring out the less conscious biases and agendas of the committee, which may affect the individual weighting given to different characteristics of the candidates.
- It is important to think in terms of competencies and tasks in the interview situation and not just emphasise ideologies and attitudes.
- There is difficulty in assessing values and attitudes in an interview situation. Case vignettes, on which candidates are asked to comment or about which they are questioned, are quite often used in the human services. Candidates are asked how they will handle particular situations, but more 'sophisticated' candidates who are well practised in giving the 'correct' answers may successfully disguise the fact that they have quite different attitudes. Experienced selectors may be able to overcome this problem, but the use of the case vignette technique needs to be handled with care.
- The skills of the various members of the selection committee should be maximised, with members given clear roles and good pre-interview preparation. The role of the chairperson is crucial.
- The whole process of interviewing, including the relationship of the outcome to what the selection committee set out to do, should be used as an opportunity for the organisation and the committee to learn about themselves, not just the candidate.

Experiential selection methods

Various 'experiential' methods have been regarded favourably by some larger organisations but they are usually too time-consuming or expensive for smaller agencies. They require expertise that normally means the need to hire consultants. Methods vary from elaborate residential programs, with stimulated problem situations and tests of 'leadership qualities', to more limited role-playing exercises.

The validation of these methods has been limited by the lack of follow up to test their success in predicting suitability, and also in the lack of ways of finding out whether those rejected would have been less suitable. For these reasons we have not included simulations in our discussions of selection, although we consider that they have some value in assessment and training once an appointment has been made.

The next section details the recruitment and selection process followed by one small community-based organisation in appointing a coordinator. The agency had three staff, including a clerical/administrative position. This coordinator needed skills in overseeing the service delivery carried out by a number of volunteers, as well as having overall responsibility as senior staff member.

RECRUITMENT AND SELECTION FRAMEWORK

This framework is provided to show that a quite formal process *can* be followed to achieve positive results and can be well worth the expenditure of time and effort involved. Though large organisations are prepared to formalise these processes, small organisations often regard them as unnecessary and time-consuming. The negative consequences of such a limited approach tend to show up at a later stage.

The time spent on this particular exercise had benefits that went beyond the task itself. In the process, those taking part needed to think through such major issues as the basic goals and objectives of the organisation, what its service was about and what qualities it took to deliver the service. In addition, the process was a learning experience in itself in such areas as the analytic, interviewing and recording skills required.

The staff recruitment and selection process followed the following steps:

1. Discussion by the Board of general details and conditions, ending in final approval and appointment of a panel to carry out recruitment and selection.
2. The panel of four consisted of three members of the organisation acting in a voluntary capacity—the president, the treasurer and a resource person with human resource management experience. In addition the current coordinator was a part of the team.
3. The panel discussed the general criteria and decided on the wording of the advertisement. The advertisement appeared in a major daily newspaper and a local paper.
4. Enquirers were sent some preliminary information consisting of:
   • basic information about the job, including job description and personal requirements.

- information about the specific nature of the service delivery, clientele and so on.
5. Written applications were considered by the panel and the following action was taken.
   - Each application was individually graded by each member into A, B, C and D, with grading based on criteria decided by the subcommittee. Some criteria were rated as essential, others as desirable.
   - Each application was then jointly considered by the group, taking into account the above gradings.
   - Clear negative gradings were eliminated, for example, where all members rated the candidate as D.
   - Clear positive gradings were set aside for interviews, for example, for candidates with one or more As or all Bs.
   - Borderline decisions were re-discussed.
   The number of applications received was 47. The final number for interview was eight.
6. A letter was prepared and sent to all the unsuccessful applicants at the same time as the eight interview times were arranged.
7. Interviews were held over two days. These were normally for one hour, with half an hour between each interview for discussion.
8. After discussion of all the interviews, the shortlist consisted of three applicants plus two supplementary candidates.
9. Two referees were contacted for each of the three shortlisted candidates and one referee each for the two other candidates.
10. A final meeting was held to decide which candidate would be offered the position, based on the complete picture of applications, interviews and referees' information. The total process took three days, including final discussion.

The president organised the selection process, with the resource person chairing the interview program and following up the referees, who were contacted by phone. It should be noted that the time of all participants was unpaid, except that the coordinator was involved in some staff time.

Before the interview process took place, the selection panel members were given a framework for the interview assessment process. The resource person formulated this framework, after discussion with the panel. It was closely related to work that had already been done by the agency on performance appraisal.

Although the following framework for assessment was used as a basis for the interview and as guidelines for the panel, there was some flexibility in the interview process itself in response to differences in applicants and questions were not allotted to particular members of the committee. There was general agreement during pre-planning about the emphasis that would be placed on particular points, and also on how the particular skills of individual committee members would be used. Some interviewers are better at obtaining factual information; others are able to draw out the material that is indicative of personal attributes, such as flexibility. It was agreed that the resource person would have a clear chairperson role.

Framework for assessment of job applicants

(Prepared for panel members)

Instructions for interviewers

The following framework is a guide only and not all aspects will be covered in the interview. Some sections of the framework may not be dealt with in depth in the interview situation, especially the more intangible qualities (these may be explored in discussions with the referees). Some of the material will be available in the application material. There are three sources to be used—application material, interviews and referees' information.

A separate sheet is provided for notes based on the framework. The first column could contain a check mark indicating that the basic quality existed, or in some cases a grading, A, B, C or D, will be given (to be decided by the selection panel). The rest of the space could contain explanatory comments. There is a danger that the framework is 'pie in the sky' but it can be used as a general reference point.

The sections are not watertight and there will be overlap, such as between the 'skills/competencies' section and the points devoted to 'qualities'. The last section is different from the others as it refers to information to be *given to* the applicant rather than information *about* the applicant.

A. Skills/competencies

1. *Communication*
* Written: report writing, submissions, etc.

- Oral communication skills at an individual level, including 'counselling', and group level, including public relations.

2. *Training*
- Teaching, training, developing.

3. *Dealing with diversity*
- Relationship skills with different ethnic, socioeconomic, generational, physical and mental characteristics of individuals and groups.

4. *Mediation*
- Skills in dealing with conflict.
- Problem solving.

5. *Organisation and administration*
- Office organisation.
- Planning skills and ability to generalise.

6. *Social*
- Interrelationships in social situations, e.g. group activities.

7. *Supervision*
- Ability to supervise, develop staff and delegate.

B. Personal qualities

1. *Appropriate value base*
- Positive orientation to the specific characteristics of the service users
- Observance of fundamental values, e.g. confidentiality.

2. *Ability to work alone*
- Ability to be 'self-sustaining'.

3. *Ability to avoid inappropriate roles*
- This means roles which are not a part of the coordinator's job as designated, e.g. inappropriate social action roles and other roles which are specific to the volunteers.

4. *Personality attributes*
- Energy, enthusiasm, and confidence.
- Assertiveness.
- Humour.
- Warmth; outgoing characteristics.
- Self-awareness.
- Resilience; ability to cope with uncertainties and lack of visible 'results'.

5. *Thinking and learning*
- Quickness in both thinking and learning.
- Clarity in thinking.

6. *Level of health*
- Level of health that is appropriate to the job requirements.

C. Structural aspects

1. *Time availability*
- Any possible problems in the on-call situation.

2. *Tenure questions*
- Questions over tenure including contract questions.

3. *Ability to work with the Board*
- Understanding of the Board's role.

4. *Networking*
- Knowledge of local networks.
- Ability to use networks.

5. *Usage issues: resources*
- Use of car, phone/answering machine, pager, mobile phone.

6. *Accommodation*
- Issue of accommodation in region.

D. Knowledge base

1. *Knowledge of theory relating to the specific service delivery*
- Literature and research.
- Principles and practice.

2. *Legislative and policy context*
- Legislation.
- Structure of government departments.
- Legal implications.

E. Information for the applicant

- Use of car.
- Question of 'on-call' and what it means.
- 'Overtime', working week and question of time in lieu.
- Probationary period.
- Salary and superannuation.
- Future planning regarding staffing levels.
- Award and contract.
- Annual leave, award provisions and public holidays.
- Clarification of material already distributed, such as job description and accountability channels.

This was the agency's first use of the process detailed above. One of the most valuable exercises was the discussion that took place after the selection. It was decided that there would be some changes in the future but that, as a whole, the selection process was successful and also provided valuable learning, as was hoped.

The final section dealing with the information given to the applicant is often neglected. Confusion can arise later if applicants have misunderstood the job information they were given during the interview. If there is a probationary period it must be quite clear what this means. Some organisations might never have used the period as a 'try-out on the job' and regard it as not really relevant. It should be made clear that it may be used and that the probationary period is not tokenism, so employees do not feel betrayed if it is implemented and they have to leave. There is a reluctance to appear negative at the initial interview and this may result in distortion, or the painting of too 'rosy' a picture. This can cause disillusionment when the realities of the job become clear.

Another area of increasing complexity in selection is that of changing industrial relations. For example, many not-for-profit organisations are, like public sector organisations, moving to workplace enterprise bargaining agreements as a replacement for awards. Philosophically, many community-based organisations may find that this form of industrial practice does not sit well with their commitment to social justice and collective bargaining. These issues need to be clarified before selection.

SERVICE VOLUNTEERS

Some time has been spent on the recruitment and selection of staff and Board members, but we have devoted less space to service volunteers. This is not because their recruitment and selection is regarded as less significant or easier to carry out successfully. The reasons are briefly as follows.

- This area has, generally, been recognised as important in organisations, and there is a significant amount of material available.[3]
- Service volunteers are closely related to the particular service of their agency. Recruitment and selection is therefore tied in

with the requirements of that service, and is usually quite specific.

- It is possible to use the orientation and early training periods as a form of selection.

Using orientation and early training programs as a form of selection is much more possible in the case of service volunteers, in contrast to the situation with staff. The luxury of a 'try-out on the job', apart from the laid-down probationary period, is not as possible with paid staff as it is for service volunteers, for reasons of job security and industrial regulations.

Some organisations expect to lose quite a number of their volunteers during training, and stress that this is not a negative result. They expect many will find the work is not what they expected or too demanding, but still find the orientation or training programs of interest. This expectation should not be overdone and there should still be a recruitment strategy that minimises losses and regularly evaluates its own success.

It is interesting that some very demanding volunteer programs are able to have quite a sophisticated selection process. This is due to an extensive recruiting campaign, the high profile and value placed on the task and the demands of the work. Examples are court counsellors and volunteer firefighters. These are usually recruited by larger organisations with funds, which the small not-for-profit organisation does not have. The small organisation therefore usually relies on the follow-up processes, rather than elaborate selection.

A common problem is the sudden influx of prospective volunteers when there is publicity over some crisis. Some organisations play up some non-typical aspects of their work to get volunteers and then have to cope with people unsuited for the particular tasks they have to perform. It is important that publicity is used carefully, as taking on the wrong service volunteer can have serious consequences for the organisation and its service users.

CONCLUSION

The processes of recruitment, selection, induction and orientation are all interrelated. Each depends on the other and if one is done badly all the others are affected. Poor recruitment efforts will inhibit the possibility of obtaining enough suitable people to make a significant selection possible. Induction and orientation must build on what has been developed in the first two processes. Induction and orientation will be considered in the next chapter.

NOTES

1. See, for example, Drucker, P. (1990) *Managing the Nonprofit Organisation*, HarperCollins, New York; and Milkovich, G.T. and Boudreau, J.W. (1988) *Personnel/Human Resource Management*, Business Publications Inc., Plano, TX.
2. See, for example, McSweeney, P. and Alexander, D. (1996) *Managing Volunteers Effectively*, Arena, Aldershot.
3. See McSweeney, P. and Alexander, D. (1996); Handy, C. (1988) *Understanding Voluntary Organisations*, Harmondsworth, Penguin; Knapp, M. (1990) *Time is Money: The Cost of Volunteering in Britain Today*, Volunteer Centre UK, London.

3

BECOMING PART OF THE ORGANISATION

• *Orientation and induction* • *Particular aspects of staff appointment* • *Orientation information* • *General background to be covered in the orientation process* • *Specific areas to be covered in the orientation process* • *Conclusion*

A practitioner who had never been a Board member was invited by a colleague to join the Board of a not-for-profit agency. She was apprehensive, but was assured by her colleague that she would be particularly welcome because of her practice experience. There was no election as she was invited to fill a vacancy until the next Annual General Meeting.

She was invited to come to the agency for an 'orientation session' before her first meeting. This consisted of a meeting with a staff member who took her around some of the buildings and introduced her to a number of different people. The names of the people soon became a blur and she found it difficult to remember what part they played in the organisation. She was then taken to a room and given some material to look at, consisting of annual reports, policy documents and general 'mission' statements. The staff member then returned and took her to morning tea where she met more people. Everyone was very welcoming and told her how much the work of the Board was appreciated, but no-one asked her about herself or seemed interested in her potential contribution.

Her first Board meeting was extremely confusing, everyone spoke in acronyms and there seemed to be hidden agendas and concealed meanings behind all the comments. Controversial matters were being discussed and she felt that she had a responsibility to know what the issues were. Her colleague told her to 'vote the way I do, I'll explain later'. Finally she realised that she had been invited to join because her colleague wanted to strengthen the vote for her particular agenda and thought that she had the 'appropriate' views.

The new member decided to discontinue, although she would have been a valuable Board member. There was no accepted orientation procedure that could have overcome the negative beginning.

In the previous chapter we separated the target groups of Board, staff, volunteers and service users. In this chapter we are combining these in the discussion, as many of the aspects relevant to orientation and induction—key aspects in helping someone become part of an organisation—are sufficiently common to all four groups. Often the difference is only a matter of emphasis and we indicate where these differences exist.

ORIENTATION AND INDUCTION

There is a tendency in small human service organisations to neglect the importance of orientation of both staff and Board members, although there is often a relatively elaborate program for service volunteers. This may be because an organisation sees the volunteers as the front line, the group that has the direct contact with the service user and is therefore the top priority for orientation and induction.[1] The importance of the service volunteer is acknowledged but not all organisations acknowledge the importance of the induction process for Board volunteers and staff. Organisations also vary in their provision of induction for service users as Board members.

In this section we group induction and orientation together and define them as 'a recognised and designated period after appointment'. In the case of staff the period usually lasts until the worker is a fully functioning member of the organisation and does not therefore apply to ongoing training and supervision. Orientation includes any time that the worker operates with restricted caseloads or workload.

In the case of a Board member the end of the orientation

period is not as clear-cut but every attempt should be made to identify a sequence of activities clearly as 'orientation'. One problem is that in a small organisation it is not always possible to have a number of Board members going through orientation together. However, there is usually sufficient commonality to devise a general program which can be adjusted to individual needs and used more than once. The balance between what is covered in the orientation and what is covered in the ongoing training program needs to be carefully monitored. Orientation overload can cause confusion and anxiety. The quality and success of the orientation will depend on the availability of knowledgeable, competent and sensitive personnel to conduct it and the receptiveness of the new recruit.

There are similarities in the needs of staff, volunteers, Board members and service users, but each group does have specific requirements that will affect the content and time allowed for orientation. Staff in relatively large organisations can be protected while they are new staff members. Their orientation is often seen as the beginning of a total training program and is not treated as a separate stage. In small organisations it may not be possible to have such a graded program and it may be necessary to strengthen the emphasis on orientation.

While service delivers can be eased gently into their role, Board members and some staff are usually involved in managerial practice and decision making from the very beginning of their appointment. This means that basic information that allows them to perform this function must be provided *as early as possible* in the orientation period.

PARTICULAR ASPECTS OF STAFF APPOINTMENT

There are a number of scenarios in the appointment of staff to the management role that will lead to different approaches to orientation. These include situations where:

- there is an *overlap* between the outgoing manager and the new appointee
- the new appointee starts *immediately* after the departure of the former incumbent
- there is *a gap* before the new manager takes up the management role, which is filled by an existing staff member in an acting capacity.

The first situation (overlap) is in some ways an ideal one, but is uncommon due to the inability of most organisations to cover the costs of a double salary. In addition, many managers, once they have decided to leave, would be reluctant to spend time training their successor (particularly if the parting is not a happy one).

The second situation (immediate appointment after the incumbent leaves) is the one that most orientation programs are in place to address. This is a real problem in the small organisation. If there are no staff members available to initiate the new manager into their managerial role this may be undertaken by a Board member, particularly the chairperson or another executive member.

The third situation (the gap) usually means that the new manager is not yet in the agency. Someone fills the managerial position in an acting role, and that person will usually provide the orientation. Whether this process turns out to be positive will largely depend on the attitude of persons in the acting role. For example, a failed applicant for the management position may be reluctant to pass on knowledge and assist the new appointee. A less usual situation is to have the gap and an overlap with an acting person. This means that the new manager joins the agency but the acting person stays in the role for a designated period. This can be a very useful arrangement.

In one agency the gap and overlap arrangement worked very positively. An acting director was willing to remain in the acting role for three months after the new appointee arrived. This enabled the new director to become familiar with the organisation and the managerial role before taking managerial responsibility, thus avoiding inappropriate decision making. The time was also used to take advantage of a well-planned general orientation program, as well as the preparation and presentation of a report by the new manager which became the basis of further planning. The possibility of using this type of approach could be considered by many small organisations.

ORIENTATION INFORMATION

The following list summarises the information to be given in an orientation program, which we will discuss in more detail.

These apply to Board members and staff, although to different degrees. There will also be variances for different staff, depending on their previous work experience and particular position in the agency. Many of the orientation topics are relevant also for the orientation of service users, as they are active participants in the organisational life of the agency and the reason for its existence.

General background
• Theoretical, policy and value base of the organisation and its programs
• History and culture of the organisation
• How the organisation plans
• General structure, including accountability, reporting requirements and the organisation of work
• Legal aspects, including incorporation

Specific areas
• Physical resources
• Recording
• Monitoring and evaluating
• Information systems
• Finances
• Service users
• Service providers (staff and volunteers)
• Environment, including legislative context and network systems

In figures 3.1 and 3.2, the orientation topics are assessed according to their relevance for each target group in the organisation, that is, whether this information is generally essential, valuable or optional for the particular group. Organisations would vary this ranking according to the particular backgrounds and experience of those going through the orientation program. The placing of service users at the bottom of the chart does not indicate their degree of importance but the fact that they will generally be the least involved of the groups in orientation.

The listed points will be discussed in detail on the following pages. The general discussion applies mainly to Board members, staff and service users and less to service volunteers, for whom the orientation emphasis is more specific to the particular service delivery.

Figure 3.1   Orientation topics by target group: general background

	Theoretical and value base	History and culture	How the organisation plans	General structure	Legal aspects
Staff	***	**	***	***	**
Board	***	**	**	***	***
Service volunteers	**	**	*	*	*
Service user	*	*	*	*	*

Figure 3.2   Orientation topics by target group: specific areas

	Physical resources	Recording	Monitoring and evaluating	Information systems	Finances	Service users	Service providers	Environment
Staff	***	***	***	***	**	***	***	***
Board	**	**	**	**	***	***	***	**
Service volunteers	*	*	*	*	*	***	*	*
Service users	*	*	**	*	*	***	*	*

Key: *** = Essential; ** = Valuable; * = Optional, depending on organisation

GENERAL BACKGROUND TO BE COVERED IN THE ORIENTATION PROCESS

Theory, policy and value bases

Organisations are often quite effective in orienting new Board members and staff about physical and factual aspects of operation. This can be done by providing annual reports, financial statements and tours of buildings. In contrast, the less tangible features such as basic values and organisational culture are often neglected. This can have serious consequences—the Board members may have a perception of the organisation which is incorrect or there may be a conflict with their own philosophy and values that they need to recognise as early as possible.

In addition, a new Board member may join with the express purpose of attempting to change some aspects of the organisation. For example, a particular constituency may have voted in or sponsored a new member with a particular 'platform' of reform.

Much of this reform activity may be undertaken on an individual basis but lately there seems to be a much more sophisticated use of group pressure, along with knowledge of the technicalities of meeting procedures, to achieve the reform group's objectives. Older Board members are often bewildered by what they see as 'takeover tactics', and feel that this is a betrayal.

If new members do pursue a deliberate change process, they must be very clear on the legitimation of this change role. They need to be able to answer the question 'What right has been given to you, by what authority, to bring about the particular change?'. Obviously what is considered legitimate by one group may not necessarily be seen as such by another. It is a question of values or ideologies.

Although Board members need to have some knowledge of the theoretical base of the organisation, such knowledge must be much wider in the case of staff so that their practice reflects theoretical consistency. It cannot be assumed in planning orientation programs that all staff have the same theoretical knowledge, particularly if they come from a different discipline and/or qualification and training base. Many employers are reluctant to accept these differences and say, 'We expect our qualified staff to know their theory', assuming that this 'theory' is common to all such staff.

In the case of values, staff would generally require as much information on the values of the organisation as Board members. This is often not recognised, due to the assumptions of commonality in relation to theoretical knowledge. For example, there are different understandings about confidentiality in different professions and disciplines, and on issues such as the duty to disclose to a third party. This has become very noticeable, for example, in the case of HIV infection.

In many ways, service users also need to know about the theory and values of the organisation if they are to make informed choices about becoming a user of the service that the organisation is offering. There are cases where an organisation has a monopoly on providing a particular service or where service users are, for various reasons, compelled to use the service (such as receiving family therapy before a child in care can be released home). Though the service users' choice may be limited, there is an ethical obligation for the organisation to inform them about what they may expect from their experience as a service user.

History and culture

Although Board members and staff may not need a great deal of historical material in the orientation phase, they need sufficient information to place their organisational activity in its proper context. This includes information that helps them to understand many of the other areas that will be covered in their orientation, such as the history and politics behind the agency's funding, and guidelines on eligibility for the service.

Staff are often neglected when information about the history and culture of the organisation is given, with a concentration instead on practical aspects of service delivery. There is insufficient acknowledgement of the interrelationship of practice and context. From the earliest time staff need to know that there are certain work practices that follow expected patterns. This is particularly important when an organisation changes its practices. Such change may include, for example, changes to eligibility requirements or changes in type of service. If workers do not know the history they may not understand the community's attitudes and expectations.

For the same reasons, service users may need to be informed of some aspects of the history of the organisation, particularly if there have been changes in eligibility or in the service itself. One agency changed from a relief-giving, financial assistance role to an emphasis on counselling. This change was not sufficiently explained to service users and the result was a great deal of resentment and misunderstanding—'I've always got help before, why won't you do it now?'

How the organisation plans

Both Board and staff should be familiarised with the strategic plans of the organisation, including the processes by which those plans were formulated. Strategic plans chart the long-term strategic course for the organisation and are usually framed to cover a three to five year period. Operational plans translate the broad direction of the strategic plan into more immediate goals, targets and ways of achieving them. It should also be clear what levels in the organisation will be involved in the ongoing planning process. Although staff need to be acquainted with the organisation's strategic plans and the planning process, in general terms the details required for staff involvement can be covered once they have commenced work. Service users can be consulted about strategic plans and informed of subsequent decisions through newsletters, noticeboards and so on.

General structure

At orientation, Board and staff should be familiarised with the organisational chart and its significance in relation to accountability, reporting requirements and the organisation of work. Staff should be quite clear about the hierarchy—to whom they are responsible and what this means in terms of supervision and other personnel practices.

Staff who have not worked in a small voluntary organisation need to be introduced to the Board's role, and may find they are surprisingly unfamiliar with the processes involved. Some of the mystery of Board elections, tenure and voting procedures should be removed during staff induction, and recognised as being of significance in the functioning of the organisation.

This information will need to be updated continuously, and particularly as circumstances change. Many small organisations feel this is bureaucratic and not necessary, but confusion and ambiguity can have serious results. A good example is the need to be clear about spheres of influence of Board members. Sometimes Board members believe their role allows them to influence staff directly, and quite often in the direction of the member's own particular preferences. The orientation period should make it clear that Boards are about general policy and planning and not directly involved in day-to-day administration or service delivery. However, the division is a subtle one as Boards have a general monitoring responsibility to see that policy is being implemented.

In general terms, service users will need to know about the structure of the organisation, particularly if it is a multi-program agency in which case they need to know how they are expected to move between programs. It is often difficult for staff of an agency to decide how much should be communicated and at what stage. When service users come to the agency, sometimes in a distressed state, they may only want to know how they can get help for the immediate problem. Finding the appropriate time to give service users more general information about the agency is one of the staff skills that needs to be part of training and ongoing evaluation.

Legal aspects

There are a number of legal aspects related to the operation of small organisations that need to be covered in an orientation program. For Board members, it is particularly important that they be given information about the extent of their legal liability in the organisation's provision of its services. Questions they will want to be answered include:

- What are the obligations under the legislation which governs the organisation?
- In what circumstances can a member of the Board be charged with an offence under relevant legislation?
- Can a Board member be sued by a service provider if the organiser is unable to pay all its debts when they fall due?
- Can a not-for-profit organisation apply for exemption from certain State and Federal taxes?
- How do they obtain a copy of the orrganisation's constitution documents and the legislation that is relevant to the organisation?
- Is there a grievance procedure and how does it work?
- Can a member of the organisation be sued personally if an injury is caused by the negligence of the organisation?
- What insurance arrangements are in place to protect the organisation and its members?
- Have appropriately experienced lawyers and accountants been retained to assist the organisation in complying with its legislative obligations?

There are grey areas in relation to the legal aspects of operating some not-for-profit organisation and care must be taken to acquaint members with the law that is relevant to them.[2] Typical of the sort of information that staff need are:

- 'duty to disclose', under a variety of Acts in areas such as mandatory reporting in child protection and in relation to public health
- the right to maintain confidentiality in court proceedings.

Service users should also know what their rights are in relation to disclosure and confidentiality. Service users will feel betrayed if they give a staff member information in confidence and then find that it has been passed on to others, including official authorities. Another area that is rarely made clear to service users is the extent of the service deliverers' direct accountability to the user, or to other levels in the agency or outside bodies, and the complaints or appeals processes available to the dissatisfied service user. As is the case with other types of information, the decision has to be made about the timing and the way this information is to be given.

SPECIFIC AREAS TO BE COVERED IN THE ORIENTATION PROCESS

Physical resources

Information on physical resources is often thought to be so basic that it can be neglected—people will find out where things are in their own time. But there is still some information that should be given in the orientation period. Knowledge of the main building environment is useful for Board members who can then familiarise themselves with the other physical resources over time. New staff, however, will need to know the location of key facilities, access to computers and equipment, car parking, transport and other information that may affect their ability to be integrated into the organisation. Similarly, service users will need to be acquainted with the layout and range of facilities that they will use while in contact with the organisation.

Recording

This is a matter of more concern to staff than Board members. From the beginning, staff should be familiar with the major systems of recording in the organisation. The excuse that 'I didn't know'—when communication breaks down, or even legal action is taken—cannot be accepted. Instruction on the keeping of records cannot be left for later training programs (assuming that they exist), particularly if the new recruit must function from day one as a responsible staff member.

The level of information about recording that needs to be given to the new Board member will depend on that member's role and can usually be comparatively simple.

Service users will need to know the extent of the information being recorded about them and the organisation will need to resolve the following issues:

- Do service users have access to their own files?
- Can they make entries in their case records?

- Can they, as with some home care-based programs (such as for people with AIDS), keep their records themselves, to be accessed by workers as necessary?

Monitoring and evaluation

Most issues in relation to monitoring and evaluation would be covered in a general staff development process. At orientation staff need to be told the ethos and approach of the organisation in terms of evaluation, so that they are able to make sense of the monitoring tasks with which they will be involved almost immediately.

If Board members are to take their employer role seriously they should at least know that such monitoring processes exist.

Service users should be acquainted broadly with evaluative procedures used in the organisation, especially those that affect them, such as the completing of 'satisfaction' questionnaires.

Information systems

Board members are often horrified at the amount of paper they receive when they join an organisation. 'I didn't think that all I'd be doing would be reading reams of material' is often the plaintive cry. Some attempt should be made in the orientation period to explain the documentation to the new member and help them prioritise their reading.

They need to know that their understanding of certain material is vital in order to make informed decisions. This is particularly relevant to finances (see the next section) but also to the many other decisions that have to be made, for example, concerning priorities and service standards. Staff often complain that they go to a lot of trouble to let committee members know what is happening, that they make recommendations, and then 'they don't read it'. The reading and understanding responsibility for both staff and Board members should be made clear from the beginning.

Finances

The actual techniques involved in financial aspects of the organisa- tion do not have to be understood to the same depth by each member of the Board. There should be experts on the Board, such as a treasurer and a finance subcommittee, to deal with the technicalities. However, *all* members of the Board are responsible for its management and should understand the general financial trends and their relationship to overall goals.

At orientation a member who is struggling to understand some financial aspects can be helped by a more experienced and knowledgeable member. Normal committee meetings should not be dominated by orientation of new members. This should be handled as part of a distinct orientation program.

This is an area of greatest importance to Boards but is also very significant for staff in terms of its consequences. Staff with management roles need to know about budgeting and this is dealt with in chapter 6. Though other staff levels may not be so involved, all staff need information on many aspects of the total process in order to understand the rationale for decisions that affect their day-to-day practice. In orientation they need to be informed about certain financial aspects and how they relate to the overall goals, values and service delivery practices of the organisation.

Service users

Information on the clientele is often neglected in the orientation period for Board members as it is assumed that new members know who the service users are and what the organisation is all about before joining. In practice, they might have only a vague idea about the service users and what the service is, and may even have the wrong impression, sometimes coloured by ideological preconceptions. An advocacy organisation, for example, may attract members who see the agency's role too narrowly as concerned only with individual advocacy and do not realise that its function is a broader one that may involve an educative role. This may happen even though such a role may be spelled out in official documents, such as the constitution.

Staff usually have a fairly clear idea of the actual and potential clientele before joining an organisation but need to relate the current service users to the past history.

Service users know what they want and what their particular problem is, but they still need to know about the more general aims of the agency so that they have an opportunity to decide, if there is a choice of agencies, whether this particular agency is the one that they wish to use.

Service providers (staff and volunteers)

New members of the Board may have only the vaguest perception of the extent of the staff and service volunteer numbers and the general human resource policy of the organisation. The structure and correct channels of communication have been mentioned earlier but introductions to appropriate personnel are a valuable part of the orientation of Board members. They need to know which staff they can refer to, and for what purpose. Generally, this applies to service users as well, in that they need to be clear about who to contact in the organisation, and for what purpose.

Environment

Some idea of the history of the organisation should be given to the Board in orientation. In addition, members need to know what the current climate is, including service networks and the legal and policy framework in which the organisation operates.

One would expect that staff would regard this particular aspect as of great importance and would have developed professional expertise in this area, in relation to issues such as service networks, government policy and service provision. Degrees of knowledge will vary according to whether the new staff member has come to the agency from another agency in the same area of service or from a different service area. The organisation will have decided how important such prior knowledge is when formulating its recruitment policy and carrying out its selection.

CONCLUSION

Chapters 2 and 3 have covered a major part of what could be called the personnel or human resource aspects of managing not-for-profit organisations, namely the recruitment, selection, induction and orientation of people into the organisation, whether they be Board members, paid and unpaid staff or service users. The next chapter addresses the issues that arise once the people chosen have to become fully functioning members of the organisation.

In illustrating some of the processes we are aware that none of the elements is fixed, and that they will vary over time within one organisation and will be different across organisations. There are, however, basic issues that need to be addressed. Some small agencies may consider that a simple approach is preferable, but critical examination will show how improvements can be achieved, even with limited resources.

The boundaries between the periods of orientation, training and development may not be clear and, if insufficient information is given during the orientation period, then it will have to be included in the later phases. The danger is that some material, if it is left out at the beginning, will never be given or it may be left until too late.

NOTES

1. For a slightly different slant on orientation, this time for the manager of volunteers, see McSweeney, P. and Alexander, D. (1996) *Managing Volunteers Effectively,* Arena, Aldershot.
2. We recognise that legal aspects are very important, but the point needs to be made that the detail is complex and we have only given some general basic guidelines. There are many national differences and in Australia, as in some other countries, there are internal State differences. As one example in Australia, Commonwealth legislation prevails over the law of a State or Territory. Some lawyers contend that an incorporated association is a corporation within the meaning of Corporations Law and that as a consequence committee members and officers of an incorporated association are subject to the obligations under such legislation as the Trade Practices Act and counterpart legislation in each of the States and Territories. In any event, with changes in such legislation as the Associations Incorporation Act for Victoria, the legal obligations imposed upon members of an incorporated association are increasingly like those imposed under Corporations Law on directors of a company. Accordingly the lawful conduct of small organisations is very likely to become increasingly complex over time and the need for legal advice will increase.

4

MAXIMISING PEOPLE'S CONTRIBUTION

• *Training and development* • *Performance appraisal supervision and general accountability* • *Conclusion*

An agency employed a young worker who had a very good track record in direct service, but had never worked as a lone worker or been involved with a Board. He was confident and charming and had excellent references from his previous employers. At first all went well. His work with the clients was excellent and he was very popular with them and with some members of the Board. But after the 'honeymoon period' he found himself unable to keep up with the demands made on him.

Gradually he fell behind in his records, letters were not answered and filing was hidden in drawers. There was some part-time clerical assistance but that worker was unable to fill in the gaps. At Board meetings the worker could not answer many questions. In addition some members of the Board were critical of his behaviour with the service users, particularly for being too 'involved' and not working with the 'community'. Eventually the criticisms became personal, involving appearance and general manner.

As he grew more insecure he became visibly more upset and stressed and eventually some members of the Board said that he must take leave and 'get help'. The Board was now interpreting all the problems as due to the worker.

An outside consultant was able to help the Board and worker identify the sources of the problems, to help restore the confidence of the worker, discuss job redesign and establish more realistic expectations for lone workers. Although it was not yet clear whether the worker could fulfil the requirements of the particular job, there was a planned process to test this out. There was also development of a mentoring program for the worker.

We have already looked at the first part of the personnel process—how to get the right people and then induct and orient them into the organisation. In this chapter we look at the next step, that is, once people join the organisation, how you can keep them and help them work as effectively as possible. Part of this, as we will see, is achieved by creating an organisation that is a place where people want to be. Later chapters will deal with the effectiveness of the program in areas such as service delivery and financial management. Programs, however well designed and financed, depend on people to implement them. That is why, in considering effectiveness, we start with the people working in the organisation.

This chapter also looks at training and development programs that can be put in place to help people contribute to the organisation to the best of their ability. The divisions between various people-management processes are often not watertight in practice and there is value in seeing the phases as a continuum, each based on what has happened in the other areas. Poor selection will affect training and development, and a lack of adequate orientation will mean that training will have to be expanded. Performance appraisal is concerned with, among other things, seeing whether experiences such as training are having the desired effect.

It is possible to group together the staff, Board and service volunteers in some of the discussion following. However, in the case of training and development, the differences are such that it is better to discuss the processes as they apply to each group separately.

It is worth noting that we have not included service users as a separate group. In small organisations, service users are not usually involved in people management, although we recognise that service users can be involved as individuals, such as on the Board. There are exceptions to this general pattern, though they are not numerous. Some organisations do involve service users as a group, controlling policy and having significant people management responsibilities, particularly the self-help agencies.

TRAINING AND DEVELOPMENT

The Board

Board members are often expected to function at full pace as soon as they join the organisation, but they will only be able to achieve this if orientation and induction have been satisfactorily carried out. It can be frightening for new Board members to be faced with decision-making and planning processes without adequate preparation. In the same way, ongoing training and development can make the Board member both more confident and more competent. This training can be achieved in a number of ways, for example, through a mentoring system and by way of workshops, seminars and retreats.

A mentoring system can be put in place in which an experienced Board member is allocated to new members to assist them in being as productive as possible in their Board role. This mentoring arrangement will vary from being short term, and linked closely with induction and orientation, to arrangements that may stay in place for a longer period. Some members may seek longer term assistance to acquire the intellectual skills needed to cope with Board functioning. Another situation where help could be needed is where Board members are drawn from a constituency that is unfamiliar with Board processes.

Board members can also be trained through workshops, seminars and retreats. These should not be seen as spasmodic but as part of an ongoing training and development program. The purposes of these events may vary from team building and familiarisation of roles to those designed to help the Board carry out its work more effectively. An example of the latter would be a workshop addressing changes to employment legislation and practices that would affect the Board's role as an employer.

Workshops and seminars should be carefully planned, preferably over a twelve-month time frame. The planning should involve the whole Board (and subcommittee members) who can indicate the most suitable arrangements for themselves. This is necessary to overcome the danger, faced by all voluntary Boards, that their good intentions are not realised because planning was not sufficiently realistic.

A suggested range of workshop/seminar topics could be:

- those based around the acquisition of new skills, such as learning to undertake strategic planning in a community-based agency. New Board members may have had more bureaucratic experience and be unfamiliar (or uncomfortable with) community consultative processes. You will often hear from such people, 'All this talking only slows us down and stops us from getting on with the job'. Workshops emphasising the value aspects of consultation, as well as techniques for doing it, can go some way to countering this sort of view.

- those designed to keep the Board up-to-date on factors in the external environment that will impinge on the agency's functioning, such as case mix, service agreements, tendering, accountability requirements, and other changes to funding arrangements.

- those aiming to familiarise Boards with the work of the agency. This is a very important purpose that is of value to the Board and staff. Staff often feel that Board members do not appreciate sufficiently the realities of their day-to-day service delivery practice. These sessions should be part of a total familiarisation process that could include visiting facilities and meeting service users. If done in a workshop/seminar format, similar benefits can be achieved by the use of experiential methods, for example, getting Board members to work through some aspects of the 'case' decision-making exercise, alongside staff. In practice, Board members usually enjoy this process of learning to appreciate the down-to-earth decisions that the agency staff have to make.

Staff

The wide literature on staff training and development should not be accepted without careful examination to assess its relevance to the small organisation. One problem is that few of the training programs available address the specific characteristics of smallness, and much of the material is of limited use.

There is a danger in small organisations that the training and development of staff in any planned sense is neglected, and is handled in an informal and ad hoc way. This is often due to the lack of both time and financial resources. This can be seen particularly in performance appraisal, which we discuss later in the chapter.

It is important to note that many of the ways that can be used by managers to maximise the contribution of staff to the organisation can also be used by managers themselves to improve their own performance. For example, managers' self-reflection and self-awareness in their management practice can be improved by recording and monitoring their decisions in terms of:

- How were they were made?
- Were they based on planning decisions?
- Did they have the requisite amount of consultation?
- Were they based on accurate and complete knowledge?
- Were they done in a suitable time frame and not, for example, rushed?

Managers can also analyse what their time is spent on, and what is avoided. Is there a particular item or type of decision that regularly finds its way to the bottom of the in-tray?

Another valuable area to analyse is to identify behaviours that are outside the manager's 'comfort zone', and to work out how change occurs around that zone. There is a theory that change is only possible if people move outside their comfort zones. This often leads to the belief that all changes must generate discomfort, conflict, 'turbulence' or even 'chaos'. Though most changes may generate some discomfort, if this is not internalised and does not become part of the comfort zone, the continuing anxiety can be disabling and contribute to poor performance. This relates to the earlier discussions of managing change and stress. If changes are internalised the effects are likely to be stronger and more persistent.

This last point is particularly significant for those in the human services who feel uncomfortable with many of their management roles, perhaps because of deficiencies in their training and selection processes. They may see some of their roles as managerialist, authoritarian and patriarchal in terms of values and processes. There are two issues to consider. First, is the managerial role with which the person is uncomfortable in fact inappropriate and therefore should not be incorporated into an expanded comfort zone? In other words, is the organisation asking the manager to behave in a way that should not be demanded in accordance with accepted professional practice? Second, is the role legitimate in terms of the organisation and accepted practice and, if so, should the manager who is uncomfortable with it stay in that job? This question is relevant both from the organisation's point of view and the perspective of the mental health of the manager.

Many organisations are too small to provide an internal career path. There needs to be some unselfishness on the part of such an organisation if the training and other opportunities it has provided lead staff to move on and which enhance their career beyond that particular organisation. This means an acceptance of staff turnover that may create problems in continuity. As a consequence, it is important that the Board itself provides continuity, and this responsibility for continuity needs to be accepted by the members of the Board.

A clear consequence of smallness is the limited range of expertise within the organisation and therefore the need to call on outside people. Some small organisations have had little experience in this process and need guidance on how to use outside assistance effectively and make the best possible use of scarce financial resources.

Using consultants

Many large and small organisations are now using consultants to undertake a range of tasks, including selection of staff, provision of training and development, facilitating planning, research projects, and designing and evaluating programs. These organisations typically use consultants for two main reasons:

1. Their staff do not have the expertise to perform certain necessary functions.
2. Their staff do not have the time to perform the function, either because it needs to be done at a time when competent staff are engaged in other duties, such as service delivery, or it needs to be done more quickly than can be achieved by, for example, deploying other staff on a fractional basis.

Both reasons, but particularly the former, can be a source of tension when consultants are brought in. Staff might believe that they have the skill to perform the task the consultants have been brought in to do, and it is demoralising to be told that they do not. A different complaint arises from staff who believe that they do the mundane work while high-priced consultants do the more interesting work in the organisation. There are some basic questions, therefore, which managers need to ask themselves before bringing consultants in:

- Does the organisation, through its existing staff group, have the capacity to do the job?

- Is it a function that ought to be done by an external person, even if the competence exists in the organisation?
- Is the decision process that has led to engaging a consultant understood by organisation members?
- Why is time an issue? Can it wait until someone is available from the organisation?

These questions address the legitimacy of engaging an external consultant.

Once managers are sure that it is a justifiable decision, there are a number of factors to consider when it comes to the point of engaging a consultant.[1] These include:

- What similar work has the consultant done previously, with what results, and who can be asked about it, apart from the consultant?
- Who will actually do the work—the person engaged, a more junior person, or a subcontractor?
- Is this person the sort of 'presence' wanted around the organisation? Would people in the organisation be able to work with her/him?
- Does the consultant accept the values and philosophy of the organisation?
- Does the consultant seem capable of focusing on the task? How many other jobs do they have on, and what capacity does the team have to handle the workload?
- Does the intervention, as outlined, represent value for money? Some staff might resent the high fees commanded by some consultants (particularly when those hiring the consultant erroneously convert the fee to an annual salary!) without understanding the real savings and other benefits that may result from more efficient and effective practice.
- Does the contract allow for either side to renegotiate the scope of the consultancy, and who bears the cost, if any, of any variation?

Having made the decision and engaged a consultant, the manager needs to consider how the consultancy will operate and how the consultant's material is to be used, for example:

- What provision has been made for regular reporting by the consultant? Does this reporting include the opportunity for transfer of knowledge to staff from the consultant, if the reason for the hiring was lack of relevant expertise among the staff?
- What is the implementation structure, if any?

- What is the implementation process? Is it clear who the consultant actually reports to—the Board, manager, whole staff group, service users or public meeting—and what is to be reported on?
- Has the organisation/manager/Board made any commitment to implement recommendations from the consultant, or will there be a separate recommendation review and planning process?
- What role will the consultants or their firm play in implementation? Too often consultants play little, if any, role in implementation, leaving many organisations without a clear implementation process. Failures are often, therefore, laid at the feet of consultants, not the organisation. Much of the cynicism about consultants ('pay them a lot of money to tell you what you already know') comes from the lack of follow-up.

Using mentors and resource people

There is some confusion in practice, and in the organisational and management literature, about the role of mentors and the differences between supervision, mentoring and consultancy. In addition there is confusion about the advantages and disadvantages of internal as against external consultancy, supervision or mentoring.

We have discussed the bringing in of consultants to assist the organisation in dealing with specific problems or to help in particular developments, such as planning. A method that has not been used so often is the bringing in of consultants to help with individual development on a one-to-one basis. Such consultancy could be regarded as *external individual mentoring*. This use of the word 'mentoring' is more common in the US than in Australia or the UK.

The general tendency is to use 'consultant' to refer to the outside organisational role, although some organisations also use the title 'human resource consultant' where the 'consultancy' is internal. Mentoring has been defined as a deliberate pairing of a more skilled or experienced person with a lesser skilled or experienced one, with an agreed goal of improving the lesser skilled person and developing specific competencies through this arrangement.[2]

Mentoring and supervision

The particular feature of 'mentoring' is that it is a pairing. Another important aspect of mentoring is that it is not 'supervision'. The differences between the two are important.

If the mentor is an internal employee, the distinction between these two processes must be clearly laid down. A 'supervisor' has an organisational administrative role that involves elements of assessment and may influence such aspects as promotion. The supervisor is in a more senior organisational position in relation to the other employee, and usually has some defined responsibility for what that employee does.

A supervisor may also have a developmental role similar to that of a mentor, but the 'supervisory' factor is the prime one. In the same way the mentor, as defined above in relation to the organisational role, has some responsibility for developing competencies. The difference between the two roles shows up in the detail and the ultimate goal. For the internal mentor role to succeed, there are essential characteristics that must be demonstrated and which illustrate clearly the difference between supervision and mentoring:

- The role must be spelled out and clearly understood by both parties.
- The relationship must be entered into voluntarily and there must be mechanisms laid down for termination by either party.
- The process must be confidential, as trust must be the foundation for the relationship.
- The material must *not* be used for promotion or disciplinary purposes.
- The relationship is *not* a therapeutic one as the basic aim is enhancement of organisational functioning, often with a particular emphasis on 'grooming', succession planning and the sharing of managerial practice, wisdom and expertise.

This last point does not mean that there is not a strong supportive element to the relationship, and this can create problems if it borders on the therapeutic. A great deal depends on the skill and integrity of the mentor. If more than support is needed—for example, if it is recognised that treatment on a personal level is required—this is a separate issue. The appropriate decisions will be those that have been developed and accepted by the organisation's management and the employees. This relates to a number of organisational programs concerned with, for example, health or alcoholism.

Use of outside mentors/consultants

The use of outside mentors is an interesting development that has arisen specifically because of the smallness of some organisations. It has been neglected in the general literature on mentoring, although in human service organisations such a process is not uncommon but it is usually called 'supervision'.

Some human service organisations recognise that they cannot provide internal 'supervision' for a number of reasons, such as lack of staff or particular expertise. They therefore call in outside people on a sessional basis. The word 'supervision' is so common in the human service area for a wide range of one-to-one roles that it is still used for the role of all persons based outside. What is often not clarified is whether it is really a mentor role. It should be clear whether the organisational supervisory aspects are included, such as assessment and reporting on competency, or whether it is entirely the mentoring/consultancy aspects, such as help with skills, support and development.

It is less common to find consultants/mentors being used for management tasks. It is apparently quite acceptable to bring in outside expertise to assist staff in their service delivery role, but not in managerial or administrative roles.

In one small organisation some staff members wanted help with their managerial tasks. The organisation had in the past paid for service delivery 'supervision' but was quite negative about the request for administrative/management assistance for staff. It was willing for staff members to attend expensive workshops on administrative aspects of practice, which often had very doubtful value, but not for the individual sessions.

The official reason given was lack of funds, so the consultant offered to draw up individual programs on a voluntary basis. Privately some staff members said they would like to pay for the sessions themselves. The organisation was still reluctant for the staff to have this 'supervision', and the resultant discussion illustrated some interesting fears about this type of consultancy.

At first there was a denial that staff needed assistance in the particular area, sometimes expressed negatively and inferring that staff should not be managerially 'incompetent' or need help. Finally a basic fear was revealed that sensitive organisational matters would be raised and considered by someone from outside the organisation, including planning, priority decisions and 'private' disciplinary matters. It was not recognised that these aspects would inevitably come up in the service delivery supervision or when staff attended workshops, if they were the factors impinging on the employees' work.

The same organisation employed a sessional consultant for staff assistance with service delivery, a process they called 'supervision'. This consultant complained that she was supposed to be talking about the service problems and 'all they wanted to talk about was the administrative issues, but they are not my concern'.

In contrast, another organisation used the managerial consultant in an individual mentoring role, covering managerial/administrative aspects. A spin-off was the agreement of the staff that certain aspects that arose out of the individual sessions could be presented in general terms to the organisation. These were items, for example, related to planning, priority setting and so on. This was an additional benefit both to the agency and the staff.

The above example illustrates how important it is for the consultancy/mentor role to be carefully developed. There is a need for understanding on the part of all those involved before any program is attempted. The consultant should have recognised the fears of 'managerial' mentoring that existed in the management in the first example above. Also, the overall benefits to the organisation could have been stressed. It was too easily assumed that, as the agency already employed an outside consultant, the different focus would not be such an issue.

Once the organisation has accepted in principle the 'managerial' consultancy role there are important steps to be followed:

1. The mentor must be carefully chosen, and trusted by all involved in the process. Different skills are required when the type of consultancy involves one-to-one processes—it is not the same as running a workshop or carrying out a review program. Also, developing competencies in a managerially focused individual program is not the same as 'counselling'.

2. Purposes and procedures must be in writing and understood by all. This includes the basic goal of the mentor program as understood by the organisation, the employee and the consultant/mentor.

3. Confidentiality is of prime importance and the responsibilities of the consultant/mentor must be understood in regard to confidentiality.

Pros and cons of internal and external mentors

The advantage of internal mentors is that they are familiar with the organisation and the organisation may feel more secure with them. The disadvantage is that the supervisory role may be confused with the mentor role and could negate any mentoring role. This confusion could develop if the mentor has a power position in relation to assessment and/or promotion.

The advantage of external mentors is that the relationship can be a trusting one, and entered into voluntarily, due to the mentor having no organisational role. It can therefore foster development more easily. Without an organisational position, the mentor can also be more objective. The disadvantage is that distrust may be felt by the organisation and a fear of undue influence from 'outside'.

The final choice of internal or external mentor will be influenced by many specific factors, such as:

- the size of the organisation, for example, are there sufficient suitable mentors in the organisation?
- the costs—can an outside mentor be afforded?
- a wide variety of current issues, for example, is the organisation insecure about its own functioning and therefore unwilling to risk outside involvement?

Advantages and disadvantages of different forms of consultancy

The question of costs needs to be considered. This is difficult to analyse objectively as the follow-up to workshops and training programs is usually inadequate. Little assessment is made of how much the functioning of the staff has been improved by attendance at the workshops, and therefore whether the costs are justified. Assessment should not be based on whether staff have enjoyed the experience, feel good, or gained some networking advantages, although these aspects have their benefits.

In assessing benefits one needs to prioritise which benefits are needed. Real benefits are difficult to see over a short period. Individual improvements in competencies are best seen over a period of time, with spaced sessions that involve constant follow-up and developments, rather than the limited time span of the workshop.

There are, however, other advantages to the workshop in the sense of the interaction with other managers and people with similar responsibilities. Ultimately an overall development plan should be drawn up which will emphasise different processes at different times and with different staff, and the expected costs balanced with the expected outcomes.

Service volunteers: training and development

Many organisations have comprehensive orientation and induction programs, for example, telephone crisis counselling services and Citizens Advice Bureaux. This is because most of the applicants will be without formal training and therefore the training responsibilities of these agencies are recognised and accepted.

The need for further training, that is, after induction and orientation, is not so readily recognised. There are two phases to this training:

1. provision of *follow-up* training and development, on a regular and planned basis
2. setting up of methods of *monitoring* the actual practice of service volunteers.

Difficulties in establishing the necessary systems may arise due to two factors: lack of resources in the small organisation and resistance on the part of some volunteers and denial of the need for ongoing training. This resistance may be due to a number of factors such as the fear of 'professionalisation' and 'supervision'. On the other hand, many volunteers recognise the value and support function of ongoing training.

The Board of one not-for-profit organisation recognised that there was increasing emphasis on training and accountability by funding bodies and the community, but were unsure that volunteers would accept this change. Rather than resisting the training program, as expected by the Board, the service volunteers were very positive and were prepared to give a surprising amount of time to the proposal. The reasons they gave for their acceptance, apart from the knowledge gained, were as follows.

• The program was based on the organisation's own

practice. It was not a 'package' produced for use with any organisation.

- The program followed on from the orientation and was not repeating material already covered.
- Although some outside consultants were used, the staff of the organisation played a major role in the program. The service volunteers, in getting to know the staff better, particularly appreciated this. They also felt that the agency staff knew the realities of the service.
- The program was seen as recognition of the importance of the work of the volunteers and the willingness of the organisation to spend time and money on their training.
- As one would expect from a program planned for group interaction, the participants found this a particularly valuable benefit, as many of the volunteers often felt isolated from one another and from the organisation as a whole.

It is important to have training and development programs, but it is also necessary to know whether they are succeeding and, in general accountability terms, whether the organisation's practice is achieving its goals and at the required standard. Too often in the small not-for-profit organisation it is assumed that people who work in this setting have the right commitment and are therefore 'doing a good job'. This is not enough and some attempts have to be made to 'appraise' the work done.

PERFORMANCE APPRAISAL, SUPERVISION AND GENERAL ACCOUNTABILITY

The term 'performance appraisal' normally refers to appraisal of the performance of individuals, not to appraisal of the organisation's goals and programs. There has been a great deal of discussion about the purpose and value of performance appraisal and we accept the importance of the individual emphasis and its value in enhancing the functioning of organisations. Although it is also possible to assess the effectiveness of a group, such as a Board or a group of staff, we will focus on individual performance appraisal at this stage.

Individual performance and the work of the organisation as a whole are interrelated in that individuals should be appraised within the framework of their role in the organisation. An organisation is accountable for the individual performance of its personnel as well as its stated organisational goals. Prisons are a particular example of the need for monitoring and performance appraisal of individual staff at all levels, especially prison officers. As well as maintaining security, prisons should have a stated goal of rehabilitation of prisoners. If prison officers are not trained appropriately in relation to rehabilitation and not assessed as to their performance in terms of the stated goals, then the prison is not carrying out its legitimate role.

Appraisal should also be distinguished from supervision. Performance appraisal is usually carried out at stated intervals and supervision is usually an ongoing process integrated into day-to-day practice. We will be looking at the wider context in chapter 9 (Program effectiveness), particularly where monitoring and evaluation are examined.

In addition, there has been a great deal of controversy in practice over whether the appraisal is solely developmental or whether it can be used for structural purposes, such as promotion and pay issues. In general, the emphasis is that appraisal is for accountability and assessment purposes, and the developmental factor is supplementary. The essential point is that staff should understand the purpose and that the structural role should not be hidden. In one organisation the support/developmental and non-threatening aspects were stressed and staff were angry when they realised that the appraisal affected their career prospects.

There are some philosophical and ideological questions involved, particularly in those small organisations that want to function in what they see as a less hierarchical and more democratic way. Such agencies may use peer review alone as a means of standard setting, or may develop a salary structure based on equality rather than function or qualifications. The essential point is that the agencies have to be consistent, they cannot function in what they see as a more 'democratic' way in some of their activities, but be hierarchical or authoritarian in other ways. In addition, there may be external demands placed on the organisation if funds are obtained from government sources.

Purposes of performance appraisal

In all organisations there must be accountability; appraisals are a necessary part of accountability in that they assess whether the performance of individuals is meeting the organisation's requirements. The general purposes of appraisals are:

- to ensure that individuals are performing agreed tasks in accordance with agreed standards
- to ensure that staff are performing their work requirements in accordance with the goals and priorities of the organisation
- to see whether the staff are maximising the results of training programs
- to provide an opportunity for individuals to review their own performance
- to provide an opportunity for individuals to identify their training and development needs and set goals for satisfying those needs
- to improve communication
- to increase work performance satisfaction
- to reward/praise staff.

Although performance appraisal usually refers to staff, the principle of individual accountability for performance should also be applicable to Board members and service volunteers.

Appraising the Board's performance

In the case of staff the tasks and expectations are usually laid down, but this is rarely done in the case of Board members for other than the Executive, even when Board members have been recruited and selected with a particular contribution in mind. Confusion about accountability, as distinct from general responsibility, is more noticeable in Boards, as is the issue of individual responsibility of Board members, particularly the executive or chairperson.

Appraisal is linked, therefore, to the question—who has the right to judge performance, a particular person or the Board as a whole? When a Board member is performing badly, even dangerously so, when decisions have to be made or when confidentiality issues arise, some Boards are hesitant to do anything about it for a variety or reasons, expressed in emotive statements such as: 'Their heart's in the right place'; 'It would be devastating to them not to be part of the Board any more'; 'They (or their family) set up the program and we can't reject them now'; 'They are putting so much money into the program, how would we manage without them'; 'They are so well known in the community that it would be bad for our image if they were not on the Board'.

Ideally, Boards should have the strength and objectivity to deal with these problems, with the overall good of the program and the service users as the basic goal. Even if rules about performance are drawn up they are probably ineffectual unless there are 'sanctions'. There is a general attitude that Board volunteers are hard to find and, because they are volunteers, the imposing of restrictions would work against filling the Board positions. There is also a reluctance to suggest that any Board member should be asked to leave.

It is possible, however, to devise some accepted performance standards for Boards and it should be possible for an organisation to apply the concept of accountability to Boards as well as staff. In reality compromises may be made but, if so, the group must minimise the dangers of the Board functioning less satisfactorily.

Some Boards have rules and regulations about one aspect of performing, that is, attendance at meetings. This appears to be the only one that is common to most Boards and it is rarely carried much further. However, it is possible to lay down some additional performance criteria, for example:

- attendance at meetings, that is, a designated minimum attendance without leave of absence
- membership of committees or task groups
- attendance at seminars, retreats and workshops
- submission of individual participation plans for each year.

Another problem facing Board members is in deciding on their differing responsibilities to their constituencies. Are they representatives or delegates?

As representatives, Board members are there to put a point of view which is 'representative' of the group that has nominated them. They do not have to report back automatically or to seek guidance on voting on all issues. (There have been cases where representatives put forward views with which members of their organisations have not agreed. This has to be sorted out between the member and their constituency.)

On the other hand, delegates are 'delegated' a specific role and must put the point of view which their organisation has instructed them to present and must vote appropriately. In small organisations members nominated by outside groups are usually representatives rather than delegates.

Confusion and conflict arise about judging peoples' performance in these roles unless it is clear what these roles are. Staff representatives or union representatives on Boards have special difficulties in sorting out their roles, firstly as a Board member and secondly as a representative of a group. There are philosophical and ideological issues involved, but there are also legal and organisational implications. Each organisation must clarify how its representative or delegate stands in relation to Board expectations. The Board has the final say as to whether it accepts delegates or representatives, and if the groups concerned are not happy with the Board's expectations they may not wish to have members of their group on the Board. On the other hand, the Board may want the contribution of certain members and may be willing to modify their expectations. The essential point is that the expectations must be clearly understood by all members and must be consistent.

Difficulties with performance appraisal in small agencies

There are several reasons why performance appraisals of staff in small agencies may be difficult:

- Closer personal contact creates a danger of over-personalising, which then means there is insufficient objectivity in assessing performance.
- Because of the small number of staff available to carry out programs, there is limited time to spend on activities other than the one-to-one contact with service users. The value of spending this time on appraisal and its contribution to service effectiveness is sometimes not recognised.
- The background information that needs to be available in the agency for performance appraisal and the recording time required are often not accorded sufficient priority.
- The increasingly popular technique of peer appraisal has problems when there are few peers available and where there are close staff interrelationships. These may result in over-personalising.

A summarised example from a small not-for-profit agency illustrates the difficulties of performance appraisal, the way one agency overcame these and the related benefits that arose from the exercise.

The Board decided that what it called a 'Staff Appraisal Review' should be carried out. Simple statistics had been

collected on service user contacts and visits, but it was recognised that they were insufficient for providing any idea of the *quality* of the work done. Also these figures did not give any indication of the variety of the tasks, such as community contacts and education.

A small group/task force was formed to look at ways in which a more satisfactory appraisal could be carried out. This group was made up of the three executive members of the Board.

It was soon realised that this group was too restricted. After some discussion the group was expanded to seven, and included two more interested members with some expertise or experience in the process, a service user who was also a member of the Board, and the senior staff member.

The agency had already identified its goals, objectives and strategic plan. The group (called a task force) then identified the agency's key activities, which were based on the goals, plans and so on.

The task force drew up a plan for assessing the standard of the work done on the tasks. The final result became the assessment instrument (referred to as 'the instrument'). The instrument consisted of a chart drawn up to show:

- the tasks required to carry out the key activities
- the personnel who would carry out these tasks, designating which staff and, if applicable, any Board members
- the expected outputs and outcomes of the tasks as identified by the task force.
- the processes required to measure both outputs and outcomes in terms of success
- the methods used to assess the quality of the above, including statistical measurements and graded assessments of quality
- the data required for the assessments to be made— records, diary recording, independent assessments and reporting—including service users' input.

As this exercise was initiated as a staff appraisal it concentrated on the staff tasks in the first stages. The intention of looking at the question of appraisal of Board members' contribution was expressed. During the process it was recognised that the agency records were not sufficient to provide the data necessary for the examination of the tasks. A hold was placed on the 'review' while the agency records themselves were reviewed and reassessed. This became a valuable exercise in itself and was carried out by the staff member and two others from the task force.

Issues that were revealed by this exercise were then addressed by the agency. They were the amount of time involved; the question of who would carry out the appraisal; the frequency; to whom the report would be made; the confidentiality of the process, particularly the results; and, finally, how the individual appraisal related to program appraisal.

Some consequences and conclusions drawn from the exercise were of particular importance.

- Individual performance appraisal cannot be separated from the rest of the agency's functioning. To ascertain whether individuals are 'doing a good job' their appraisal must be related to their role in the organisation and to the expectations of all the participants in the service delivery, including the funding body.
- Evaluation/assessment/appraisal must not be seen only in quantitative terms. Qualitative measures are possible and valid. Problems arise if attempts are made to use them in inappropriate aggregations or comparisons. Also, putting a figure to a vague, subjective or inaccurate measure does not make it 'objective'.[3]
- Although the first exercise may be time-consuming, once the instrument is completed the appraisal itself is not time-consuming, and becomes even less so as it is repeated.
- There were significant side benefits from the increased understanding of the whole of the agency's functioning. The people involved in the process described were volunteers, including the staff member who gave extra time.
- The development of a formalised process meant that appraisals would become a regular annual exercise that could also be used for development and support purposes.
- The quantitative elements were useful when used in conjunction with the details required by the funding body.
- As the process showed, the need to carry out performance and program appraisals helps to improve the general recording processes of the agency.

Service volunteers

The final group to be appraised, and in some ways as difficult as the Board appraisal, was that of the other volunteers, that is, the service volunteers.

Many agencies have excellent training programs for service volunteers but few have developed performance appraisal exercises or carry out individual monitoring or supervision. There seems to be a tendency to believe that because people are not paid they should not be assessed. But the issue of standards of service for the service user still needs to be addressed. Appraisal should be discussed when service volunteers are first appointed, so that it can be seen in a positive way as part of a program to ensure that they make their most effective contribution.

Even if there is some monitoring of performance, in most cases the particular program will be less elaborate than that provided for staff. Some agencies overcome the difficulties of attitudes by not using the words 'performance appraisal' or 'supervision' but speak of consultation and support. The latter are legitimate parts of the process but there are also accountability requirements that go beyond support. If volunteers are working with service users, often doing work that overlaps with the staff activities, there is the same responsibility to the service users. The staff structure issue of career promotion will not normally arise, although there are sometimes questions of volunteer 'seniority' and recognition of service.

Terminating the services of individuals

There is one final process that relates to the questions of appraisal, which has been touched on briefly, and that is the 'sacking' or termination of the services of an individual. As far as staff are concerned, there are award and industrial requirements that have to be addressed, particularly the complex area of 'unfair dismissal'.

There are also principles involved, no matter which individual is to leave the organisation. Terminating someone's services is different from redundancy, although the distinction is sometimes blurred. Various techniques such as re-structuring and 'spilling' positions are sometimes used to 'get rid of' one or two employees. This may mean hardship for many staff, which would not be necessary if the question of the fear of termination was openly addressed. Termination is a particularly stressful situation in not-for-profit and human service organisations. They are often expected to be more 'caring' and therefore less 'ruthless' and 'hard-headed', with the result that sometimes even incompetent members are 'carried'. Some general points need to be made.

- There is a reluctance to face this issue when the person is unpaid, but this cannot discount the importance of accountability and responsibility, no matter what role is played by the person.

- The ultimate goal of the best possible service to the service user has to prevail. If the person providing the service is harming the service user the decision is more clear-cut, but there is also the obligation to provide the best possible service. How far this should be weighed against the needs of the provider is a matter of balance that should be constantly re-examined.

- No decisions about termination should be made without a laid-down procedure that is known to all concerned. This includes the use of the probation period.

- All processes should be open and recorded. Appraisal, the use of supervision and mentoring are all aspects of the one overall process. Termination, if necessary, is part of that total process. They will reveal whether the person is intrinsically unable to do the work at a satisfactory standard or, for example, is influenced by circumstances, either structural or personal, that can be modified.

- Decisions need to be made as early as possible and as honestly as possible. People should not be faced with decisions 'out of the blue', or with dishonest and fudged reasons. If they have been in an organisation for many years they are justified in being angry to hear that their work is unsatisfactory if there are no records of this in the past. The lack of records is often one of the most significant factors in the managerial inability to deal with the problem of terminating an employee. This has been recognised in regulations now in place in some organisations, which prohibit the termination of employees unless there is evidence of a certain number of interviews, sometimes ambiguously called 'counselling sessions'. The records have to show that the employee understood that the work was unsatisfactory. Whether the interviews are part of the general appraisal system or prompted by a particular problem, they are an essential part of the termination process, and a protection for both the employee and the organisation.

CONCLUSION

The processes that we have described in this chapter often reveal problems that are preventing people in the agency achieving their greatest potential. Even with the best recruitment, selection, induction, orientation, training, development and monitoring programs, some problems and difficulties will arise.

Organisations are dynamic and constantly face stresses from both inside and outside. In the next chapter we will look at some of these obstacles to effective performance and at ways of overcoming them.

NOTES

1. Many of these points are drawn from the excellent set of guidelines provided in Popovich, I. (1995) *Managing Consultants*, Century/Random House, London.
2. Murray, M. (1991) *Beyond the Myths and Magic of Mentoring*, Jossey-Bass Publishers, San Francisco, page xiv.
3. For a very good discussion of these issues of measurement and the development of an organisationally appropriate appraisal style, see Brody, R. (1993) *Effectively Managing Human Service Organisations*, Sage, London.

5

OVERCOMING OBSTACLES TO EFFECTIVE PERFORMANCE

• *Time management* • *Meetings* • *Stress* • *Communication* • *Conclusion*

A visitor to an agency was surprised to see the staff in the tea room taking out notebooks and writing on them at various times during their conversations. Some acted as if they were enjoying a private joke, others were writing rather surreptitiously. He eventually asked what was happening and was told that it was a 'time study'.

The staff of the agency were recording their work activities as part of a study, which involved noting each activity as it changed, with no units of less than five minutes. They recorded the times, what the activity was, for example, an interview, meeting, informal conversation, phone call and so on. In addition, they recorded a brief description of the main purpose/content, such as 'Office interview with x to arrange referral to y for post-trauma counselling'. The period covered was one week and even in that short period staff became adept at providing succinct statements that were informative and often entertaining,

It was surprising how much information was obtained from the exercise and even those who had been sceptical were interested in the results. What appeared to be minor interactions turned out to be unexpectedly significant. The exercise showed, among other things, how much was achieved and how much support was given from informal contacts. It illustrated how important it was that staff should not be isolated in their own rooms and should take advantage of their interaction with others over cups of coffee/tea.

The final discussions were particularly valuable and staff became so involved that they suggested the exercise be repeated at different times of the year for comparison purposes, for example, the Christmas period. The essential factor in its success was that the exercise was in no way a 'control' one; it was not to 'check on people' individually but to gain information in general terms in order to improve the service. It was a matter of team cooperation. Other exercises, such as the keeping of time logs and diaries, would have a more individual emphasis and be part of monitoring.

Through performance appraisal and supervision it may become apparent that there are barriers to people's ability to maximise their performance in the organisation. These barriers may be organisational or individual, and will need quite different strategies to enable people to continue to work effectively. The following barriers will be discussed here:

- people's use of time
- people feeling that they are working under unacceptable levels of stress and that they are 'burned out'
- communication problems, which may be symptomatic of problems in interpersonal relations or in the structure of communication in the organisation.

TIME MANAGEMENT

Techniques for improving time management are harder to apply in small organisations than in large ones because they usually have to be developed by the individuals themselves. That is, it is a matter of self-management. The large organisation often provides a protective framework that ensures that the individual follows certain time-management practices. As an example, a larger organisation may set aside specific times for face-to-face contact with clients, that is, duty work, and establish guidelines which require reports to be written by certain dates and in certain ways. In addition, there are expectations about time allotments, such as service user workloads, as well as allotments to specific activities, such as requirements for the direct practice worker to spend time on community development.

In small organisations the decision regarding time allotments and workload control may be set by the Board, but often depends on the worker's own decisions, based on values, analytical ability and managerial skills. One of the major problems is that, in a small agency, the staff, (there may even be only one staff member in the organisation or branch) are trained as service deliverers then find they need 'managerial' skills. The response of that worker may be 'I serve my clients, I haven't got the time to meet the other demands such as recording and reporting', or 'I don't like making all these general decisions, I just want to do the best for each client'.

In the smaller organisation the excuse of immediacy and lack of time is often used, rather than recognition that the problem is one of time management. Where the agency is a 'crisis' one, that is, where the consumer is typically facing a crisis situation, the pressure for the worker also to function continually in 'crisis mode' is very strong.

Time management can be seen as involving two levels:

- the level that is influenced by values, priority and policy; one of the commonest examples is where there is a policy decision about the time given to community development as against individual service delivery
- the basic day-to-day time management techniques that affect the efficiency of the agency's working.

These two levels are different and workers who are competent in one may not be competent in the other. This is very significant in small organisations where the one worker may be responsible for both levels. Worker stress can be so high in this area that the situation of a lone worker—coping with service delivery, community contacts and Board interrelationships—should always be avoided. Such a situation needs at least two workers so that there can be some division of tasks and colleague support.

There is a large amount of literature about day-to-day time management techniques and endless brochures, modules, video-tapes, training programs, workshops and seminars. The authors have found however, that the most valuable learning experience is hands-on. What the wealth of material does indicate is that time management is perceived to be a problem by many practitioners and managers and many are seeking quick solutions.

It is rather like being overweight and constantly searching for the diet that works. Like dieting, overcoming time management problems is most often a matter of discipline and willpower, although people tend to blame factors outside themselves or beyond their control. This does not mean that there are never situations beyond the individual's control, but the effort has to be made to find out the causes of time management problems, and separate out the different techniques for different causes. Some particular issues related to small not-for-profit organisations are:

- As the 'product' of a human service organisation is not an inanimate object, time management has an extra element of unpredictability.
- Emotions are involved in human service delivery and therefore it is more difficult to impose time constraints (as in a crisis agency).

In spite of these factors some attempt has to be made to manage time. A few ways of doing this are as follows:

1. Keep a time log and carry out a time study of designated periods. Some professions, of necessity, keep a time log permanently, for example, to assess costs for different contracts. If that is not possible, certain periods should be covered.
2. Conduct a time analysis to find out what are the time-consuming tasks.
3. Further analyse the time log to see whether the time priorities are dictated by the worker's preferences or the consumers' needs. Keep records of the results.
4. Start the day with a list of prioritised tasks. At least 15 minutes could be dedicated to sorting this out. Some prefer to do this at the end of the day in readiness for the next day, but doing it when one is fresh is preferable if possible. Any task not completed goes automatically onto the next day's list.
5. Use a year planner for major, regular tasks. A colour code for priorities and urgencies is valuable.

This is a relatively simple list. There are refinements, for example, extra categories could include:

- whether a task could have been delegated
- the source of the task—where the work comes from—to see whether the source could be controlled by channelling referrals in certain circumstances.

Many workers would say that they must give priority to the service user and therefore don't have time to carry out any time analysis. It is surprising, however, how much can be done once it has been practised. Some of these activities were carried out successfully in the following example.

One agency where the stress level on the overworked staff was causing concern, there had been a belief that nothing could be done: 'that's the way our agency is'. Apart from the techniques above, staff analysed why they treated certain situations as a crisis, the possibility of shortening the hours when staff were available and providing a 'buffer zone'. It was finally accepted that such activities were not a betrayal of the service user and would benefit them in the end in the quality of the service given.

MEETINGS

The title of the well-known training video made by John Cleese, *Meetings, Bloody Meetings*, says it all. Many of the complaints about the 'waste of time' are directed at the time spent on 'meetings' or group activities of various kinds. One agency complained that every time it rang another agency the staff 'were having a meeting—when do they do any work?'. The meeting times were seen as unrelated or peripheral to the concept of 'work'.

A meeting is a gathering of two or more persons and may vary from small informal groups through to structured and formal situations. No matter what the group or the purpose of the meeting, 'rules' and expectations of behaviour develop. In certain circumstances these are enshrined in regulations or are required by law. Our concern here is not to delve into the detail of meeting procedures but to consider some ways to improve the use of meetings.[1]

Purposes of organisational meetings

There are a number of purposes of meetings, including:

- fulfilment of legal requirements, for example, in relation to Annual General Meetings, elections and so on
- for ongoing management or governance of an organisation

- to achieve a specific task
- to provide support, development and training.

We do not add 'for therapeutic purposes' as this is not the usual situation. It is also arguable whether such group meetings should take place within the organisation or should be referred out, for example, in the case of therapeutic meetings dealing with alcoholism.

The essential factor in every meeting is that the *purpose* must be clear and open and must be kept in mind at all times. It must be clear, for example, whether or not a particular meeting has the power to make decisions or recommendations and where and how these will be acted on.

The importance of particular values for volunteers is not always acknowledged as legitimate by agencies. Meetings often have an additional significance for volunteers. There are instrumental purposes such as increasing knowledge and using the volunteer's community input. In addition there are expressive purposes such as providing an opportunity for social interaction among the volunteers. Service volunteers in particular may feel isolated from the organisation and meetings are a way of reinforcing their connection to and providing an additional link with the organisation. The different purposes often mean that trying to combine them in the one meeting causes confusion and conflict.

One agency had a Case Committee, consisting of 'community' volunteers from outside the agency. The committee met monthly to discuss 'problem cases' and to make recommendations about aspects of future case planning. These meetings required a great deal of preparation, including administrative and clerical time, as well as the time of the case workers. This involvement was resented by staff who felt they spent a great deal of their time 'talking about what they were doing', when they should be 'getting on with their job'. They resented that people coming in for one discussion a month should be able to say how the professionals should act. The committee members were very positive about the committee as they said it helped them understand the work of the agency, and they felt they could make a contribution. When the conflict finally became obvious and dysfunctional, the agency brought in a consultant/facilitator to help the committee and other groups involved to clarify the purposes of the committee and the different expectations of the groups. The negatives and the benefits were analysed and various options drawn up that would maximise the benefits and minimise the problems.

Maximising the value of meeting time

Constant analysis and monitoring

There should be constant analysis of the meeting patterns to decide whether they are necessary and warrant the time involved. Are they achieving their purpose(s)? Are there alternatives? The purpose must be the group purpose, for example, it must not be for the personal benefit and support of one or two members.

Competent leadership

Whether it is a chairperson, a convener or a facilitator, someone must be responsible for leading the meeting processes. A leaderless group will develop its own power structure and, if it is not formalised, dominant members may covertly and inappropriately control the group. Some groups like to rotate the role of chairperson in order to develop the members and to be more 'democratic'. This is only suitable in some circumstances and should be carefully examined. Is the development of individual members the prime purpose of the group? Does this purpose outweigh the need to have skilled and focused chairing, and to achieve specific tasks?

In the case of more formal groups, at least, it is essential to have continuity in the chairperson's role and the success of such groups depends to a great extent on the chairperson's competence. It is also necessary to recognise that different skills are needed for different chairing roles, and a person who is used to informal group processes may be the wrong person to lead a task-oriented organisational meeting. There often seems to be a reluctance to accept that poor chairing is a serious problem that needs to be addressed. Some people want the power or status of the chairperson or president role without recognising the competencies that are required, including skill in handling meetings.

Recording and handling material

There is some reluctance and suspicion on the part of small groups towards the recording of details of meetings. It is feared that spontaneity will be lost and that it is a waste of time.

A staff group said that it did not want its meetings recorded. One member said that she accepted that there should not be any group records, if that was the group decision, but that she found it difficult to function without any record and asked permission to take her own notes. After a few sessions there was a disagreement about a past discussion and the member was asked what she had recorded. After a few more weeks and more instances of referring back to the member's notes, the group decided that there were advantages in having the meetings recorded and minutes were taken from then on.

Minute taking is a very important skill and the records can be used to enhance the working of the group, for example, by setting aside a column for 'action to be taken'. If the minutes are to be of value in this way they need to be circulated as soon as possible after the meeting, not at the last minute before the next meeting. Some organisations tape meetings and this can be invaluable if used correctly. It is not a substitute for minute taking and is only used for back-up purposes, for example if there is a query about a minute. It can also assist the chairperson in understanding the group process. There needs to be agreement about the keeping of any of the taped records and about their use.

Another use of minutes can be the insight they give about general issues and also the processes that lie behind the decisions. This can have a number of benefits, such as:

* ensuring continuity in the decision-making patterns;
* increasing the understanding of new members about the reasons for past decisions;
* providing information for planning, reviews and consultancies.

If there are varied uses and the minute taking goes beyond the simple record of the final decision or motion, special skills are required which include writing and persenting skills and the ability to summarise, as well as an understanding of process. In certain circumstances minute taking can be used to help clarify what is happening. In one agency the person taking the minutes would ask for clarification or verification of a point and this questioning helped the group to be clear about what they really wanted. Although this might seem to be taking over the chairperson's role it can be a support to the chairperson.

The circulation of material and the devising of an agenda are tools in making meetings as productive as possible. One Board asked that any member who wanted an item put on the agenda should do so well before the meeting time and should also provide a summary of the reasons for asking for the item to be included. In the same way there are systems of 'starring' items, or grouping items, so that they can be given priority. The spending of a disproportionate amount of time on insignificant matters is a familiar problem and the system of allotting time to certain topics can be useful. One organisation that did this ruled that the allotted time could only be exceeded if requested by a member and approved by the group. Such a request could not be debated, only approved or otherwise.

Staff meetings

Staff meetings deserve special attention as they are another user of time but are also very important in enhancing the functioning of the organisation. Face-to-face communication has much more value than written memos and allows for interaction and feedback. If they are planned carefully, staff meetings have value in increasing communication, sharing ideas, improving service delivery and providing group support. If they develop into complaints sessions or are tense and conflictual, they will be of little value and this should be avoided wherever possible. Another danger is that they become one-way, with the chairperson, such as the senior member, using the time to convey information 'downwards' and not listening to the communication 'upwards'.

Annual General Meetings

Annual General Meetings (AGMs) are laid down in constitutions and vary in their benefits. The comments that have been made about other meetings also hold, that is, the need for planning, and competent chairing. AGMs can also be useful for communicating with those outside the agency, such as the general community and the stakeholders.

AGMs are an occasion when some formality needs to be accepted. There have been situations where the lack of basic knowledge of meeting procedures, or of relevant legislation, has had serious negative effects on the decisions made. One organisation, for example, passed a constitutional change by a simple majority when a two-thirds majority was required.

The time spent on meetings should not be seen as an alternative to time spent on other aspects of the agency's functioning, such as service delivery. They are all of importance. One member of a group added up the time spent at a meeting, looked at the salaries of the staff concerned and said, 'This meeting is costing $x'. This was an incorrect statement. The salary was paid in any case and the cost was an *opportunity cost* in that it 'cost' the time away from other activities that may or may not have been of more value to the organisation. If overtime were involved then that part of the time would be a dollar cost.

STRESS

Another obstacle to the most effective performance of people in organisations is the negative influence of stress. It may originate with, or be exacerbated by, factors relating to any or all of the following:

- the personality or personal circumstances of the staff member
- aspects of management practice
- the organisational structure and the political/policy context

Burnout and dysfunctional rates of staff turnover are two of the consequences of stress. This is not to suggest that stress is always harmful and it is part of the manager's analytical skill to differentiate between stress that may even be stimulating (sometimes defined as pressure) and stress that is harmful either to the individual or the organisation (sometimes defined as strain).

There is a danger in some organisations of equating the lack of stress and conflict as a sign of a healthy organisation, when in reality it may be apathetic and functioning well below its potential. On the other hand, there are those who see conflict and stress as necessary and never negative. Some consultants have deliberately generated stress and conflict because they believe they are of value in themselves. Such tactics are part of turbulence, chaos or conflict theories.

Personal factors

Interrelationships in small organisations are of a more intense nature than those in large ones and people are often expected to engage with one another as personalities rather than through the organisational roles that they occupy. This creates greater stress if there is friction in the relationships. When relationships become more personalised, organisational actions, such as approval of leave, may be interpreted as personal approval or disapproval.

Traits that can be accommodated in the larger organisation, such as insecurity or the need for privacy, will be challenged in the small organisation.

Managerial factors

There are a number of managerial characteristics required which, if lacking, can create stress. These include the following:

- *Consistency.* This is one of the most important requirements. Staff will often manage to cope with decision making, relationship patterns and communications that are not necessarily ideal or popular—as long as they are consistent. It is the uncertainty of inconsistency that is particularly stressful.
- *Clarity.* Insecurity and stress are heightened when decision making is not clear. Organisations talk increasingly of the need for 'transparency' of their processes, particularly decision making, where those affected by decisions want to know both the 'who' and the 'why' of decision making.
- *Understanding staff needs.* Without an ability to understand staff needs, they will not be met because they will simply not be recognised.
- *Sensitivity to signs of stress.* If the managerial characteristics noted above—consistency, clarity and understanding staff needs—are lacking, then it is unlikely that signs of stress will be picked up by the manager or recognised for what they are.

Organisational factors

Unclear organisational roles can create stress. 'We are all a team, there is no-one in charge' is a misguided philosophy that can cause confusion when organisational decisions (particularly difficult ones, such as budget cuts) have to be made.

Less secure or more competitive funding arrangements can heighten uncertainties. Examples can be seen where organisations have to bid for funding in competition with their colleagues in other organisations, often to carry out their core business.

Agencies are also finding it difficult to adjust to functioning in a more complex policy environment. Constant changes and lack of consistency in funding authorities due to policy, legislation and organisational reviews have created a climate of uncertainty.

Recognising burnout

Burnout is a consequence of stress and is a complex phenomenon. Analysis and recognition of both its causes and consequences are necessary if the impact of burnout is to be handled appropriately. Among other things, it is important to recognise whether burnout is caused by personal factors outside the work situation or by factors within the organisation, such as the type of work, organisational patterns and the speed of change. These are not necessarily separated, and burnout can be caused by the interaction of each set of factors with the other.

The term 'job burnout' is often used when the cause lies in the workplace. In addition, personal burnout, though caused by outside factors, may still have organisational consequences.

Burnout is often expressed by:

- emotional exhaustion, cynicism and apathy
- alienation, expressed as a feeling of not being connected to other workers and service users
- over-involvement, rather than withdrawal or alienation, may be an indicator of burnout in some workers, as indicated in recent studies in health-related areas such as AIDS
- low self-esteem, particularly about the value of one's work contribution
- feeling of a lack of control in the work environment
- a range of physical symptoms, such as lingering minor illnesses; gastrointestinal disturbances; behavioural symptoms such as irritability and increased alcohol use; and cognitive/affective symptoms, such as indecision, inattention and depression.

The organisational consequences of burnout are:

- deterioration in individual work performance
- low morale of the individual which may then spread to other staff
- a general climate of distrust and repressed conflict, particularly if a number of staff are suffering from burnout from organisational causes
- high staff turnover.

Origins of stress

People experience stress, such as bereavement and marital conflict, in their personal lives. The issue is whether these affect people in their work situation. The difficulty is in recognising whether the precipitating factors of stress are in fact personal or are related to the work itself, such as work overload and stressful supervision. One danger is that work-related causes may be denied by management with a consequent 'blaming of the victim'.

The stresses faced by lone workers have already been mentioned. Unfortunately there are also circumstances where the 'victim' may not feel able to acknowledge an organisational cause because of fears of being penalised or not believed, and may identify their stress as 'personal'. This often happens in situations of supervisory conflict and sexual harassment. A less recognised projection can occur with work overload, where workers do not want management to think that they are incompetent if they cannot cope.

There are at least three types of job-caused stress and the distinction is significant when the question of dealing with the consequences is addressed. Stress can occur when:

- the nature of the work itself is stressful, such as in child protection and working with the terminally ill.
- the person doing the job is working under an additional burden because they do not have the skills necessary to do the particular job. This lack of competence may be transitory; the work might have changed but people have not had a chance to be re-skilled for the new tasks. It may, however, be more permanent, for example, in cases where the wrong level of staff appointment was made.
- there are organisational factors independent of stress caused by the *type* of work, as mentioned earlier. These are variable, such as work overload, poor working conditions or monotonous and repetitive work.

Dealing with stress and burnout

The approach to handling burnout will depend on what has caused it. If the cause is job related, either intrinsic or consequential, then it is important to do something about the job situation. If the cause is personal and external to the organisation, there is controversy about the extent to which the organisation is responsible for dealing with such causes or whether the problem should be referred on, for example, by providing marriage guidance. In small organisations it is difficult to refer such matters on, and there is strong temptation to deal with the cause on a personal basis within the organisation.

114

Much advice is available on how to alter the job situation through work redesign, provide more information and sign up for stress management programs. These include techniques for the individual as well as many group interventions for managing and alleviating stress. There is a danger that, because so much information is available about individualised approaches, there will be a temptation to concentrate on the symptoms rather than dealing with organisational causes. Such causes are often more difficult, time-consuming and expensive to deal with.

Table 5.1 details a number of models for managing stress in staff, including professional supervision, emotional support or counselling, stress reduction activities and the management of the work context. It is important to note that the choice of model will depend on the culture of the organisation as well as on the nature of the problems. A stress reduction approach that is entirely foreign to the workers and to the usual functioning of the organisation may be met with scepticism or, even worse, become a source of stress in itself.

Methods for manipulating the context in which people work are noted in table 5.2. Some of these, such as discouraging people from working alone or in isolation, may not be possible to implement for practical reasons, for example, in the case of a single worker agency, and equivalents will need to be found. It may be possible to encourage the worker to identify a group of peers from other small organisations, to use as a support group. Similarly, it may not be possible, in the small organisation with limited staff resources, to vary the type of work that people do, if that work is stressful. In these cases it is important to work out what is an acceptable workload to minimise stress.

COMMUNICATION

Communication problems are often symptomatic of other problems in organisations although they can also be problems in their own right. Where communication problems exist they can seriously impede people in organisations, at whatever level they work, from performing effectively. It is sometimes assumed that there will be fewer problems of communication in small organisations, but geographical and physical proximity are not necessarily factors that prevent communication problems.

Table 5.1 Models for staff stress management and prevention

	1. Professional supervision	2. Emotional support/ therapeutic counselling	3. Stress reduction/ management	4. Context management
Facilitator	External or internal	External or internal	External or internal	Not applicable
Nature	Individual or group ('team')	Individual or group ('team')	Individual or group ('team')	See below
Regularity	Regular or irregular (on demand)	Regular or irregular (on demand)	Regular or irregular (on demand)	Continuous
Duration	Ongoing	Ongoing or limited duration (e.g. crisis management)	Ongoing or limited duration (e.g. crisis management)	Continuous
Frequency	Weekly, fortnightly or monthly	Weekly, fortnightly or monthly, or on request	Weekly, fortnightly or monthly, or on request	Not applicable
Composition	Same or mixed professions	Same or mixed professions for groups	Same or mixed professions for groups	Applies to all staff
Content	Case review, professional monitoring, Skills assessment	Ventilation, emotional support, team-building and restoration	Relaxation strategies, including meditation, visualisation, massage, shiatsu and exercise, seminars and classes in, for example, time management, team-building, and so on.	See table 5.2

Source: D. Miller (1995) 'Models of Management for Occupational Morbidity and Burnout', in L. Bennett, D. Miller and M. Ross (eds) *Health Workers and AIDS: Research Intervention and Current Issues in Burnout and Response*, Harwood Academic Publishers, Switzerland, p. 183.

Table 5.2 Context management for prevention of staff stress

Procedural/structural initiatives	Environmental initiatives
Limiting working hours	Normalising the experience and expression of work-related stress
Providing pre-work orientation and training and on-going staff development	Recognising the impact of the particular sort of work done, such as multiple loss, or domestic violence
Enabling expression of work successes	Providing opportunities for skills development
Training in stress recognition and management	Providing a work space where staff can relax
Enabling work variation	Providing a pleasant work environment
Discouraging working alone	Actively encouraging that holidays be taken
Planning time away from work	

Source: D. Miller (1995) 'Models of Management for Occupational Morbidity and Burnout', in L. Bennett, D. Miller and M. Ross (eds) *Health Workers and AIDS: Research in Intervention and Current Issues in Burnout and Response*, Harwood Academic Publishers, Switzerland, p. 186.

Factors affecting messages

If communication is understood as interaction that conveys a message from a sender to a receiver, then a large number of influences on this process can be identified.

Medium or channel

Messages can be verbal, written, physical or non-physical. The medium of communication can be as varied as the environment itself. The medium can include face-to-face communication, whether verbal or non-verbal, through to more distant communication that requires a whole range of technical channels, such as phones, faxes and satellites. All these variations have a major effect on the message. In small organisations verbal communication is used more frequently but this can result in confusion if messages are not confirmed in writing. 'But you said . . .' and 'No, I didn't' are familiar refrains.

Intent

A message may be sent unintentionally or unconsciously by someone, who may be quite surprised that a message has been perceived and has had an interpretation placed on it. For example, some body language could be interpreted as hostile or aggressive when this was not the intention of the sender (even unconsciously).

Distortion or 'noise'

There may be gender or cultural differences that distort people's perceptions of each other. The different cultures may be ethnic in origin or may be group or organisational cultures. People moving from one cultural pattern to another need to recognise the differences and learn how to accommodate these differences if they are to communicate effectively in the new setting.

Accuracy checking

In order to verify that a message has been received accurately there is a range of methods, such as feedback techniques and duplication of channels, and what are often called 'fail-safe devices'. This is one of the most important features of communication yet small organisations in particular neglect to set up proper techniques, believing that their smallness makes it unnecessary.

The dilemma in communication is to achieve a balance between efficiency and effectiveness. In order to make sure the message is received two channels may be used, such as verbal with confirmation in writing. In addition, formal or informal confirmation and feedback may be required. In sheer efficiency terms this may be uneconomic but can provide a safeguard for effectiveness. The more significant the message in terms of consequences, the more safeguards should be built in. This is particularly relevant in the human services area where lives may depend not only on the communication being precise and timely but also on it being clearly understood. This holds whether the organisation is small or large, but seems to be more accepted in the larger organisation, sometimes being seen as unnecessarily 'bureaucratic' and time-wasting in the small agency.

Communication patterns

There are two major patterns of communication in human service organisations which may interact but which have some specific characteristics:

- communication external to the organisation, such as that between
  — service users and service providers
  — the organisation and other organisations
  — the organisation and the community to which it relates, whether this is a community of people with a specific interest or a geographic community
  — the organisation and the political structure, including its government funding source
- intra-organisational communication, such as that between:
  — management and staff
  — staff and Board of management
  — staff members (e.g. within peer groups) and paid and unpaid staff
  — service users and other personnel.

We will concentrate here on the latter group of communications, by identifying some common communication problems and how to handle them.

The complexity of the relationship between communication problems and human resource management more generally can be seen in attempts to identify what is cause and what is effect.

In one organisation, the authors were brought in with a brief to examine communication and 'personnel practices' in the light of a series of personnel problems, including high levels of staff turnover in particular sections and explicit conflict between the Board and staff. It soon became apparent that poor communication was not the core of the problem but a symptom of a wide range of personnel problems, such as lack of role clarity, and fundamental differences in perceptions of goals and aims between members of the organisation.

Another organisation also saw its difficulties as due to poor communication and the consultant decided to commence with an exercise that required the staff to draw up a communication chart. The wide divergence in staff perceptions of the communication is shown in figures 5.1 and 5.2. They illustrate two extremes in staff perceptions. The first is very brief and showed that the particular staff member was thinking in simple hierarchical terms. The lack of reference to communication upwards was significant. The second example was much more complex and

Figure 5.1

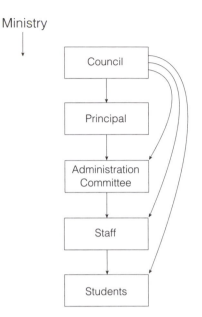

illustrated a more sophisticated understanding of the organisation's communication interactions.

Analysis of all the staff charts revealed major differences in perception.

- Some staff showed the communication as hierarchical, with varied views as to the relative positions.
- Some drew the pattern as a circle, again with varied views as to who was in the centre. The placing by one participant of an administrative staff member in the centre was significant and was accompanied with the comment that this was an inappropriate position.
- Some groups or individuals outside the staff group were not included or were seen as peripheral. This was illustrated by the varied positions allotted to unions, students, parents, and the Council.

The charts were accompanied by comments and the material was discussed in a number of meetings. Finally, suggestions and recommendations about the various levels of communication were made, as well as comments on some of the other organisational aspects that were revealed by the exercise.

Figure 5.2

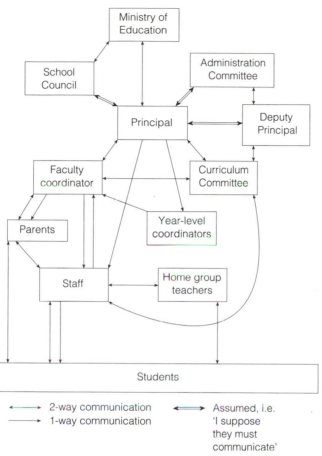

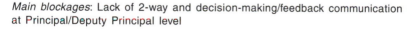

Main blockages: Lack of 2-way and decision-making/feedback communication at Principal/Deputy Principal level

Roles and communication

Sometimes people know to whom they report but are not made sufficiently aware of what that person needs to know. In addition, skills in communication are necessary in order to suit the purpose and the particular characteristics of the person or group that is the receiver. This means that the sender must try to become familiar with the receiver or target. This is one of the most neglected processes, perhaps because it is often the most difficult part of the communication cycle.

Problems can arise when the purpose of the communication is not clear and therefore those involved in the process may not fulfil their roles. As an example, if the sender sees the receiver as having a role in decision making there will be frustration and misunderstanding if the receiver merely regards the message as for information purposes only. If it is not clear that action is expected, the sender can become angry because nothing was done about the information.

Communication between staff and Board

A number of problems can arise if communication is poor between Boards and staff. Suspicion, fear and insecurity can result when either group is unaware of, or unclear about, both the intent and content of what each is doing. Very often the tendency is for each group to think that it is the other group that is not communicating.

Distortions of practice can occur if staff do not carry out the policy intent of a Board because this intent has not been conveyed clearly to the staff. This may result from Boards not understanding sufficiently how their policy may be made operational. Failure on the part of the staff may be perceived by the Board as deliberate intransigence, rather than a result of poor communication or confusion. Obviously this situation will be worse if there are other relationship problems between Boards and staff.

Lack of skill and knowledge of communication techniques on the part of both Board and staff can cause errors in judging what the content of the communication should be and when is the most appropriate time for that communication to be effective. We often hear 'You should have told us earlier' or 'If only you had explained more' in defence of something perceived as resistance or incompetence.

Intra-staff communication

When the management style is authoritarian, communication may be limited and information not shared because of fear on the part of management that it will lessen its power. In addition, communication may be limited by a lack of encouragement of anything other than top–down communication. Communication techniques should be a vital part of any manager's repertoire of skills and managers who lack these skills will not be able to maximise either their own or other staff's potential.

Problems in communication between peers may include:

- not sharing information on resources and skills. This could be brought about, for example, when there is no climate of cooperation in the organisation. This can also reflect staff members' lack of skill in communication rather than any negative intent.
- not informing colleagues about what they are doing because of a fear of others encroaching on their areas of responsibility, that is, a territorial issue.

Communication and gender differences

A particularly important aspect of communication is gender difference in style.[2] These differences are not uniform—for example, when people of the same occupational group are communicating professionally, particularly in technical terms, differences would not be evident. However, gender can influence the general way of presenting ideas, orientations towards problem sharing, listening and working style.

Presenting ideas

Very often, through socialisation as children and reinforced by school and adult experiences, women learn that they are more 'acceptable' if they frame their ideas as suggestions and downplay their certainty. Men, on the other hand, learn to downplay their doubts so as not to appear weak and indecisive, particularly when they are in a leadership role. In this way, women's ideas may not be given the credence that men's ideas are, because it is wrongly believed that they are more tentative and less thought-through than they really are.

Problem sharing

Women tend to talk to each other more, particularly about problems, not just to find a solution as men tend to, but as a way of sharing and developing relationships between the group. Men's tendency to share problems only when they want solutions means that they may miss out on some of the benefits of consultation that could help them, in some cases, frame the problem differently. Women's tendency to share problems in the workplace may mean that they are seen as having more problems than men, and also that they are incapable of solving these problems themselves. It is important that this sort of labelling does not happen.

Listening

Men and women tend to listen differently. Men tend to listen to the surface material, that is, the facts and opinions, whereas women will pick up on the 'feeling' aspect of the communication as well. In addition, women tend to be more active listeners, giving a lot of feedback to the person to whom they are talking. Men tend to be more passive as listeners. One problem with this is that, when men talk to women, they may misinterpret women's encouragement of the speaker as agreement.

Working styles

Men will often adopt an oppositional style in presenting arguments, whereas women will work on building rapport with colleagues and may feel alienated from what they see as an unnecessarily aggressive way of behaving on the part of male colleagues.

Many of the problems identified above can be dealt with if the reasons for different communication patterns are understood, and allowance and respect for the differences are built in to the way the organisation does business.

Working towards clear written communication

Recognising that a lot of communication takes place via memos, policy and procedure manuals, e-mails, file notes and letters, it is important that written communication is clear and unambiguous. Below is a checklist designed to help enhance written communication.[3]

You must know:	*Before you begin to write make sure that you:*
your subject	(a) Have a clear understanding of the subject
your reason for writing	(b) Know why you are writing—what does your correspondent want to know and why do they want to know it?
your reader	(c) Adapt your style and the content to suit your correspondent's needs and their present knowledge of the subject.
You must be:	*When writing you should:*
clear	(a) Make your meaning clear; arrange the subject in logical order; be grammatically correct; do not include irrelevant material.

124

simple and brief	(b) Use the most simple direct language; avoid obscure words and phrases, unnecessary words, long sentences; avoid technical or legal terms and abbreviations unless you are sure that they will be understood by the reader; be as brief as possible; avoid 'padding'.
accurate and complete	(c) Be as accurate and complete as possible
polite and human	(d) In your letters to the public be sympathetic if your correspondent is troubled; be particularly polite if they are rude; be lucid and helpful if they are muddled; be patient if they are stubborn; be appreciative if they are helpful; and never be patronising.
prompt	(e) Answer promptly, sending acknow-ledgements or interim replies if necessary—delays harm the reputation of the agency, and are discourteous.

Check your writing:	*Look critically at your written work. Can you answer 'yes' to the following questions about it?*
is it clear?	(a) Can the language be easily understood by the recipient?
	(b) Is it free of slang?
	(c) Are the words the simplest that can carry the thought?
	(d) Is the sentence structure clear?
is it simple and brief?	(a) Does it give only the essential facts?
	(b) Does it include only essential words and phrases?
is it accurate?	(a) Is the information correct?
	(b) Do the statements conform with rules, policy etc.?
	(c) Is the writing free of errors in grammar, spelling and punctuation?
is it complete?	(a) Does it give all the necessary information?
	(b) Does it answer all the questions?
is it human?	(a) Is the writing free of antagonistic words and phrases?

(b) Is it, where appropriate, tactful, helpful, courteous, sympathetic, frank, forceful?
(c) Will the tone bring the desired response?

CONCLUSION

This chapter has covered a number of obstacles to effective management with some suggestions about ways of overcoming them. One of the major obstacles we have yet to cover is poor financial management. Although some may be reluctant to admit it, money is of paramount importance in the survival of an organisation. No matter how much the service users need the particular program, and no matter how committed the service providers, the agency and its programs will not survive if it is not financially viable. The next chapter deals with the much-feared area of financial management.

NOTES

1. There are a number of books about meeting procedures, tailored to different situations. Probably the most useful for the small Australian not-for-profit organisation is Renton, N.E. (1994) *Guide for Meetings and Organisations*, sixth edition, The Law Book Company Limited, Sydney.
2. This material is based on a valuable article by Zanetic S. and Jeffrey C. (1997) 'Understanding the Other Half of the Workplace' *HR Monthly*, May.
3. Every attempt has been made to locate the source and holder of copyright for this material. Could the holder of copyright please contact the publishers.

6

FINANCIAL MANAGEMENT

• Interrelationship of strands of financial management • Obtaining funds • Budgeting and costing • Conclusion

A not-for-profit organisation began to find its traditional funding sources no longer sufficient to maintain its programs, but at the last moment it received a substantial bequest. The organisation decided not to change its planning but to use the extra money to continue to carry on its programs as before. In a few years the same problems arose and at that time a special request was made to the government for extra funding. To the surprise of some other organisations, the agency was granted special funding, although it was made clear that this money was a one-off grant and was mainly earmarked for a special program. This program had been used as an argument for the importance of the work of the agency.

Shortly afterwards the executive officer left to go to another position. The new executive officer realised that the finances were in a dangerous state and began to institute new systems, based on generally accepted management practices, to try to rectify the situation. These were seen by some members of the Board, and some staff members, as a 'new broom' trying to be assertive and as a personal attack on the previous executive officer. Some members of the Board had strong personal ties with the previous officer, and also tended to speak of the agency as 'our agency'.

The changes cut across many well-established patterns and privileges, and revealed poor recording practices. As one example, expensive equipment that was used in private homes was regarded by some staff as their own property, though it was recorded as central office equipment.

Eventually the agency had to restructure completely to survive; there was a significant turnover of staff, and some bitterness, not only within the agency but also in the wider community. There was only limited acceptance of the real causes of the problem, which dated back to many years before the new executive officer was appointed.

The previous chapter dealt with aspects that concerned people, but people and resources are closely interrelated. Competent handling of budgeting, costing and financial management is dependent on people and it is therefore dependent on effective recruiting, selecting and training of personnel. In addition, if resources are not sufficient to provide an effective service, then competence and commitment by themselves are not enough. Poor physical resources, such as inadequate equipment or an unsatisfactory work environment, will have negative effects on both the service provided and the morale of the service providers. These latter aspects are discussed further in chapter 7, 'Office and physical resource management'.

This chapter discusses the management activities and techniques that are necessary to acquire funds and disburse them, and some of the issues associated with tendering and contracting. One of the problems of small organisations is that there is often a lack of personnel with financial expertise and the mishandling of funds can be a source of concern. Funding bodies are now recognising this, and talking in terms of accountability. The problem is that the ways and mechanics of the accountability processes are often inappropriate or inadequate and this causes friction between the funding body and the recipient.

INTERRELATIONSHIP OF STRANDS OF FINANCIAL MANAGEMENT

Although the elements of financial management are interrelated, some have been separated for the purposes of discussion in this chapter. Costing and budgeting are given particular attention but they are only part of the financial processes that are important in the smooth functioning of an organisation, no matter how small. An accountant commented, 'the large organisation may have an extra $000 000 added to its budget figures, but the principles are the same'.

Some of the complex financial patterns of large organisations are not appropriate for small agencies, but this does not mean that care need not be taken in the handling of smaller amounts of money. Financial management is part of the total management of the agency and, where the staff are small in number, the executive officer/general manager often has major responsibility for both financial and general management.

Even if executive officers are not familiar with the skills needed to 'keep the books', the Board, including the executive officer, has overall responsibility for the financial health of the agency. This may mean bringing in personnel from outside to help with specific tasks. There will be various degrees of delegation according to different levels of skill, but the Board is the part of the agency with the ultimate responsibility for the governance of the agency, including the financial responsibilities. The question of the various role responsibilities has been discussed previously, but financial responsibility seems to be the area about which the most fear is expressed by the average person who joins the not-for-profit organisation. In contrast, Board members of business organisations rarely admit to being ignorant about financial matters.

Although the technical procedures will vary from agency to agency, one of the major financial concerns causing many difficulties is the increased scarcity of funds.

An agency head commented that she thought she was supposed to be concerned about improving the services of the agency and its general management, but she seemed to spend all her time trying to find new sources of funds. 'They want a fundraiser, not a manager' was her complaint and there was some evidence that her reputed fundraising success in her last job had been a significant factor in her recruitment. This was unfortunate, as she had changed jobs to avoid the fundraising emphasis. It was interesting that neither the Board expectations in this area nor the executive officer's feelings about it surfaced in the selection process.

Unlike a business firm, the sources of funds in the not-for-profit agency are usually fixed for either specific or indefinite periods. The service users/customers and 'the market' are not usually a major source of funds in human service agencies. This is changing because of new demands for user-pays services but it is an unfamiliar area for many agencies. A major source has been government funding and in the past such funding was fairly steady, once funds were granted. If the agency received funding in one year it was fairly sure that this would be continued until the agency applied for more funds, for example for new projects. If there was a cut in funds this created trauma and concern. With the increased funding for specific projects rather than core grants and with contracts, time-limited funds and tendering, the uncertainties have placed agencies in different territory. The changes require skills in handling uncertainty, in forecasting and planning, and in making applications for funds. These challenges are new to many who have been working in the human services area for many years.

The difficulties faced by agencies in adjusting to the changes are graphically illustrated in a training video prepared for Board members.[1] The agency portrayed was a service for the care of intellectually disabled children. 'My father would turn in his grave' was the favourite phrase of Mr Smythe-Blameley, a member of the Board. He was the son of a 'Founder' and benefactor who was very significant when the original residential home was set up. The centre now covered a wide range of activities as well as the residential services, and included a number of staff from varied disciplines and backgrounds, as well as teams of volunteers.

Mr Smythe-Bramlay could not understand the need for policies in relation to staff matters.'We treat people as individuals. We expect people to be working for the children and not concerned with pay and leave and those things, we are not like the bureaucracies.'

The climax of his bewilderment came when the funding body did not hand out the expected grant, and also asked for a review of certain activities, in particular the residential services. 'In my father's day if we couldn't manage without getting some government money he would have gone into the department and thumped the table and come out with more not less.'

OBTAINING FUNDS

Changing circumstances have meant that some important issues need to be looked at:

* where the funds come from and how one applies for them
* tendering processes
* some funding issues that arise when the money has been obtained.

Sources and types of funds

There are a number of general questions that need to be asked by agencies in relation to obtaining funds, many of which also apply to tender applications.

Should the agency apply for funds because of availability alone?
This is a temptation that is hard to resist: 'The money is there, why shouldn't we take advantage of it to help our clients?' In spite of the attraction of this view, it needs to be resisted. A Board member commented, 'we are panicking and applying for everything that is going'. Examples can be seen of agencies applying for funds although they cannot provide an adequate service. Their staff cannot be retrained to carry out unfamiliar tasks, or tasks for which they are basically unsuitable, due to different approaches in their past experiences. Staff who are used to functioning in a specialised setting do not always adjust to community programs that make different demands on them. A quick training program is not going to change the way staff work after years of operating in a different way.

How much should trends be followed?
Another question relates to planning and refers to the time element involved, in particular. How much can agencies find out about trends and changes taking place in the community so that they can apply for funds in accordance with those changes and be prepared? There is a difference between trying to go along with the 'flavour of the month' and the process of adjusting to changes that are based on improved knowledge. The importance of planning and analysis is a constant theme in all managerial practice and the vignette at the beginning of this chapter illustrates the dangers of a lack of planning and of not looking at the future.

How much can independence be preserved?

The source of the funds, whether government or non-government, may affect the independence of the service. Unacceptable restrictions may be placed on the agency, or can be implicit and not evident until programs have been commenced. Values of the agency as they relate to the particular funding source need to be taken into account. Agencies need to be clear about their attitudes, which must be open and formulated and based on the goals and practice of the agency and not on the personal opinion of particular individuals or groups.

Many examples can be given of possible conflict that is glossed over at the initial stages because of the desire to obtain the funds. Some agencies find it difficult to apply for funds that they know come from activities of which they disapprove. Common examples are funds derived from tobacco or alcohol taxes or levies, which may be directed to an agency or a specific government department to be disbursed to community organisations or for research into the prevention of health-related harms. In many countries, a levy on electronic gaming machines is collected and paid into a community support fund, to be drawn on by community agencies.

Again, the agency must be clear about its policy in relation to such operations. Some organisations will refuse to compromise their values by accepting 'tainted' funds. Others might feel that their distance from the source of the revenue created by a 'third party' distribution agency is enough to appease their discomfort.

Links between designated funds and projects

The purpose for which the funds are to be used should be clear to all parties and adhered to in practice. The vignette at the beginning of the chapter illustrated a situation where funds are given for one purpose and then 'fudged' in their application to the agency's programs. There are particular dangers when money granted for specific projects, often with strict time limits, is used to cover core activities. Staff may be employed to work on a particular project but see themselves as agency staff with continuing employment. There is bitterness if they are terminated when a project finishes, if such a contingency was not made clear at the time of their appointment.

The above questions relate to general issues, which should be clear *before* an application is made. When the decision has been made to apply for the particular funds, the process that follows is in effect an example of the agency's planning ability, as well as its technical competence in the actual grants submission or tender application. The following section deals with some of the processes that should be observed when preparing the material. There are many formulas available that are tailored to various fields, but some general points can be made that can be adjusted to the specific situation. The essential feature is that the smallness of the amount requested does not mean that the principles to be observed are any different from those applied to larger, more complex organisations.

Submissions and applications for funds

The following example illustrates the common features that should be present in all funding requests.[2]

- *Developing the idea.* This is the first step in making the application. As stated earlier, it is important that the proposed program is in accordance with the purpose and goals of the agency, and fits in with the long-term plans as well as immediate needs.
- *Assessing the resources of the agency* and their ability to achieve the goals of the proposed project. This is where the integrity and honesty of the agency is tested. It is particularly important to assess the capability of the personnel involved.
- *Identifying the most appropriate funding source.* This is relevant where the submission is part of an overall funding plan, which then leads to finding the appropriate source. (In the case of tenders the source is determined.)
- *Planning the writing of the proposal.* Unfortunately, advertisements asking for submissions often completely underestimate the time involved and this encourages poor submissions. This problem is related to the point made earlier about planning and anticipating trends. It also highlights the responsibility of the funding agency to allow sufficient time for well-prepared submissions, and sufficient time for the carrying out of the program. One of the problems is that funding bodies are often unaware of the internal functioning of non-government agencies, and the importance of including Boards in the process. This means that time has to be allowed for Board members to be involved. As volunteers, with outside commitments, they cannot be expected to be available and prepared to participate at very short notice.

    There are many other aspects to the submission, for

example, the use of appropriate expertise—some staff are better than others at submission writing. Another crucial element is the involvement of those staff who will be responsible for the program. It is no use hearing later, 'we could have told you it wouldn't work'. The person or group responsible for the proposal must be convinced of its value and enthusiastic about implementing it. Tokenism is ultimately destructive.

- *Honesty in budget estimates.* The budget for the project, like all budgets, is 'notional'; that is, it is what is expected but not necessarily known—an 'informed guess'. Though certainty may not be attainable, the estimate should be as honest and informed as possible. For example, one agency did not include the funds that it expected to gain from payment fees from service users and this omission was revealed later in the project. (This is relevant to the general Service Agreement that an agency may have with the funding body.)
- *Writing the proposal.* Although the form of the proposal or submission is dictated by many outside criteria influenced by the funding source, there are some general principles involved, as follows.
  — Use simple language.
  — State clearly the objectives and goals of the project.
  — See that the above are reflected in the title and abstract.
  — Include a statement of need that is realistic, well supported and credible. This support should be in the form of up-to-date statistics that provide a clear demonstration, rather than assertion, of need.
  — Spell out the procedures in a way that accords with the program goals and objectives.
  — Describe available resources, whether physical or staff, as honestly as possible. This means not overestimating staff capabilities or underestimating the staff resources required in order to gain the funds.
  — Include a detailed and competent budget, including a time frame.
  — Include an evaluation procedure that is not mere tokenism.
  — State the advantages of this project in the context of assuming that there will be competing claims from other agencies for the same funds.

The above criteria are guidelines and are not always easy to achieve. As an example, it is stated above that one should use simple language. The problem is that what is 'simple' to one group may not be seen in the same way by others. One story circulates that a funding body stated (perhaps jokingly?) that it had decided in favour of one agency because it 'couldn't understand the language and assumed therefore that it was learned and expert'. This is a dangerous precedent to follow. The importance of clear communication—of language that the receiver can understand—was highlighted in the checklist at the end of chapter 5.

An interesting comparison with the above points can be seen in the framework developed by a business school to help organisations unused to applying for funds in a competitive environment, and unfamiliar with 'business' concepts. The application is expressed as a 'Business Plan' and the following is a simplified version.

- Details of the *Opportunity*, what the product/service is to do.
- The *Market*. This includes secondary data, customer/user details, competitors/other suppliers.
- *Marketing strategy*—product/promotion/place/package.
- *Operational strategy*, how it will be achieved and the resources available.
- *Financial projections.*
- *Financial requirements.*
- The *Champion*/Entrepreneur/Team, including details of their expertise, commitment, 'track record'.
- *Benefits* not only to the user but also to the funding body.

Three of the above points are worth special mention. The first is the part played by the 'champion'. (The word 'entrepreneur' has been so discredited, at least in human services agencies, that other words are often used.) This 'champion' could be one person or a small group acting as the driving force. This does not mean that there should not be wide participation in many of the processes, but there needs to be a core person or group committed to the implementation. They must have a 'passion' for the success of the project, otherwise it will not achieve the hoped-for success.

The second and less familiar aspect is one that is often neglected. The applicant may be able to illustrate that the funding body itself will benefit from the proposed project. For example, the particular project could enhance the activities of the funding body by complementing some aspects of the funding body's services, providing an extra benefit not actually listed as a requirement.

Finally, the different use of some words is interesting. Many of the funding bodies are beginning to borrow terms from the

135

wider industrial setting, such as 'business plan', without being clear what is meant. Apparently this is because the funding body wants the agency to be more 'businesslike'. Not-for-profit agencies are now 'businesses' in an 'industry'. Does a 'business plan' refer to the overall strategic plan for the whole agency/business, or the particular project or program? This might be ambiguous and needs to be clarified. The word 'budget' is not used in the list above but would be a substitute for financial requirements, including limited financial projections. Business organisations tend to use 'budget' only for the total financial plan of the agency rather than for particular projects.

Tendering

The section above dealt with submissions in general but there are some points that are specific to the *tendering* process. There are similarities but there are also some differences. Many agencies that have been familiar with grants applications are facing new challenges in coping with the tendering process.

Competition

The competitive element in tendering is often claimed to be its greatest advantage. It is believed that competition will improve the service, cut waste and be of advantage to all concerned. There is, to date, little practice research on the benefits of competition, although there is some evidence that the process does encourage a more critical and evaluative approach to practice. There may have been some competition for grants in the past, but quite often agencies had a particular niche which was their own area. The significant basis of a tender is that a number of agencies are applying, knowing that there is competition and that they need to have an advantage over others.

On the negative side, this has created an atmosphere that is unfamiliar and frightening to many in the human service area, in particular where there has been a tradition of cooperation. One executive was heard to say, 'The clients are suffering too from the change in atmosphere, it affects all our interchanges, the way we refer. Now we keep secrets from each other, we are frightened to tell agency X about our services, as they may have an advantage over us at the next tender'.

It is sometimes difficult to be sure that the competition is real. There have been claims that agencies have been encouraged to apply in order to create the appearance of competition when in reality only one agency is going to be considered. Another complication has been the issue of 'Competitive Neutrality', which has caused some confusion. In the interest of equality of competition some funding bodies are attempting to cancel out non-government agencies' advantages, such as tax concessions and other supports in order to work out the real costs. These agencies see themselves as being penalised for savings that they have always regarded as their right. They consider the savings are a legitimate advantage because of their particular approach and values, which they believe enhance the quality of their service.

Uncertainty

Because the tendering process is relatively new in the human service field there is a great deal of uncertainty about what is required and what will bring success. Some believe that a glossy document brings the greatest success, though others put their faith in content. It is believed by many that the actual document is not so important and that it is an agency's reputation that counts. As an indication of agency uncertainty and the need for help, a number of people are developing roles as tendering consultants, that is, helping in the preparation of tenders.

Competence of the funding body

This book has been written for the not-for-profit agency, but there are issues that are important in relation to the performance of the *funding agency* which, in turn, affect the *recipients* of the funds. For instance, competence in managing the tender process varies between funding organisations and there are also variances within the one body. Many of the problems may be due to lack of familiarity with the process, but agencies need to be assured that the funding body, or service purchaser, is competent in the tendering process. Problems can include the following.

- The process is often just as new to the funding body as it is to those applying. This can mean agencies have to deal with people who know little about the tendering process, yet they feel that 'these are the people who are deciding whether we get the money or not'.
- The staff turnover in the funding bodies means that, even where there are people with experience, they often do not remain in the job long enough for the agencies to develop

confidence in them. Those responsible for preparing the tenders and deciding on results may be unfamiliar with the particular service represented by the agency.

- There is often a lack of training for staff in many of the funding bodies in relation to tendering. This includes training on how to encourage the best value from the applications and how to make the choice that will bring the greatest benefit to the community and the service users. As an example, if tenders that are superficial are not examined from the point of view of quality but judged on the lowest cost alone, then the results can be harmful.

- Evidence of consistency about the bases of the grants is difficult to collect. Some agencies believe it is on the basis of least cost, others that it is dependent on 'who knows whom'. Another suggestion was that the idea was to 'spread it around, and give everyone a go', that it did not matter if an agency had the best application—if it was seen as having had 'too much' of the available funding, some other agency would be funded.

  Another story describes how an agency's tender for a training program was accepted on the basis of the expertise of certain people, who happened to be known to the funding body, and without adequate examination and follow up. There were no mechanisms to ensure that the people whose presence in the bid had influenced the choice had more than a minimal role in the final product and, in fact, their subsequent participation was almost non-existent.

- Preparation of the information given to the agencies seems to vary greatly in standards. The material varies between extreme detail and unreasonable demands, through to insufficient indication of what is really wanted. In addition, the time allowed for the agencies to respond after the documentation is received is often much too short. This could be a positive outcome in that it means that the agency responds quickly and does not spend too much time on the tender application. But it needs to be assessed carefully against the negative results of hasty submissions.

- Lack of interaction and feedback means that many agencies feel they are working in a vacuum. Few of the funding bodies encourage agencies to give them feedback on ways that would help the agencies and improve the whole process. Any criticisms or comments tend to be put down to 'sour grapes'. Some funding bodies seem to feel that they must keep the basis of their decisions a secret to avoid too much argument.

- The level at which the decisions are monitored is unclear. When the decisions are made at a devolved and relatively junior level a great deal of variation and inconsistency can be seen. It is often not clear to applicants whether there is any overall monitoring by senior and more experienced staff.

The consequence of these problems, whether real or perceived, is that in many cases there has developed an adversarial atmosphere between the funding bodies (the purchasers) and those applying for funds (the service providers). There is a positive development when experience improves in the funding bodies and briefs become much more sophisticated about what is required. This relieves some of the uncertainty and raises the standard of applications. There is unfortunately a negative aspect that needs to be watched in this improvement. More experience and confidence can result in a more prescriptive approach, which places limits on the flexibility that is allowed to the agencies at the same time that 'creativity' is officially encouraged.

Tendering and the privatisation process

There are many degrees of privatisation but a particular development is causing concern to small agencies, or small units of government agencies. It concerns the calling for tenders for work that they have done previously on a permanent basis. Such staff find the process very difficult and psychologically they often resent having to apply for their 'own work'. Comments are made, such as: 'We are being judged by people who don't know anything about the service and we have been doing it all our lives'. The funding body would say that the value of the process is to bring fresh blood into the service, but this does mean that the 'new blood' must be able to provide a better service, not merely a change.

As we have noted before, privatisation is not new. The difference, when tendering is added to the picture as a way of distributing funds, is that it is seen to place competition at the forefront of the process and to clearly indicate that competition is a good thing. This sort of thinking, characteristic of the economic rationalist approach, is based on a belief that the same principles of competition which are believed to make the market strong ('only the best products will survive healthy competition') also apply to a field such as the human services. This market-driven view ignores, among other things, the often high degree of regulation, either by government or fields of business themselves, that exists to protect players in the commercial world. No such regulation exists in the human service area, and while individual agencies or types of service, such as residential care and child care, may be regulated, there is no regulation of the competition itself to protect small players.

In essence, the issue with tendering is that any positive benefits it may have, as a method of distributing funds, have not been clearly demonstrated. On the other hand, many of its negative effects are clearer to see.[3]

Fragmentation of services

Fragmentation of services is another result that causes concern to many agencies. Rather than having one agency carrying out a total integrated process there seems to be a tendency to split a project between a number of agencies, resulting in a lack of cohesion of tasks, philosophies and goals. As one agency complained, 'There are lots of bits and pieces from different agencies with very different levels of competency and different philosophies'. If the differences gave the service users a choice there would be some advantages but the result is usually that different users merely receive different services on an arbitrary basis.

In contrast to this criticism, some agencies are working with others to an extent that was not common in the past. In these cases the funding bodies have encouraged joint projects and cooperation, with the benefits of shared expertise and improved services. The overall picture is not yet clear and there are different perceptions in different groups. There is also a contra pattern to the fragmentation picture in that there appears to be an alternative trend to ask for 'mega' tenders from major agencies. It is not obvious how this will develop and there are variations throughout the regions and the States. It is to be hoped that if there are central agencies the monitoring of the services will not suffer, and systems for monitoring sub-contracts and accountability at all levels will be developed. The constant danger is that the only account-ability will be for easily measurable physical and financial aspects and that quality monitoring will fall into the 'too hard' basket.

Ways of overcoming the problems

In spite of the problems noted above, the tendering process appears likely to remain. Therefore, it is necessary for agencies to find methods for dealing with the difficulties. These methods include the following.

- Approach the tendering process as positively as possible, seeing each exercise as a learning experience and as part of the agency's general planning and priority setting.
- Do not see the failure to win a particular application as completely negative but evaluate each application to bring about improvements.
- Develop skills in all the processes, encouraging those who can contribute most, including a number of different individuals and groups.
- The use of consultants has increased as agencies and funding bodies struggle with unfamiliar processes. The techniques for using consultants for tendering are the same as they are for other purposes. The danger is that the agencies do not learn as much from the process as they should and that the aim of training internal staff to do the job wherever possible is not followed. In some cases the consultants prepare glossy, well-presented but stereotyped documents that are not based on staff participation and are often removed from the real situation.
- One of the skills to be developed is that of working within very tight deadlines. Agencies need to develop skill in working fast and accurately. Safeguards should be built in to ensure that tenders are not missed because there was a virus in the computer, the photocopier broke, the only person with the whole picture was off sick, the courier got lost, the tender box was moved to another building, and so on. All of these reasons, we know, have contributed to agencies failing to submit tenders on time and therefore missing out on necessary funds. The process is hard enough without these problems.
- Limit applications to those projects that suit the agency's particular expertise, commitment and overall plans.
- Form some consortia of agencies to bid for tenders and do not let the funding body determine the nature of the relationship between agencies as primarily a competitive one. Of course, there will still be competition between agencies, but agencies can use the process to reduce the negative consequences of competition and, indeed, use the process as a vehicle with which to form strategic partnerships for the benefit of their clients.[4]

The agencies may also be of benefit to the funding body by giving the funding body feedback on its own performance. When such a suggestion was made, one practitioner said, 'They don't want our advice. Our jobs depend on it, so I just keep my head down, keep quiet, and do the best I can'. Hopefully, if the adversarial situation can be acknowledged and dealt with, benefits will be felt by both 'sides' addressing the problem.

Funding and accountability

When the funds are obtained a number of additional issues need to be considered. These are closely related to the question of accountability.[5]

As noted at the beginning of this chapter and in the introductory vignette in chapter 1, there is an increased emphasis on accountability in general and on the relationship between accountability and funding in particular. The tendency to contract out services to non-government agencies, coupled with an increase in privatisation, has meant that many more agencies are now applying to carry out programs with government funding. This is another new process to some agencies. It is particularly relevant to those small agencies that have not previously had in place the reporting and recording processes necessary for providing the required level of accountability.

In the definitions presented in the Introduction, a distinction was made between accountability and responsibility. This distinction becomes significant when processes are considered. If an accountability role is prescribed, or accepted voluntarily, it is necessary to clarify to which group the agency is 'accountable'. In addition, and most importantly, there need to be mechanisms in place to ensure that this accountability is observed. It must be clear whether the accountability is embedded in the structure and whether there are legal implications and/or requirements. This means that there must be adequate reporting processes that indicate whether there are any sanctions if the body to whom the agency is accountable is not satisfied.

Accountability without sanctions has some advantages but it can be a 'toothless tiger'. A particular example is that of health care for the elderly where agencies are meant to be accountable in return for funds, but there are many misgivings about the way this is carried out. The reporting procedures and supervision of the day-to-day practices are often suspect in terms of ensuring that proper care is given. When agencies say they are 'responsible' to various groups, such as consumers, 'the community', or 'stake-holders', but cannot show how the process is carried out, this can only be seen as a vague generality and in no way as effective accountability.

Although the trend towards accountability for funds received is an encouraging one it is only of value if the funding body is able to make demands that will improve the service given and which are achievable. Many times agency staff complain that 'they don't understand what we do and the records and results they ask for are meaningless. They will be a waste of time and we will only fudge them because we know that they are useless'. Too often, the funding body takes the easy way out, such as asking for simple figures. All those practising know that the figures fail to indicate the reality of the service given and, in particular, the standard of the service. Asking for interview numbers in a counselling agency, or the number of 'matches' in Citizen Advocacy programs, is useless in maintaining standards unless there are quality assessments. There may be a lack of quality assessment of service delivery but it is even more rare that questions are asked about management competency. There is little recognition of the importance of management competencies in their effect on service delivery, except in relation to financial matters.

Accountability *for what* is the issue. It can be for (a) standards, (b) effectiveness related to goals, values and philosophy, and (c) efficiency, particularly in financial aspects. In this chapter we are concerned with financial aspects, while the issues of standards and effectiveness are discussed in chapter 9.

As the definitions in the Introduction illustrated, efficiency and effectiveness are interrelated. They are so closely paired that they are rarely mentioned separately, but it is doubtful whether many understand that there is a difference. It seems that it is recognised that efficiency alone is not enough and it is the 'done thing' to add effectiveness, without much understanding of their interrelationship. It is also doubtful whether many think beyond cost efficiency when using the word. The use of the case mix method of financing services in the health area is an example of some of the problems where the link between efficiency and effectiveness has been oversimplified. It is inferred that the achievement of 'efficiency' will automatically bring about effectiveness.

What happens to the funds after they are received is an area that has often been poorly managed in the small agencies. There seems to be a 'fear of figures' and a belief that it is all too difficult and should be left to the experts. In the section following we cover some of the basic procedures that are necessary for the small agency in particular.

143

BUDGETING AND COSTING

Some of the basic practice issues involved in budgeting and costing will be considered here. Several publications offer further discussion if needed, for example, of philosophical and ideological aspects of budgeting.[6] It is necessary also to recognise that budgeting is more than the simple listing of items of cost and expenditure. The budgets referred to in this section are those of the agency as a whole, although the general process is similar for single projects, whether this is called a business plan or financial plan or whatever. In some single-purpose agencies the budget for the single program is almost the total agency budget.

Budgeting

It has been stated that budgets are 'political' documents that answer the central question 'Who gets what, when and how?'. As funds are limited and have to be divided among competing uses, the budget becomes a mechanism for making choices between alternative expenditures. When these choices are coordinated to achieve desired goals, a budget reflects a plan. Budgetary decisions are *planning* decisions, stated in monetary terms.

If the questions who, what, when, and how are asked, the process of budgeting can be simplified.

Who?

The Board has the final responsibility for approving the budget and it is important that this is recognised. Although not all members of the Board have equal knowledge of financial matters, all must understand what they are approving and the general trends and priorities. The Board must also understand the mechanisms that are in place to monitor expenditure.

A rather public disagreement was aired between some members of the Board of a human service organisation. One member of the Board complained that the general members of the Board were not involved in decisions regarding expenditure and 'only told after the money was spent'. The response of the president was that 'we have confidence in our excellent executive officer'. However, the president, when questioned, could not remember which matters were discussed and approved, or state what was the accepted pattern of reporting, delegating and approving.

Another Board/committee of management of a small, self-help agency that received government funding saw any formality and monitoring of expenditure as an insult to the staff members and an indication of lack of trust. The committee was devastated when it finally became obvious that there had been a serious misuse of funds, with money used for unacceptable personal expenditure and 'favours to friends'.

The appropriate degrees of delegation must be clearly laid down, as well as the mechanisms for monitoring any delegated responsibilities. These should be recorded so that there is no ambiguity and the processes are accepted by all the parties involved. The following sample CEO Budgeting Policy and the sample Budget Cycle can be adapted to an agency's particular needs.

Sample CEO Budgeting Policy

Policy
It is the responsibility of the Chief Executive Offficer (CEO) to research and develop the organisation's overall annual operating budget. The annual budget should be soundly prepared reflecting a mix of ongoing operational and capital requirements and the organisation's critical strategic issues as identified in the strategic plan. The budget should reflect both expenditure and revenue projections.

Procedures
1. The annual budget is a reflection of the organisation's annual operational plan and as such should be presented in partnership with the plan showing the relationship between planned-for events and associated costs and revenues.

The annual budget shall:

2. contain sufficient detail to allow an accurate projection of revenues and expenditures

3. present a true cash flow position, which does not confuse or mislead any audit trail
4. contain projected expenditures, which meet the projected reasonable estimate of revenue during the period covered by the budget
5. comply with the Board's stated objectives and priorities
6. be presented in such a way as to make it easy to interpret and complying with standard budget presentation formats.

The CEO is responsible for:

7. the annual presentation of budgets (capital and revenue) and for providing such additional information to enable the Board to make its approval
8. submitting to the Board explanations for variances from the approved budgets
9. ensuring that any application to the Board for expenditure, which has not been specifically budgeted for, is supported by precise costings and a recommendation as to how the new expenditure can be funded.

Policy reviewed every 3 years

Source: Kilmister, T. (1993) *Boards at Work: A New Perspective on Not-for-Profit Boards,* NFP Press, Wellington, p. 146.

When?/How?

These are related. There are differences of opinion about the timing of budget preparation; for example, what times are allowed for preparation; when budget variations and modifications can take place; what reporting-back procedures exist; and how often cash flow information is circulated. These details will depend on the requirements of each agency and the availability of staff and resources. The following is a suggested Budget Cycle for a not-for-profit organisation which might seem complex but can be simplified by agencies for their particular needs.[7]

Budget Cycle

Program and budget planning
Needs assessment and feasibility studies
Program planning
Cost estimating
Budget development

Funds procurement
Budget request submission
Negotiation with funding source
Re-budgeting and re-submission
Award and acceptance

Fiscal management
Designation of cost and responsibility centres
Internal funds allocation and re-budgeting
Establishment of restricted accounts
Financial transactions, recording and accounting
Operations monitoring and reporting
Cost control and containment

Assessment and audits
Performance audit, that is, program evaluation
End-of-year financial statements
Financial audit
Cost analysis

Recycle
Program re-planning
Continuation budgeting
Cost finding and rate setting

What?

The sample Budget Cycle indicates the when and how, but also includes some material that the small organisation may not require, such as the complex cost/expenditure information. The way the costs are listed and monitored can be very varied. The particular method of linking costs to programs or departments may vary from agency to agency, and the degree of sophistication of the costing section of the budgetary exercise will depend on the complexity of the agency and the expertise available.

Some years ago, a municipal council allotted all the building maintenance and repair costs for its day nursery to its central maintenance department. Another council allotted the maintenance and repair costs to the day nursery where the work was done. The government department which provided some of the funds for the day nurseries wanted to know why the nursery in one municipality 'cost' so much more than the other. The spread of administrative costs was even more variable.

Basic processes in budget analysis

The above example highlights the problems of achieving accurate budget analysis and control of expenditure. Executive officers, or whichever staff members have the responsibility for financial management, should be familiar with four basic processes involved in budget analysis, that is, ratios, comparisons, trends and projections.

- *Ratios.* This is a simple way of showing the relationship of two items to each other. Cost of services supplied to service users in relation to income received would be one ratio; or, for example, administrative costs in relation to total costs. Changes in ratios need to be noted and discussed, or adjusted if necessary.

- *Comparisons.* This is the process of examining the costs of an item in one year and comparing them with the costs in the previous year, or over a period of years. Cost increases or decreases revealed by the comparison cannot be analysed in isolation but are the trigger for further analysis to discover the reasons for the changes.

- *Trends.* Various methods are used for illustrating trends over months or years, the most popular being graphs or other pictorial methods. This exercise is important, as otherwise trends may go unnoticed and planning may be inadequate. As these can be presented visually they are more easily understood by many members of the Board.

- *Projections.* These are the basis for future budgeting and are, as all budgetary processes, a notional exercise. Projections may be optimistic, pessimistic, or a middle-of-the-road expectation. Skilful personnel develop a balance that is in accord with the agency's goals and objectives; the essential factor is that the budgeting process should not be endangered by inexpert projections. Sometimes projections are used to set up contingency or variable budgets, particularly in times of rapid change, but this should not be used too often as it can create uncertainty and insecurity.[8]

It is important to tailor techniques to a particular agency, while at the same time learning from other experiences where it is appropriate. Although it is not advisable to develop unnecessarily complex systems, it is also dangerous to oversimplify. Using an incremental budgetary system, that merely looks at what was done in one year and adds or subtracts arbitrary amounts each year, will eventually backfire. Ignoring the need to examine costs and expenditures regularly, such as at monthly intervals, will result in crisis spending or cutting back at the end of the financial year. Such transactions are not based on proper analysis but are the result of inefficient and hasty expediency.

Various methods of budgeting have come and gone over the years. For example, zero-based budgeting was favoured for a time by governments of a number of countries and agencies had to become familiar with the method. The pros and cons of the various methods will not be discussed here but the choice made by the agencies will, to some extent, be dictated by the information required by the funding source.[9]

To summarise, budgeting is a forecasting exercise based on knowledge, monitoring and appropriate recording. It involves ways of 'dollarising the planning' and is part of the general financial management of the agency. Costing is one of the techniques in the budgetary exercise, which provides information for the 'dollarising' process.

Costing

Costing is only part of the budgetary process but, because of the mystique of numbers, it seems to occupy a central role and create some problems in a number of small agencies. The methods of recording costs/expenditure need to be simple enough to be understood by all levels involved. With the improvements in technology, there is a temptation to install systems that are much more elaborate than is necessary for the financial management of the agency. Complexity tends to confuse those who should be able to understand the process in order to make the appropriate decisions.

This section will include a simple costing framework as an example but will not cover the bookkeeping details of flow charts, balance sheets and so on. The Board is ultimately responsible for the efficient financial management of the agency, but relies on the CEO for general advice. Most not-for-profit agencies have a subcommittee of the Board that deals with financial matters and which usually consists of the chairperson, the treasurer and the CEO, as well as any other member who may have expertise in the area. This subcommittee should ensure that the Board receives all the information to enable it to make appropriate decisions.

Most small agencies do not have a full-time accountant or finance director, but all agencies need some accounting expertise, whether it is a part-time staff member or a consultant. A most successful arrangement has often been the assistance given by volunteers. This can be a member of the Board, often the treasurer, or an interested member of the community who is willing to give some specialised assistance. Whoever gives the advice should recognise that not all business procedures are applicable to small agencies. Confusion can be caused by the non-recognition that funding bodies' requirements influence the way records are kept. Whatever method is used, complexity should be avoided. If the process is too complicated the CEO or Board members may opt out of understanding the financial aspects and therefore may not fulfil their decision-making responsibility.

The following is a simple system that excludes salary costs and separates other costs into direct and indirect costs.[10] The direct costs are allotted relatively easily to departments (or programs) but the indirect costs may not be so easily allocated. As in the municipal council example above, the method of portioning out such costs, particularly administrative 'spread', may be arbitrary.

Costing Framework

A. *Direct costs* (listed below are typical examples of such costs).
1. Materials or merchandise purchased.
2. Transportation (travel, car, upkeep for staff).
3. Utilities (power and water).
4. Telephone (usually listed separately).
5. Insurance (especially for private agencies).
6. Office equipment expenses (for computers, printers, scanners, calculators, dictaphones, and so on).

7. Office supplies (paper, printer cartridges, toner etc).
8. All other supplies (non-office, such as cleaning materials).
9. Services purchased by the agency.
10. Miscellaneous.

B. *Indirect costs* (expenses that cannot be charged directly to a department).
1. Overhead charges (accounting expenses, central administration, and so on).
2. Training and development (including seminars, workshops, conferences).
3. Fringe benefits.
4. Taxes.
5. Advertising, cost of publications, printed reports.
6. Depreciation (on equipment serving all departments).
7. Rent.

Salary costs are often separated out from all other costs as above, particularly when they are the major expense of the agency. They would be added to the direct departmental costs in some cases, but would also include central costs, for example, for salaries of administrative staff. Such items as superannuation depend on the particular requirements laid down by legislation.

'Miscellaneous' is sometimes used for minor items that do not fit into the other categories and seem too small to be itemised separately. If too many items are included in 'Miscellaneous', they should be clustered into categories, to avoid it becoming a 'wastepaper-basket' category. Some suggest the category should be avoided altogether.

The important point about the method used to allocate costs is that the result must be credible to the staff concerned. Even simple items can be confused. For example, an agency used a category 'staff amenities' and it was not until the costs were queried as being too high that it was found that this item referred to drinks and biscuits that were also used for morning tea for service users. The staff usage was minimal.

Wherever possible, the process of planning the allocation of costs should involve the contribution of those affected by the outcome. This includes various levels of staff, and also service users. The mechanics of sharing the information and encouraging input and feedback are part of general management, and illustrate the need to relate financial management to the other agency processes.

CONCLUSION

The use of these relatively simple concepts is not so easy for some agencies because their recording methods are not allied to their planning requirements. Poor recording was mentioned with reference to performance appraisal, and is discussed in the next chapter when office management is considered.

The interrelationship of good management techniques is stressed throughout this book. Good managers apply the principles of 'constant critical appraisal' to all their work and recognise the importance of planning and of systematic and useful recording, no matter which part of the managerial task is under consideration. The next chapter discusses some of the management tasks involved in the smooth functioning of the agency, that is, managing the office, including the physical resources.

NOTES

1. The video *Any Other Business* is part of an excellent Board of Directors' Resource Kit developed by Denise Picton of Oz-Train Pty Ltd, PO Box 361, Glenside, South Australia, 5065.
2. Derived from Hall, M. (1971) *Developing Skills in Proposal Writing, 2nd Edition*, Continuing Education Publications, Portland, Oregon.
3. For an excellent discussion of the impact of tendering and competition on the human services, particularly smaller organisations, see de Carvalho, D. (1996) *Competitive Care: Understanding the Implications of National Competition Policy and the COAG Agenda for the Community Services Sector*, Discussion Paper No. 11, Australian Social Welfare Commission, Canberra. See also *Turning People into Commodities: Report of the Public Hearings on Competitive Tendering in Human Services*, People Together Project, Melbourne.
4. This concept of strategic partnerships is discussed in commercial operations in, for example, Lendrum, T. (1995) *The Strategic Partnering Handbook*, McGraw-Hill Book Co., Sydney. The human services could benefit from familiarity with this sort of thinking, challenging as it does the orthodoxy of competition.
5. Although a number of commentators on the community service area

have rightly taken issue with its 'uncritical' analysis of competitive tendering and contracting, the Industry Commission's Report No. 48, *Competitive Tendering and Contracting in the Public Sector* (AGPS, Canberra, 1996) contains some very useful guidelines for ensuring that the process works, particularly on p. 349.

6. See, for example, chapter 9, 'Finance and Budgeting' in Donovan, F. and Jackson, A.C. (1991). See also Simon, H. (1976) *Administrative Behaviour, Third Edition,* Free Press, New York, pp. 192–97.

7. This has been adapted from Vinter, R. and Kish, R. (1984) *Budgeting for Non-profit Organisations,* The Free Press, New York.

8. See Ehlers, W., Austin, M. and Prothero, J. (1976) *Administration for the Human Services,* Harper and Row Publishers, New York.

9. See chapter 9, 'Finance and Budgeting', in Donovan, F. and Jackson, A.C. (1991) for a discussion of a range of budgeting methods. Terms are constantly changing in popularity, although the concepts are not always new. See, for example, Boxall P. (1988) 'The Revolution in Government Accounting' in *Australian CPA,* April, which deals with 'accrual-based reporting', and 'whole-of-government reporting'.

10. This is adapted from Ehlers, W., Austin, M. and Prothero, J. (1976), p. 310.

7

OFFICE AND PHYSICAL RESOURCE MANAGEMENT

● *Office management* ● *Physical resources management* ● *Conclusion*

Information from a service user's file held in another agency was urgently required by a particular agency for a case planning session at which important decisions had to be made. An expected report had not arrived, but the outside agency was contacted for some essential facts and up-to-date information on recent developments. The worker concerned was found to be on leave, and the file was marked out to another worker who was unavailable. The latter worker's files were checked but the relevant file could not be found. Decisions had to be postponed, a result that had unfortunate repercussions for the service user.

Later it was revealed that the second worker had handed over the file to another worker but had not altered the central record. When the agency was queried about the situation, the excuse was made that heavy case loads, a concern for 'people not paper', had brought about the breakdown in communication.

In this chapter, two broad areas are covered under the heading 'Office and physical resource management'.[1] The physical resource aspect is sometimes seen as low-level, 'practical' knowledge and does not need to be formalised. In addition, it is seen as 'commonsense' that does not need to be discussed in general terms. We do not agree with these views and regard the two areas as significant and needing attention for two fundamental reasons.

- Basic management skills, as outlined in this chapter, play an important part in influencing the general standard of service delivery.
- Some of the negative attitudes towards management that are mentioned in this book apply particularly to the knowledge and skills area of day-to-day management and need to be addressed.

As the vignette above illustrates, 'I am interested in people, not paper' is a familiar phrase. The thinking behind this emphasis needs to be corrected to ensure managerially competent service delivery, that is, for it to be recognised that paper affects people.

OFFICE MANAGEMENT

At a seminar on administration, participants asked about ways of improving their relationships with administrators, and the point was made that competence in office housekeeping could bring about improvements in such relationships. It is sometimes irritating to be appreciated for doing reports and statistics well and submitting them on time, rather than for other aspects of service delivery. However, it is worth capitalising on a competency that can be relatively easily acquired.

Those non-physical aspects that are dealt with in this chapter inevitably overlap with a number of the other sections in the book, but the emphasis here is on practical office management. A number of human resource management issues could be included under the general heading of office management, for example, 'time management', but the 'people' emphasis has led to its inclusion in chapter 4, 'Maximising people's contribution'. This does not mean that it is not recognised that office management includes human resource management, a point sometimes neglected when the qualities for an 'office manager' are being considered. There are inevitably grey areas; for example, task management and filing systems are difficult to categorise but are included in this chapter because of the significance of the physical resource aspects.

The following example illustrates the interrelationship between office management and personnel aspects.

In one agency a staff member was appointed with a clear mandate to upgrade the office procedures and 'professionalise' them for greater efficiency and effectiveness. The problem was that the roles of all staff had not been carefully designated and the new staff member was expected to 'tidy up' only a part of a situation that needed to be tackled as a whole. It is important to take account of the wider area of human resource management, not merely the question of office procedures. A set of new rules and regulations cannot be laid down and expected to work automatically if those who have to observe the rules are members of a group unused to this type of process. In this case, some senior people saw themselves as being outside the particular process, which immediately undermined the total exercise.

In a similar case, a new staff member in an agency was recognised as having an interest in this area and was given the task of reorganising the office procedures. This person was relatively junior in the hierarchy and recently appointed, and it soon became clear that she was encountering problems in undertaking this particular role. The resistance of some staff and the difficulties that resulted were sufficient to cause the new staff member to withdraw from the exercise.

In both cases, one of the areas of contention was the attempt to get all staff members to notify the contact point, that is, the reception area, of their movements. There were a number of reasons for the difficulty of instituting this process and each had to be addressed specifically. One was that staff members were disorganised and had difficulty in planning their movements and notifying reception of their prospective pattern. But another reason was the perception of this as a restriction or control issue. Some staff believed that members were unwilling to notify movements because they were behaving inappropriately in that time, and this was one of the negative feelings of suspicion that existed in the particular agency. There were additional problems caused by increases in job-sharing, part-time work and more work done at home.

In contrast to the negative example above, another agency gained full cooperation in carrying out the exercise, though many staff found it difficult due to the nature of their work. After a time, however, they managed to anticipate their movements and develop a pattern that was satisfactory to the whole group. This had quite dramatic effects on the whole office, particularly as it enabled administrative staff to make appointments with security and service users, knowing they would not be kept waiting indefinitely owing to some unforeseen crisis. Back-up and 'fail-safe' patterns were developed in those areas that were found hardest to predict.

In the cases described earlier, it was found that an agency's attempts to bring about improvement in 'efficiency' depend on recognition of the expectations of staff that they will be involved in the decision making. Attempts to enforce regulations, or to develop 'control by paper', will only fail and will not bring about the desired ultimate improvement in office procedures. It will create only routine adherence to some rules, and some distortion, especially where the staff can 'get away with it'. Without consultation, including with service users, office procedures will not achieve the goal of greater efficiency and competence.

Although this emphasis on discussion and participation may appear to require increased time, in the long run such participation in the early stages is repaid by a greater efficiency in the later stages. The ability to provide and maintain a secure administrative framework, and at the same time allow for flexibility, is essential to good management and is not a simple skill. Too often, either one or the other is seen as possible but not both.

As well as the need for carrying out major tasks or projects, there are the day–to-day managerial tasks involved in running an office. Some of the difficulties managers encounter in carrying out tasks that appear simple might arise from a personality or attitudinal matter, rather than from a lack of the basic skills. There is also a belief that some people have administrative ability and others have not, and that there is nothing one can do about it. One staff member in an agency was heard to boast of an inability to observe routines as if this were evidence of greater sensibility. In contrast to these views, we consider that there should be an expectation of a certain level of competence in carrying out basic tasks or procedures, and that these *can be learned.*

Standard operating procedures

Procedures are usually formalised into what are called standard operating procedures (SOPs). No matter how small the agency and how simple its activities, when there are a number of people involved there should be a record of the general office patterns.

'No-one told me about doing that' is all too often the excuse when mistakes happen. How much is recorded and made routine is often a matter of contention, with such a process sometimes seen as not taking account of individual differences and flexibility. There are a number of points that can be made about SOPs:

- Their development should be seen as a participative process.
- There should be regular re-examination to ensure that the situation has not changed and the routine is still relevant and not carried out for its own sake.
- Provision should be made for accepted degrees of flexibility and/or exceptions. These should not be based on personalities but should be within clear guidelines.
- The procedures should balance the needs of the service user, the service deliverer and the agency.

The above may be the general goals in producing SOPs but in practice there are a number of problems which have to be overcome. Many agencies are afraid to allow flexibility to staff because they do not have confidence in the staff's discretion, or fear the impact of undue influence. Because of these fears they insist that staff 'follow the rules'. This can be overcome by appropriate training but also by clear patterns and *monitoring of exceptions*. Another advantage of allowing certain exceptions is that the rules can be re-examined when it is seen that the exceptions are becoming too numerous. It must be completely clear who has the power to make exceptions and why. They should all be recorded so that they can be monitored and, in addition, any patterns can be seen. It is the fear of exceptions and flexibility that causes the rigidities that are so frustrating for those dealing with the 'bureaucracy'.

Some problems relating to standards in office behaviour and procedures are more evident in small rather than large agencies, because of the more personalised approach.

An agency insisted that it was 'a family' and therefore some of the behaviour of staff was accepted because they were 'family'. This meant that a casual attitude to timekeeping, maintenance of records and the keeping of appointments was seen as permissible. This casual attitude was also shown in the general office management and appearance. The effect on the service users was not considered. In particular, the agency failed to recognise that some service users saw the approach as a denigration of their importance, which was especially unfortunate as the group was already vulnerable. The service users didn't necessarily consider the noisy and untidy reception area as a friendly place and many felt that they were not regarded as important enough for care to be taken.

There should be a constant balancing of the needs of the organisation, including the staff, against those of other stakeholders, including the service users. Ensuring that simple procedures are observed—such as answering messages, replying promptly to mail, seeing that people are not kept waiting at the reception area—not only improves efficiency but conveys a message of consideration of other people's needs. It may mean tighter rostering but ways can usually be found.

Task management

Some time has been spent on the process of making grant or tender applications and in some cases such applications represent the first time that a formal planning exercise has been undertaken. Similar planning should also take place within the agency when tasks are being allotted or changed, or new projects are undertaken. All tasks should be part of the agency plan and should be evaluated and analysed constantly. The complaint often arises of there being no time to give to such a process but this is a question of sorting out priorities and recognising the long-term effects of poor planning. The following examples of planning and task management illustrate the process.[2] In particular, the points raised under 'Incorporation of new tasks' are often neglected.

Personal planning: key elements

A. *Understand the limiting and fixed factors*
- How much time is required to achieve the goal and what resources are available?
- What are the obstacles (negative constraints)?
- What are the unknowns (recognition and identification of possible situations)?
- What actions of others might affect the achievement of the goal?

159

B. *Design a plan to deal with the above*
- Use your own and others' experience.
- Use simulation by analogy.

C. *Assess feasibility*
- Can the goal be achieved, considering the first analysis (see A above)?
- Has the planner the capability of achieving the goal?

D. *Identify and use checkpoint to evaluate*
- Revise plans if necessary.
- Modify goals if necessary.

Task management procedures

Having first defined the task and listed and clarified the assumptions behind the definition of the task, a number of other steps can be followed to manage the task.

1. Place the task in the context of the total system by asking:
   - What is its purpose and is it necessary, that is, why is it being carried out?
   - Does it contribute to or enhance the overall goal(s) of the organisation/group?
2. Determine who will be affected by the task.
3. Clarify what resources are required:
   - people
   - materials
   - time.
4. Analyse the feasibility of successful completion of the task and possible consequences of non-completion of part of the task or the entire task.
5. Consider the various alternative methods of achieving the task.
6. Make an action plan, that is, place the plan in a detailed (proposed) time schedule.
7. Keep records while carrying out the task so that it can be a learning experience as well as achieving the particular task goal.
8. On completing the task, record possible future follow-up action and the basic information required for those further processes.

Incorporation of new tasks

When considering accepting new tasks, it is worth asking the following two questions:

- What will need to be deleted to fit in the new task?
- Does the new task mean a major change in priorities?

The following action should then be taken:

- Make your own time estimates and then double them. (New tasks are usually underestimated and the estimates of those making the request are usually gross underestimations!)
- Obtain in writing what is specifically requested. Note the assistance you could expect to receive.
- Avoid taking on too many new tasks at one time.
- See whether you can make an exchange in return for accepting the new task.
- Don't accept new tasks just because you are flattered at being asked.

Timelines and work schedules

Work schedules can be drawn up in a variety of ways but quite simple techniques can make a great deal of difference in the functioning of an agency. Details such as working backwards from the final date, not underestimating final revisions and allowing emergency time for illness can help ensure that tasks are completed on time. A simple adjustment that brought about improvements in the delivery of reports is illustrated by the following example.

An agency required reports to be written by certain dates for courts or for case reviews. The court or case review dates were put up on a board to remind the staff of the date by which the reports had to be written. Staff did remember these dates but did not take sufficient account of typing time or preparation time, with the result that reports were constantly being rushed at the last moment. The date posted on the board was then changed to one which subtracted a designated typing time. The final date was the time the material was to be ready for typing, not the time the report was due at the court or the meeting. This simple process of altering the visual date that workers saw as they passed the board improved the functioning of the agency. For all applications or reports a timeline schedule should be drawn up that is visible and always allows a 'fail-safe' period to allow for illnesses, computer glitches and other unforeseen hold-ups.

Recording and reporting

There are various levels of recording and reporting, including:

- individual 'case' recording
- generalised records and subsequent reporting that arise out of the case recording
- recording and reporting that does not relate to the individual service delivery but to other factors, such as the processes of decision making and the formation of policies
- recording that is part of managerial accountability, such as monthly and annual reports
- personnel records.

Individual case recording

A significant amount of attention has been paid to the keeping of records related to individual service users, but some of the old, inadequate chronological records are still in use. These give no indication of the purpose of the actions, the planning involved, nor do they provide regular summaries of significant information. Chronological records are usually descriptive and result in a large volume of material that has to be waded through before the relevant information can be obtained. Such records are of little value in providing information that enables an assessment to be made of the success of the process.

An agency should develop records that illustrate the planning process, and also develop a self-critical approach to its service. This could include:

- a statement of the proposed outcome, drawn up with the service user
- a statement of the actions proposed to achieve the outcome
- regular summaries of progress
- any modifications to the initial plan due to changes in the process.

Generalised records

Not only do such 'case' records enable assessments to be made of the individual service, but they can also be used to provide information for the generalised agency records, the second type of recording. These include factual information about numbers of contacts and types of help given—material now usually stored in the computer system. The type of information depends on the agency's needs, but even a small agency with limited functions needs some generalised information. This can illustrate such aspects as changes in the composition of the clientele or changes in the type of problem being presented.

The keeping of general records means that information is not only available for submissions and tenders but also for communication on issues that arise. Agencies may be asked by the media, or other agencies, for information about their activities. Very often vague statements are all that can be made. Intelligent anticipation of what the public, the media or other organisations may want to know is part of the agency's responsibility to communicate with the wider community and stakeholders.

Records for policy and planning

The third type of recording is the one most neglected in the small agency, that is, information related to policy and decision making. Whether this is stored manually in a filing system (as is common in the small agency) or in a computer system, there should be a record of policy decisions. This should be kept up-to-date and summarised. New members of Boards, in particular, should not have to pick up details of policy in a haphazard way, sometimes even receiving incorrect information. It is not only important that the policy be up-to-date but there should be records of the process, for example, why the decisions were made, by whom and when. If the time has come for a reconsideration, or a new member wishes to change or challenge a policy, the background information is essential for informed debate.

Records and regular reporting

Another use of the generalised records is as a source of information for the reporting that is part of the agency's communication pattern. This includes the standard annual report, which is part of any AGM, but most agencies usually have other reporting requirements as part of the Board processes. The various comments about submissions and tendering, the discussion of communication and the data collection for performance appraisal are all relevant to managerial reporting. The same basic sources are used—for example, diaries, logs, case records and general and policy files. The Board should make it clear what it requires and how often, but it is also important that the CEO shows what can be done with the available resources.

Some agencies rely on case vignettes or 'stories' to bring life to their reports and these are valuable records when used with discretion. However, they should not be used alone, without generalised information. They should not be seen as alternatives to more formalised information. Consider these questions first: Is the dramatic and heart-warming story a typical example of the work that is done? How does it fit in with the agency's goals and priorities? Does it raise any issues that should be dealt with in agency policy?

Presentation of reports

Reports should not be discursive and anecdotal, apart from the 'stories' mentioned above. They should contain information that gives the Board a clear picture of what is done in the agency, and should wherever possible highlight the successes. The development of computer technology means that the information can be presented graphically, for example, with pie charts. Time should not be spent in the meeting reading out reports. They should be circulated well before the meeting so that the Board can consider them and ask questions. The data should not simply be a list of statistics. One agency asked the senior staff member to highlight the *issues* involved, indicate the trends that the figures illustrated and, finally, make recommendations about action if necessary. The interaction of data can be seen and if the system is well planned the same data can be used for a number of purposes.

Personnel records

The type of personnel records that are kept will be determined by the agency's personnel policies, including its performance appraisal program. The essential feature of a personnel record is that it is not a secret dossier that cannot be seen by the worker. On the negative side it is sometimes claimed that records that are seen by workers will not be honestly maintained. This says something about the people keeping the records. Some people find it extremely difficult to deal with reactions to negative comments and to handle what should be a normal process. A great deal depends on how the records are used and the interrelationships that exist. The confidentiality of the records is also important if they are to be seen as a potentially positive factor. Personnel information should not be disclosed to others without the permission of the worker, and in accordance with laid-down procedures.

As with all records about individual situations, the generalising of the material can be useful for managerial purposes. The aggregation of data can reveal changes in labour patterns and turnover and indicate where recruitment and selection processes should be adjusted. The complete information should be available in a way that is easy to access, that is, there should be an adequate storage and retrieval system.

Storage and retrieval systems (filing)

The current term for what used to be called 'filing' is useful in indicating that there are two processes:

- decisions about storing information and the physical process involved—this includes both manual and computer systems
- the process of retrieving that information in order to use it.

How the information is stored will, of course, have a great effect on whether it can be retrieved efficiently. Many agencies spend more time on storage and retrieval of individual service user/client/patient records than of information needed for other purposes. However, many have a wide contact with community resources and extensive interaction with other agencies, all of which require information systems that enable these contacts to be carried out effectively.

Each organisation must decide on a system that best fits its own functioning. There have been many examples of inappropriate transferring of packages, whether manual or computer, based on a belief that if it works in one place it will work in others. There may be fundamental differences between two agencies that appear superficially to be similar.

One of the factors often ignored is the different level of expertise and therefore the amount of training that may be needed. There are some fundamental questions that need to be asked, whether software is being chosen or a manual system is being considered. We offer some guidelines below for the requirements of a manual system. There is much material available about computers but little about manual systems, yet many small agencies rely on manual systems for their generalised information. It is also sometimes forgotten that the ability to group and categorise material manually is a sound basis for intelligent use of computers. There is often a naive hope that 'when we computerise it will all work out'.

Guidelines for storing and retrieving files

Essential elements
- Consistency.
- Cross-referencing.
- Grouping and categorising.
- Accessibility of information.
- Continuous and up-to-date maintenance.

Choice of particular systems
- It is preferable to use a numbering system for files for referencing and indexing purposes.
- A general card index is necessary for a manual system.
- Cards should be in alphabetical order under groupings or categories.
- Enclosures within the files should always be numbered and filed chronologically.

Use of title for files
- 'Wastepaper basket' or miscellaneous files should be avoided.
- Chronological filing is lazy. Files should not be opened and shut every year to avoid large files. If files are too large it is preferable to break them up by category.
- Consistency with groupings or categories is essential. For example, categorisation could be either by committee or function/issue. In the example given below, if categorisation is by committee it would be the *Council of Social Service (COSS)*, if by function it would be *Housing*. The categories would then be:

COSS (committee)	*Housing* (function)
Alcoholism	Aboriginal and Islander
Benefits	Council of Social Service
Drug addiction	Housing Department
Housing etc.	Shelter etc.

- Whichever grouping is used, cross-referencing is important and overloading should be avoided. If a committee has a very wide function, there should be subcategorisation.
- If filing is alphabetical in the card index the first word is important. The key word should be carefully chosen. For example, for the Victorian Association of Day Nurseries, the key word is 'Nurseries'. Cross-referencing then would be to 'Day' and 'Victorian'.

Guidelines for enclosures
- Avoid loose sheets.
- Number all enclosures and attachments.
- Ensure that there is consistency and cross-referencing within files as well as across.
- File a new piece of material in the file to which reference is made. For example, in a reply to a letter always locate the original correspondence before filing.
- Where a letter refers to more than one topic, cross-reference or put copies in other files.
- When putting an extract on another file, place on a larger sheet and try to keep files relatively uniform. Small scraps of paper can be overlooked.
- Put file number and enclosure on all relevant material.
- Use letter headings that identify the file where possible.
- Use the inner cover for an ongoing summary, referring to enclosures. For noting closed files or closely related files the inner cover is also useful.
- Select the major subject of an incoming letter. This requires careful reading, as headings on letters received can be deceptive. There may also be reference to more than one issue, and cross-referencing may be needed.

Physical aspects
- Various systems are available, from cards to various types of hanging files, box files and colour-coded systems. Whatever system is used it should be as simple as possible.
- Files should not be allowed to become too bulky. Avoid bulky enclosures and loose sheets or pamphlets inside files. Box files and cross-referencing should be used.
- Card indexes are valuable as summaries and as ways of indicating action that has been taken. Cards can be used without files for short-term issues or contacts.

Central index and security of files
- There should always be a central index even if files are not always kept centrally.
- Files kept separately should be accessible and monitored carefully.
- Cards should never be taken out of the index.
- When a file is taken, an insert (signed and dated) should be placed where the file has been taken from.
- The person taking the file is responsible for its whereabouts.

For example, if you give the file to another person, you must record the movement on the insert.

Introduction of computers
- The agency must be quite clear about what it wants the computer and software to do.
- The system should be the simplest one available to do the required job, as unnecessary complexities are expensive and counter-productive.
- The ability of the staff to learn the new system, and the amount of training required, should be taken into account when choosing.
- The system should be understood by as many staff as possible.
- Discussion with other peer agencies about their computer needs, and the way they have handled them, is valuable.

If the above points are not considered the result can be serious for the small agency, as its funds are unlikely to cope with too much wastage. One large service organisation ruefully admitted that it wasted months of time, and large amounts of money, on overestimating the feasibility of adjusting a package, and under-estimating the amount of staff training required. Small agencies cannot afford such costs. The training required could unfortunately also result in having only one or two staff in the small agency who understand the mysteries of the system. This can result in problems if crucial staff are absent or leave, and can also create inappropriate power patterns based on the exclusive 'knowledge power' of one or two people.

PHYSICAL RESOURCES MANAGEMENT

Physical and non-physical aspects of management are closely interrelated. The principles that apply to non-physical processes apply also to physical processes. This means that one of the important elements is the need for the participation and under-standing of all staff in handling physical resources.

Planning the physical environment

Small agencies rarely have money to spare for glamorous office accommodation but this does not mean that they should give up on appearances. Drab colours and untidy noticeboards full of out-of-date and curling notices demonstrate a lack of effort in creating a pleasant working environment. They also convey a negative message to the service users. A little planning can also take account of the needs of all those who use the offices. Reception areas should not be used as working areas if at all possible. Public areas are noisy and lack privacy. Service users do not want to state their business in a work area or waiting room, where others can overhear what is being said. Planners and architects are often unaware of the importance of privacy in many not-for-profit organisations, particularly those in the health and welfare areas.

Noticeboards are a much under-used resource, not only as a public relations feature but also in terms of office management. Noticeboards are a useful communication tool but if they are not used effectively they will be ignored and become dysfunctional. Other physical means of communication, such as brochures and newsletters, are all valuable if they are well-produced, monitored continually and checked for response and effectiveness.

Office space

Office space is notorious as a source of contention, not only because of practical questions but also because the size, furnishings and location of an office are often seen as status issues. Many small agencies, particularly those that stress they are a 'family', are reluctant to have a system that has hierarchical overtones. At the other extreme, one organisation ranked all staff in hierarchical terms from most senior to most junior, and then allotted office space based on that ranking, grading the offices according to size and attractiveness. Whatever the method, it must be visible, understood and generally accepted by the people concerned.

One organisation had some rooms allotted to volunteers and these were prized. They gave the volunteers a feeling of belonging and a focal place for them to meet and share views. This was particularly important for volunteers, as they felt rather isolated from the mainstream activities of the agency. When some extra staff were appointed, it was decided to eliminate the volunteers' rooms. This was not discussed with them and they were notified of the change by letter, which justified the change on the grounds of the expanding of the agency's services.

It was debatable that such a change was necessary, and that some compromise could not have been found, but in any case the process was quite unacceptable. There should have been personal contact with the volunteers, reasons given for the change, and a discussion of any options available. The memo method was chosen as the easy way out, but in the end it created a great deal of bitterness that affected the agency for some years.

This example shows that it is important to take into account the particular needs of an agency and not talk in number terms only, or make invalid comparisons across agencies. One of the challenges when designing a building is that different jobs require different types of offices and workplaces. It is sometimes difficult to anticipate the number of people that will exist in the agency in the future. There is no guarantee that an office will suit the work group throughout the lifecycle of the organisation. Because of this, every attempt needs to be made to assess and revise plans to ensure that the offices will accommodate generally the demands of the job with the least amount of restructuring possible.

This refers also to work flows and the placing of certain offices close to others. In one organisation two important departments that had close relationships with one another were geographically separated, for no clear reason beyond some past personal preferences. Again, intelligent anticipation would at least have minimised some of the problems and cut down the need for so much physical change at a later date.

The question of privacy was mentioned with reference to reception areas but it is also of importance for general office allocation. There have been fashions in office design and at one stage open space was the favoured type of office accommodation. This was always of doubtful value in the small agency, particularly in the health/welfare area. It is also difficult in a noisy, communal space to prepare reports that take a great deal of thought and concentration.

In some agencies the lack of private space has led people to take work home rather than work on the material in the office. Apart from the strain this places on some people at home, there are problems when staff are absent for long periods. Many of the ad hoc informal contacts can be lost. Some agencies have 'drop in' clients or deal with unscheduled activities or crises. When certain staff are away writing reports, others have to deal disproportionately with the unscheduled activities.

This type of situation needs to be monitored, discussed and dealt with on equitable terms. The development of computers and home-based work has made this even more important and is an issue that needs attention. Organisations whose service is people based cannot divorce themselves from the need to 'be there' for people. There is also the personnel issue of isolation of staff, when the sharing of ideas and group support are so important in service organisations.

'Taking work home' is also a problem as far as the office organisation is concerned. It is serious enough if a file is lost in the office system, as was illustrated in the vignette at the beginning of the chapter, but it becomes much worse if material is lost outside the office, or cannot be accessed from a computer because of limited knowledge. The whole question of confidentiality, which has always been an issue in the human service area, is exacerbated by the separation of people from the office base. There are many horror stories: memos are lost or 'leaked', with varying degrees of culpability; personal information about service users ends up in the wrong place; important files are found 'in the street'; and personal files are discarded but not shredded.

Security of offices

Security is a particularly important issue in the small agency. Sometimes the service users may be in a distressed state or on the verge of violent or dangerous behaviour. Larger agencies might have elaborate security systems and security staff available but small agencies can rarely afford such resources. Planning can help overcome some of the difficulties, for example, the siting of various sections and the availability of security buzzers. The physical aspects need to be coordinated with the personnel practices that should take account of security matters. There is sometimes a reluctance to face this issue, almost as if it is seen as a betrayal of the service users.

Service user needs

Service user needs do not always fit in with organisational needs but it is important to weigh these up and give service user needs the priority that they deserve. There is now greater awareness, for example, of the needs of the disabled, but sometimes there is neglect of the problems of the parent with small children or elderly people who have difficulty accessing or negotiating the physical aspects of an agency.

The balancing of such needs has been acknowledged in the setting up of community health centres or neighbourhood centres. The general view is that the ideal arrangement for workers as well as service users is to locate the agency in a house, or rooms, that are seen as part of the community. One problem, however, is that such houses may be unsuitable in terms of work environment and make the carrying out of office procedures much more difficult than they would be in a modern office. Many workers prefer the homely, friendly atmosphere of the converted house and are prepared to put up with the inconveniences that result from such a work layout. It is possible here to reach a compromise by careful use of the space available.

Transport

There are various theories on the reasons for the significance of transport. There is no doubt that inadequate transport facilities for staff can have severe functional consequences in human service organisations, where movement outside the office to other organisations and to service users is so much a part of the service delivery. However, as with rooms, there seems to be an aura of status attached to certain resources. The car in the case of lower levels, and aeroplanes in the case of VIPs, are a constant point of contention among members of the organisations themselves and for the community outside the organisation. There seem to be more complaints about misuse of resources related to transport than almost any other. In one small not-for-profit agency the Board seemed to spend a disproportionate amount of time discussing the use of the car, the methods of recording that use, and how much personal use was allowed.

In one small municipal council the CEO and the city engineer had sedans and other staff had utilities. When a social worker was appointed there was some discussion as to whether she rated 'sedan' or 'utility'. Finally, it was decided that there were functional reasons for the social worker to have a sedan, on the grounds that she would be carrying passengers rather than goods. However, many in the council saw this as a status issue linking the social worker with the CEO and the engineer. The social worker had to keep careful log records of the movement of the car in the early years, as the community and the organisation monitored the use of her car very carefully, more or less informally.

Equipment and other resources

Just as it is sometimes difficult to get reasonably attractive offices because of the lack of resources in the small agency, it is often difficult to get adequate office equipment and resources. When the choice is between services for people and material goods there seems to be a reluctance to spend the money. One worker in a small agency pointed out that she was unable to do the job properly because her 'dinosaur' of a computer could only be used for simple typing/word-processing. Outdated equipment was not, however, regarded as a priority by the agency's Board but as a minor inconvenience.

There is a tendency for some Boards to debate every physical item of expenditure ad nauseam because it is a practical issue that can be easily understood. One staff member of a small agency complained that every minor item of equipment was used until it fell apart and the pros and cons of each type of replacement equipment occupied a disproportionate amount of the committee of management's time. This is a problem that should not exist if the roles of the staff and Board are clear and if priorities and time management have been properly addressed.

The use of technology is a new dilemma for agencies; the days when an office consisted of a typewriter, a desk and a phone no longer exist. The question is a balance between cost, convenience, efficiency and user friendliness. An example of the type of problem is the answering machine. They are valuable for inter-agency contacts but not necessarily suitable for service user calls. The screening of calls can help the agency cope with its workload and see that the most appropriate person deals with the situation, but it is not always the best way of dealing with particularly stressful areas of service. Constant reassessment is needed.

CONCLUSION

The concentration in the preceding chapters has been on the processes that concern the individual managers and how they can be improved to help achieve the goals of both best service and survival. The following two chapters will cover the aspects that concern the agency as a whole. Chapter 8 deals with the way information is collected and 'managed', and chapter 9 discusses how programs can be assessed and made as effective as possible. These are the final chapters because in many ways they are the most complex and, to some extent, the most unfamiliar to a number of agencies. In addition, in order to effectively tackle these areas, managers need to be familiar with the areas discussed so far.

NOTES

1. Some of this material first appeared as chapter 10 'Managing the Office and the Work Environment', in Donovan, F. and Jackson, A.C. (1991).
2. These are adapted from Ehlers, W.M. (1976) 'Unit III, Planning Lesson 3, Personal Planning', in W.M. Ehlers, M.J. Austin and J.C. Prothers *Administration for the Human Services*, Harper & Row, New York, p. 105.

8

MANAGING INFORMATION

A group of small, not-for-profit agencies, whose service users had similar needs, decided to form a loose federation or association, for a number of reasons. They wanted to avoid competing with one another, but also considered that they would be able to support one another in a number of ways. One of these ways was the sharing of information, not only to improve their tendering processes but also to improve their general management, particularly their planning.

Although their intentions were good, a number of problems threatened the success of the new association. Some problems were due to the perceived relative power role of the small agencies in relation to the 'central' body, and also the question of its financing. These problems in turn were related to the gathering of information, which was one of the reasons for setting up the association. The agencies were asking such questions as 'Why are they asking for this? What are they going to do with it?'.

It became obvious that there was a noticeable difference in skills and commitment among the different agencies when it came to collecting information. When the association tried to encourage the agencies to develop similar methods so that the information could serve a useful purpose, there was resistance. Some of the agencies 'didn't have the time', they were 'too busy providing a service for the clients', or they 'couldn't see what use it all was anyhow'. In addition, there were others who saw the material as threatening their autonomy, allowing unfair comparisons.

The result was that the association had to defer the information gathering until it had developed a program to clarify the purposes of the information-gathering role, what processes and skills were involved and how the agencies could be helped in developing those skills. A final and very important goal was to convince the agencies that benefits would flow back to them and their service users. The committee of the association, which was made up of agency and community representatives, had underestimated both the suspicions of 'centralism' and motives for information collecting.

This attitude was similar to the problems that central offices of larger government organisations have with their devolved units. Even the language was similar: 'Those people in there don't understand what we have to do and just seem to want paper'. One lesson to be learned is that, when information is gathered, those collecting it at the 'coalface' need to be convinced of its value and should receive constant feedback as to the use that is made of their efforts.

It is sometimes assumed that 'information' refers only to the material that is required by management. Also, the technical term 'information' does not mean just raw data—it refers to data that have been analysed and interpreted. It involves a wide range of material required for many aspects of practice and service delivery, for example, as mentioned in previous chapters, with reference to performance appraisal, budgeting and costing, human resource management, evaluation and planning. These are specific information requirements and there have been many examples of this type of information gathering throughout the book. This chapter deals, however, with the information that is necessary simply to do the day-to-day work of the agency.

This information about services and their users, as it is more generalised, often becomes more complex and technical. It is not necessary for all agencies to carry out all processes. How much depends on size, the type of service and the availability of funds and staff. Not all information required by the organisation needs to be collected within the organisation. A number of external data sources can be used, such as local government data sources, the Australian Bureau of Statistics (ABS), household surveys conducted by large research or government institutions, and government departments. There are dangers, however, in the indiscriminate use of outside sources of information. Different methods of data analysis make comparisons difficult or invalid, particularly the comparing of data obtained in different countries and applied in different social contexts.

PURPOSES OF INFORMATION SYSTEMS

The purposes of an information system include:

- providing developmental information for policy and planning and for continuity in service delivery, thereby avoiding ad hoc decisions and an episodic approach
- supporting accountability requirements and providing information on program processes, impacts and outcomes to all of the relevant audiences
- preventing the loss of historical knowledge of past developments, especially if key personnel leave
- substantiating funding claims or submissions by providing information which links factors, such as service user profiles, cost of service provision, and outcomes achieved
- providing community information which may include answering criticisms about service priorities in general and service to particular individuals
- providing support for public relations programs.

Whatever the unit of information might be, the purpose for which the information is collected should be clearly stated, and priorities determined. One of the major faults in information collection is the assumption that information can be used for a wide variety of purposes. Once data have been analysed and interpreted for a particular purpose the information should be used for that purpose. It is always possible to modify the data to achieve different purposes, but there must be awareness of the limitations to this process. Having said this, we need to acknowledge that information can be, and often is, used for purposes other than those for which it was collected.

Small organisations sometimes feel that they do not have

sufficient influence and control over the way that information they have provided is used. A small not-for-profit organisation might be part of a 'chain' of small agencies funded from a central source and accountable to that funding body, or to a service purchaser that is itself funded for that purpose. In these circumstances the agency may have little control over how either the purchaser or funder uses aggregated data from all of the smaller services. This aggregated data may be used to make a political point with which the agency may not agree, or may be used to make 'bigger picture' decisions with which the agency, again, may not be in agreement.

A good example of this would be the case of a decision to expand legal gambling opportunities because of an interpretation by politicians and the gaming industry that the social impact of gambling *on aggregate* is not serious. This decision may, however, miss information from problem-gambling counselling agencies showing that, in some economically depressed and socially stressed areas, women and adolescents are particularly vulnerable to electronic gaming machines located in shopping precincts. In other words, it is the analysis and interpretation of data, how they are turned into information, that is the crucial feature of their use.

Some of the types of information covered in the previous discussion on purposes above could be classified as information about:

- individual consumers
- policy
- planning processes
- resource availability and usage
- costing and budgeting
- housekeeping details
- staffing, awards, industrial aspects
- community contacts and interrelationships
- training.

Some of these have been dealt with in earlier chapters. In the following section, we will consider the areas of information needed under two main headings—for policy and planning, and for the purposes of accountability and evaluation. We would stress that there is a close interrelationship between all types of information. If case or individual service user-level information is weak, then policy and planning is negatively affected. If people recognise this interrelationship the development of information systems will not be seen as a remote managerial function contradicting the workers' desire to 'put people before paper'.[1]

Information for policy and planning

In some ways the policy and planning purpose of information encompasses all the other purposes listed earlier. This is because the information system's major objective, for the manager, is to provide material to contribute to more effective decision making and planning both in the long and the short term, through achieving the other purposes. The short-term decisions that managers need to make include:

- allocating and reallocating staff and other resources
- reorientating the services to cover any identified 'at-risk' group whose needs are not being met, where meeting those needs is seen as a legitimate part of the operation of the agency
- determining that program activities could be improved or need to be changed

The longer term decisions include:

- decisions about the effectiveness of the program or its elements, intervention methods and personnel
- identification of the need for new programs
- identification of the need for new policy, or changes to the orientation of the organisation.

Information for accountability and evaluation

One of the most important features of a management information system in any human service organisation is to ensure that information is available in such a way as to help monitoring and evaluation to become routine. The information system needs to be designed to provide a range of information covering such aspects of the agency's operations as:

- referral and admission patterns
- service delivery
- discharge patterns
- time spent in programs
- outcome.

Information about service use

One of the most difficult types of agency for which to design a relevant information system is the multiple program agency. Even small agencies may have multiple programs if they serve different target groups. The change from core funding to program funding has also meant that agencies that were previously offering only one program may take on new areas. Evaluation includes knowing how the program components relate to each other, what determines the service for each type of client, and the most effective way of packaging services. This includes understanding 'client flow' through the system.

In one family service agency that had a fairly unsophisticated data collection system, a framework had to be developed to convert these data into useful information for judging the effectiveness of the program, and to provide information for future policy and program planning. To produce the required information the agency had to first collect the data. This collection was by manual means and included both initial intake record cards and case files. Turning data into useful information involved some analysis, and interpretation. The framework shown on page 181 was applied to the data in the records, and also became, after the evaluation period, the routine case-recording framework for the agency.

One feature in which the manager was interested as part of her evaluation of 'client flow' or service use patterns was multiple use of the agency. The agency, as part of its statement of purpose, noted that it was a 'person-centred' and not a 'problem-centred' organisation. By this the agency meant that it should be able to offer services related to a variety of service user needs at the one site and time, if necessary; that is, it aimed to deal with a *cluster* of problems if necessary, rather than force people to use a number of different agencies dealing with perhaps more limited views of what those people's 'problems' or requests for service were.

Using the framework the manager was able to distinguish three types of multiple-use clients:

1. those who had a single contact with the agency but used a number of services during the contact period
2. those who had a number of contacts with the agency but used a different service on each contact
3. those who had a number of contacts with the agency and used the same service on each contact.

By analysing use in terms of the service and demographic patterns of these groups, it could be seen whether multiple-use clients were in fact different from other ser-vice users. Over one-third of the agency's service users were multiple users of one sort or another. Of these, almost a fifth were from one of the most depressed housing areas in the city. The multiple-use families were more likely than single-use families to:

- have changed area of residence between contacts
- have a higher proportion of families with young de-pendent children
- be concerned with problems of family breakdown or deterioration of relationships
- be suffering the material consequences of family breakdown, such as housing needs.

They were, in these respects, seen to be more vulnerable than single-use families.

By examining various aspects of the findings of its study of client records, the agency was able to determine the need to establish an outreach program in the area of low-status housing, which also had one of the highest rates of family breakdown.

Framework for ordering data from case records in a multi-program family agency

1. *Case no.*
2. *Date of first referral*
3. *Area of residence*
4. *Birthplace of mother:*
   a Australian born
   b Non-English-speaking born
   c English-speaking born
5. *Birthplace of father:*
   a Australian born
   b Non-English-speaking born
   c English-speaking born
6. *Description of household structure:*
   a Both natural parents present
   b Couple without children

c Both adoptive parents present
d Female-headed one parent
e Male-headed one parent
f Blended with children only of female
g Blended with children only of male
h Blended with children of each
i Blended with children of both and/or each
j Blended—unknown
k Single person household
l Non-related 'families' e.g. group house

Life stage of family:
7. Child(ren) up to 5 present
  a Yes
  b No
  c Not known
8. Children 6–12 present
  a Yes
  b No
  c Not known
9. Teenager(s) 13–19 present (dependent)
  a Yes
  b No
  c Not known
10. Teenager(s) present (non-dependent)
  a Yes
  b No
  c Not known
11. Children in long-term substitute care
  a Yes
  b No
  c Not known
12. Aged persons (60+) present
  a Yes
  b No
  c Not known
13. Parent(s) with adult child(ren) not present
  a Yes
  b No
  c Not known
14. Third generation present in household
  a Yes
  b No
  c Not known
15. *Referred by:*
  a Self
  b Relation/friend/neighbour
  c Agency client
  d Private psychiatrist
  e Medical service
  f Legal service
  g Statutory agency (welfare)

h Statutory agency (non-welfare)
i Voluntary agency (counselling)
j Voluntary agency (non-counselling)
k Other
l Unknown
16. *Reason for referral:*
  a Family relationship problems
  b Child behaviour problems
  c Emotional disturbance in adults
  d Domestic violence
  e Housing problems/homelessness
  f Social isolation
  g Child at risk/neglect
  h Emotional/physical deprivation
  i Marital conflict
  j Integration of handicapped child
  k Daycare for parent relief
  l Parenting skills
  m Preschool preparation
  n Personal development
  o Family breakdown
  p Welfare rights
17. *Assessed problem:*
  a Family relationship problems
  b Child behaviour problems
  c Emotional disturbance in adults
  d Domestic violence
  e Housing problems/homelessness
  f Social isolation
  g Child at risk/neglect
  h Emotional/physical deprivation
  i Marital conflict
  j Integration of handicapped child

k Daycare for parent relief
l Parenting skills
m Preschool preparation
n Personal development
o Family breakdown
p Welfare rights

18. *Point of entry (service):*
   a Counselling
   b Group
   c Daycare
   d Preschool
   e Emergency
      accommodation

Closed cases

19. *Reason for closure:*
   a Situation resolved
   b Problem resolved but
      basic situation unresolved
   c One client helped but
      other remains dissatisfied
   d Client chose to
      discontinue but gained
      understanding of problem
   e Client left area
   f Service withdrawn
   g Referred to another
      agency

Program use

20. *Counselling*
Months since last contact:
   a 0–3
   b 4–6
   c over 6
Code of last contact ——
No. of times this service
previously used ——

21. *Parenting group*
Months since last contact:
   a 0–3
   b 4–6
   c over 6
Code of last contact ——
No. of times this service
previously used ——

22. *Assertiveness training group*
Months since last contact:

a 0–3
b 4–6
c over 6
Code of last contact ——
No. of times this service
previously used ——

23. *Alone again group*
Months since last contact:
   a 0–3
   b 4–6
   c over 6
Code of last contact ——
No. of times this service
previously used ——

24. *Youth group*
Months since last contact:
   a 0–3
   b 4–6
   c over 6
Code of last contact ——
No. of times this service
previously used ——

25. *Daycare*
Months since last contact:
   a 0–3
   b 4–6
   c over 6
Code of last contact ——
No. of times this service
previously used ——

26. *Preschool*
Months since last contact:
   a 0–3
   b 4–6
   c over 6
Code of last contact ——
No. of times this service
previously used ——

27. *Emergency accommodation*
Months since last contact:
   a 0–3
   b 4–6
   c over 6
Code of last contact ——
No. of times this service
previously used ——

The example above shows the direct benefits of an organisation understanding patterns in its operation and being able to respond by changing the way it delivers its services. It also shows how the data were held in the organisation's information system but not acted upon for some years until a new manager started asking some new evaluation-type questions and devised an interpretive framework, allowing analysis to be done, so that patterns emerged that could be used for planning purposes.

The analysis, however, was beyond the skill level of the manager, who, recognising this, offered the agency's data to the local technical college computer studies course as classroom material, if the college would analyse it for free. They agreed. Although the task could have been done without a computer, it would have taken longer.

In addition to the uses already mentioned, this data set could be used for:

• seeing which programs had better success rates
• assessing whether the agency's public relations, in terms of the extent to which its work was known by other agencies, were effective
• informing workers about the accuracy of referrals, by matching the 'assessed problem' with 'reason for referral'.

What this framework cannot do in isolation, however, is to give some more detailed information on what the staff do on a day-to-day basis in performing their designated roles. This is important information for managers as it tells them whether:

• they have staff with the right competencies to do the work of the agency.
• the work that the Board and manager believed was the best way of implementing the policies of the agency is actually what is done.

Information about worker activity

It is important to identify whether the purpose of an exercise is for performance appraisal or program appraisal and this refers also to information collection. If information about worker activity is being collected to assess how the program is being carried out in general terms, there are useful and relatively simple ways of keeping track of what workers actually do in their day-to-day practice. One example is the use of a spreadsheet documenting worker activity over time as well as relevant details about the service user.

The manager of an agency employing social workers as case managers for people with acquired brain injury was asked to provide information to the larger agency which purchased their service on behalf of a government department funder. The information required was about the type of work done by the social workers in pursuit of their case management role, as representation had been made to the funder that nursing trained personnel should be carrying out these functions rather than social workers. The purchasing agent was asked, therefore, to provide details on these functions using a range of typical cases referred to the service provider, including older stroke patients, younger accident victims and very young patients, such as near drowning cases. The manager was expected to provide this information.

Records of twenty-four service users were compiled, to show the *intensity* of service provision (how many activities the social workers were engaged in simultaneously in relation to each case) and the *extent* of service provision (for how long the services were provided), Microsoft Excel© spreadsheets were used. The spreadsheets showed the involvement of over 120 external agencies and therapists, in addition to resource linking, case management, advocacy and counselling interventions. Crises and other significant events in the service user's psychosocial environment were listed, along with demographic details and a case summary. Figure 8.1 shows an extract from one record as an example.[2] The legend explains the notations on the chart.

As a result of this detailed analysis, linked with followup interviews and assessment of the service user after the social work intervention, the agency was able to argue for retention of the social workers' role.

As can be seen from this example, such an exercise can leave the manager not only with detailed case-by-case information on practice, but also, in the process of detailing the fields of practice activity for inclusion in the spreadsheet, allows assumptions about what happens in practice to be challenged. New insights into the complexity of practice can be gained, along with the capacity to

Figure 8.1 Sample services map

	A	B	C	D	E	F	G	H	I	J	K	L	M	N	O	P	Q	R	S	T	U	V	W	X	Y	Z	AA	AB
1	PATIENT	1	HYPOXIA					AGE 30		GENDER																		
2	WEEK	0	2	4	6	8	10	12	14	16	18	20	22	24	26	28	30	32	34	36	38	40	42	44	46	48	50	52
3	CRISIS EVENTS		IP DISCHARGE				CARER'S RETURN			F																		
4							TO WORK																					
5	ORGANISATION																											
6	WORKCOVER																											
7	TAC																											
8	DSS																											
9	CRS																											
10	TLC												[				M		M									^
11	Employer																											x
12	Norwood							[			^																	
13	Horizon										^																	
14	Westcod										^																	
15	Yooralla					[		]																			M		
16	RDNS							[		]																			
17	DRS										x																	
18	SIG. OTHER																											
19	MOTHER																											
20	FATHER																											
21	SIBLING																											
22	Partner/Spouse																^											

	B	C	D	E	F	G	H	I	J	K	L	M	N	O	P	Q	R	S	T	U	V	W	X	Y	Z	AA	AB
A	0	2	4	6	8	10	12	14	16	18	20	22	24	26	28	30	32	34	36	38	40	42	44	46	48	50	52
WEEK																											
23 CHILD																											
24																											
25 THERAPY																											
26 PHYSIO	[>																										
27 OCCUPATION	[											]															
28 SPEECH	[											M															
29 RECREATION																											
30 MEDICAL		M				M		M																			
31 PSYCH																											
32 NEUROPSYCH																											
33 DIETICIAN																											
34 SOCIAL WORK																											
35 Resource prov	91, 10, 15, 28, 24, 43, 53, 54, 57–65																										
36 # Gov'nment			66		41	88	23	49	90		46		[89 >														
37 CR					75		10	[41 >																			
38 # community link					74		72	[66 >																			
39 *							57	[61 >																			
40							18	[86 >																			
41 *								[65 >																			
42 *											[14 >													^			
43 *										[39 >																	
44 Vocational																											

#	A	B	C	D	E	F	G	H	I	J	K	L	M	N	O	P	Q	R	S	T	U	V	W	X	Y	Z	AA	AB
	WEEK	0	2	4	6	8	10	12	14	16	18	20	22	24	26	28	30	32	34	36	38	40	42	44	46	48	50	52
45	Commercial link																											
46																												
47	SW letter of support				91	10	15, 28, 24, 43, 53				54, 57–65				86	53	86											
48	Medical Certificate																											
49	Therapy letter																											
50	advocacy:																											
51	#individual						14																					
52	group																											
53																												
54	case manage				[																							
55	Key worker				Nη			Nη		SW		team																
56	Screening																											
57	initial assess																											
58	(init. by)																											
59	psychsoc assess																											
60	Monitoring																							]		[14, 50 >		
61	discharge plan																											
62	treatment plan				M	M		M		M	MM		M	M				M										
63	Family meet																											
64	(init. by)						SW	M	M																			
65	Fam involv treat										^																	
66	Agency inv treat				43		M86			M57		M																

	A	B	C	D	E	F	G	H	I	J	K	L	M	N	O	P	Q	R	S	T	U	V	W	X	Y	Z	AA	AB
		0	2	4	6	8	10	12	14	16	18	20	22	24	26	28	30	32	34	36	38	40	42	44	46	48	50	52
67	WEEK																												
68	FOLLOW UP																												
69																													
70	COUNSELLING																												
71	Patient																												
71	#Patient crisis																												
73	Depression																												
74	Patient adjust																												
75	Patient grief																												
76	: image/role																												
77	: prognosis																												
78	: terminal																												
79	Dependence																												
80	Support network																												
81	Relaxation																												
82	Pain																												
83	Financial																												
84	Behav. mod.																												
85	# OTHER																												
86	"																												
87	"																												
88	Family																												
89	# Fam crisis																												

	A	B	C	D	E	F	G	H	I	J	K	L	M	N	O	P	Q	R	S	T	U	V	W	X	Y	Z	AA	AB
90	family adjust						—			—																		
91	family grief																											
92	partner/spouse																											
93	goal setting																											
94	Guardian/Admin						▨		▨																			
95	# OTHER				**20**																							
96	"																											
97	WEEK	0	2	4	6	8	10	12	14	16	18	20	22	24	26	28	30	32	34	36	38	40	42	44	46	48	50	52

Legend

[Initial assessment of formal initiation of services provided

] Formal discharge

▨ Shading means at least one intervention in a two-week period, but can represent many interventions. Spaces between shaded areas show only that intervention has not been recorded

< Records indicate previous contact, but details are not recorded of when or how long previously

> Contact is assumed to have continued, but records do not document for how long

M Indicates presence at a meeting regarding the patient

Nη Nurse

SW Social worker

14 Resource 14 from a Resource List has been contacted by the social worker

14 A counselling intervention focus

▮ A crisis event or significant event on the environment of the patient

compare different worker styles of practice activities across a number of workers with the same type of service user, to gain better knowledge about service user requirements.

Agency-focused or service user-focused information

A major issue confronting agencies is whether the information system used is agency-focused or user-focused. Although this bald distinction may oversimplify the issue, it is clear that agencies can design a system that yields only information that, in a more or less sophisticated way, answers the question 'How much is being done here?' (quantity), which is an organisation-centred question. What is needed is information that answers 'What is being done here?', 'With whom?', 'Why?', and 'With what results?', which are more user-oriented questions.

Ideally there should be no distinction in the agency/user focus of a management information system, especially if the agency is identifying characteristics of its user group that enables it to contribute to needs analysis and policy formulation outside the program's immediate focus. An example of this would be the identification of sociodemographic trends that can point to the vulnerability of some service users for whom new services may need to be provided, either by that agency or another.

One agency realised that there were requests for help from a significant number who were officially outside its target group. It was necessary to decide whether the agency should or could modify its program, or whether it should pass on the information to another, perhaps more suitable agency, or draw the matter to the attention of the appropriate government agency. In addition, there was the question of action about referrals and public expectations. The need for this wider use of information is particularly relevant to advocacy-oriented organisations, but can form an important function for other agencies as well.

It is also possible to build what some agencies have termed 'social action' components into an information system to obtain, fairly systematically, information on factors such as income levels and family composition, in much the same way as the framework applied to the multiple service agency earlier. For example, their framework for data analysis, which later became their framework for data collection, contained a lot of categories for recording types of family structure. This was because they were keen to know what sorts of families were accessing their parenting groups, and to see whether these groups were geared towards the issues likely to be faced by the different sorts of family structures.[3]

IMPROVING AN EXISTING INFORMATION SYSTEM

Information systems should be considered a dynamic element in managing human service organisations. One requirement of such a system is that it be flexible and able to respond to changes in reporting requirements and changing information needs.

Reviewing the system

It is useful to routinely review the system in the same way that other aspects of the organisation's operations are reviewed. Some of the questions that would help in such a review include:

- Is the system still doing the job for which it was designed?
- Is it operating as economically as it can?
- Is it contributing to quality assurance, or the ability of the agency to tell whether it is meeting the needs of its users?
- Is it appropriate for the size of the organisation?
- Is it more complex than it needs to be?
- Is it more simple than it should be?
- Is it being used to answer questions about the performance of the program or simply administrative performance?

Another indicator of the need for review of the information system is when the manager has to search frequently outside the existing system. Occasionally there will be a need to step outside the system in order to obtain material for some special purpose and which in no way can be considered routine. However, some managers may find that they are consistently going outside the system for specific information. In this case there is a clear need to incorporate that information requirement into the regular system.

Improving the system

Having decided that the system needs some change, there are a number of steps that can be followed to make the changes. These steps are outlined below.[4]

1. *Assess how prepared the agency is for the change*, and how feasible the change is. This includes having as much agreement as possible from the Board and staff about the need for change,

and a commitment to carrying the change through, even though it may be inconvenient.

2. *Analyse the existing system.* This includes attempting to forecast how the system may need to change in the future and not just to relate the analysis to the limitations of the system as they exist now. At this stage, the cost of operating the existing system, including extra costs for data entry and analysis, should be calculated, if not already known.

3. *Think about the design changes necessary.* This includes thinking about the required detail of information necessary for the agency to perform its decision-making and planning functions. At this point, the requirements should be able to be translated into hardware and software specifications. The relationship of all the components of the information system to each other should be made clear at this time, including intake data on service users, worker activity records and case notes.

4. *Familiarise people with the new system.* Having decided the changes, staff need to become familiar with the new system. This may mean that the agency has to provide training for the staff, and may mean some changes to the way the office operates.

5. *Monitor the changes.* Once the system is up and running, it should be monitored to see if it is performing in the way that was hoped, and that it is having the desired impact on decision making and service provision.

Design checklist

There are a number of other general points about an information system that agencies should consider when thinking about how their system operates, or that can be applied as principles to any new system being considered.

- *It should be as economical as possible,* both in terms of staff time spent on data collection and information retrieval and the cost of establishing and maintaining the management information system. It should be recognised that economy of time is a priority decision. The possibility of sampling has already been mentioned, but constant monitoring will indicate shortcuts and improved methods involving less time. If a system is to be effective it will inevitably take some time away from service delivery.

  One significant feature is that skill increases with familiarity, and time taken should be monitored over a relatively extended period. Other earlier examples of time studies and monitoring exercises showed that the time taken lessens with familiarity and skill. It is important to recognise this, as some of the resistance to managerial processes is due to a fear of the time element.

- *It should be compatible where possible with existing databases*, such as those created through the national census and available through the Australian Bureau of Statistics or those used by regional planning authorities or local authorities. This is crucial where an organisation wishes to match its knowledge of target populations with what is known about them elsewhere. It is also important that agencies ensure that they share information with other agencies and are using systems that are compatible, for comparative purposes. There have been examples where the time spent on developing systems has been wasted because it was found that the data were incompatible with ABS and most of the material had to be discarded.

- *It should rely wherever possible on non-specialist skills to operate the system* to reinforce the notion that data collection and information retrieval are matters of routine operation of human service organisations. This necessarily involves, as noted above, adequate preparation of staff and education to ensure commitment.

- *The system should be planned to reduce human error* where a computer-based system is introduced, for example, and run with a minimum of rules and an optimum amount of both training and support.

- *Material should not distort practitioner's experience*, otherwise it will be ignored, misused or waste time as workers attempt modifications. This is one of the most difficult yet common problems. If one worker in one agency decides to distort material because it is regarded as 'meaningless', or 'inappropriate', then the whole exercise is jeopardised.

- *The system must be able to provide 'readouts' of original data*, so the raw data can be moved to another system if necessary, where different software can be used to analyse the data.

- *Staff should be able to gain access to their own data* to satisfy themselves that the information is correct and to allow themselves to conduct their own analysis of patterns. Many systems forget to allow this access.

194

ATTITUDES TO INFORMATION COLLECTION

A special feature of information systems in human service organisations is that attitudes assume a greater significance than in other types of organisations.

Negative attitudes commonly held by workers

Some negative attitudes to management in general that exist in some human service organisations have already been mentioned and information systems are often caught up in that climate. These negative attitudes can be summarised as follows.

- There is a fear that information systems will not be able to deal with qualitative material; that they only deal with quantitative material and will miss those aspects of practice not satisfactorily contained in quantitative data.
- There is a belief that generalising information or aggregating individual experience, in a way that a management information system does, dehumanises service users. There is a belief that a person's problems are unique, which has the effect of upgrading the status of that person's problem. It follows from this belief in uniqueness that people are diminished if this generalisation takes place.
- There is concern about protecting a client's rights to confidentiality, which are seen as being threatened by the sharing and dissemination of information. This issue emerges particularly in relation to inter-agency aspects of data collection where information is shared between agencies.
- There is also a concern that the design and operation of the information system will reinforce some of the excesses of the 'new managerialists' who, as discussed in chapter 1, are regarded as operating from a narrow perspective. They may be considered unable to conceptualise practice in the terms necessary to operate what many workers would consider to be an appropriate information system.
- A danger exists that, as knowledge is power, the data retrieval process and the uses to which information is put can be manipulated. This is sometimes allied to a suspicion that, even though the purpose of collecting management information may be said to be improvement of service, it is in fact a way of controlling workers.
- There is a belief that the time taken for implementing the

information system is of no benefit to the service user and therefore takes away from the scarce resource of time for service delivery.

Some of these fears can be overcome by managers involving staff in all steps of the planning and design of information systems. It is particularly important that there should be proper consultation when any change is being considered. It also helps to reduce anxiety if agencies have representation on the bodies that are designing any monitoring requirements linked to funding, if these are external agencies. Staff need to know that their concerns about confidentiality and the representation of their practice in the information system have been taken into consideration in both the design and implementation of the system.

Making information systems more user-friendly

A further way that managers can ensure better compliance with and use of the agency's information system is to humanise it, making it as user-friendly as possible. Although we often think it is computer-based information systems that need to be humanised, there is a need to make manual systems accessible and work to the best advantage of the agency in meeting the needs of users. A set of criteria for humanising a system should include procedures for dealing with:

- the users of the system
- exceptions
- information
- privacy and ethics.

Procedures for dealing with users

The system should:
- use a language that is easy to understand
- enable courteous transactions to be conducted with it
- be quick to react
- respond quickly to users
- relieve the users of unnecessary chores
- include provisions for corrections
- clearly reflect that management is responsible for mismanagement.

Procedures for dealing with exceptions

A system should:
- recognise as much as possible that it deals with different classes of individuals
- recognise that special conditions might occur that could require special actions by it
- allow for potential alternatives in input and processing
- have procedures in place to enable operators to override it when necessary.

Action of the system with respect to information

A system should have provisions to:
- ensure that data is transferable to other systems for additional analysis
- permit individuals to inspect information about themselves
- enable workers to access their own service-user data
- correct errors
- assess the relevance and usefulness of information stored in the system
- allow individuals to add information that they consider important
- be clear about what information is stored in the system and what use will be made of that information.

The problem of privacy

In the design of a system all procedures should be evaluated with respect to both privacy and the requirement to humanise the process. The decision to merge information from different files and systems should never occur automatically. Whenever information from one file is made available to another file, it should be examined first for its implications for privacy.

Ethical issues in system design

A system should:
- not trick or deceive
- assist participants and users and not manipulate them
- not eliminate opportunities for employment without a careful examination of consequences to other available jobs
- not form part of a secret databank
- treat with consideration all individuals who come in contact with it.

HANDLING INFORMATION

After the material has gone through all the earlier processes there is the final process of how the material is handled. A surfeit of material is available on techniques for handling information but here we are primarily concerned with emphasising the general issues and principles involved, such as the importance of clarity of purpose, of constant review and as widespread a level of participation as possible. Some specific concerns in handling material relate to who should be able to access it, and how confidential is the information?

Access and confidentiality

It has to be clear to whom members of the organisation are responsible for collection, storage and use of information. A wide range of problems can arise relating to client records, such as service users' access to records and their right to limit the use of information. In organisations such as community groups and self-help groups there is often a strong expectation that communication should pass freely between service providers and service users, influenced sometimes by the lack of distinction between the two groups. Board members drawn from consumer groups are particularly vulnerable to what could be considered breaches of their privacy, and often pressure to disclose confidential information about other service users.

There has been an increasing tendency in human service organisations to make records more open. This has now been formally acknowledged in freedom of information legislation, particularly as it relates to statutory agencies and human service organisations. It has made managers aware of the need to be clear about responsibility and purpose and to be careful in allowing use of records for reasons that have not clearly been stated. One danger, however, has been that, because of fears of consequences, such as criticism and even legal action, valuable information that would be useful in making more informed management decisions may not be recorded. This has to be carefully monitored and, again, safeguards built in.

There is a danger that records are unable to be used for monitoring of standards because of restrictions on them in an effort to avoid criticism. For example, negative comments might never be made about inefficient workers because of the possible repercussions. When comments are made, they should be carefully backed up by evidence that the assessor is able to justify.

CONCLUSION

We have dealt with the questions of data collection, data storage and retrieval and data analysis as they are relevant to small organisations. We have stated that small organisations, who do not require the same sophistication as large organisations, have traditionally relied on limited manual systems but more recently have had to face the limitations of those systems. There is a danger that organisations see this need for change as necessitating major updating that is beyond the requirements of the small unit, resulting in unnecessary financial commitments and inappropriate training demands.

NOTES

1. For an excellent discussion of the relationship of different parts of an information system to each other, see Jackowski, E. and Stevens, B. (1988) 'Integrated Information Systems Concepts: An Information Resource Management Approach', in J. Rabin and M. Steinhauer (eds) *Handbook on Human Services Administration*, Marcel Decker, New York. Although their discussion is geared towards larger organisations, the important point they make is that effective policy making rests on a good information system at program level, which itself rests on a good information system operating at the level of service delivery.
2. For more detail on this particular method of constructing service records, with a particular focus on worker activity, see Jackson, A.C. and Tangney, S. (1997) 'A Service Mapping Approach to the Analysis of Service Use for People with Acquired Brain Injury', in G. Auslander (ed.) *International Perspectives on Social Work in Health Care*, The Haworth Press, New York. See also Nishimoto, R., Weil, M., and Theil, K.S. (1991) 'A Service Tracking and Referral Form to Monitor the Receipt of Services in a Case Management Program', *Administration in Social Work*, 15, 3, 33–47.
3. There has been a lot of attention paid, particularly in the health field in recent years, to constructing *minimum data sets* which attempt to capture the essence of practice across a wide range of similar agencies, such as hospitals and community health centres. These are interesting, as they often contain well thought out lists of 'problems' or 'indicators for intervention' and their attendant outcomes. They can therefore become useful starting points for agencies trying to

'capture' their practice in such a way that lends itself to being recorded and compared across sites. A good example of a minimum data set is provided in Coulton, C., Friedman, B.A. and Keller, S.M. (1992) *A Minimum Data Set for Hospital Social Work*, Social Work Management Information System Monograph, Society for Social Work Administrators in Health Care, Chicago, Ill.

4. For a thorough discussion of these processes, see Schoech, D., Schkade, L. and Mayers, R. (1981) 'Strategies for Information System Development', *Administration in Social Work*, 5, 3/4, 11–26.

9

PROGRAM EFFECTIVENESS

• *Evaluation and monitoring* • *Planning and evaluation* • *Conclusion*

We have seen that organisations will run efficiently and effectively in meeting the needs of the target population by making the best use of the resources available. This chapter examines program effectiveness as a particular aspect of agency operations, emphasising the programs themselves rather than the other aspects, such as finances and human resource management.

The importance of service users has been an underlying theme in the book, although we have concentrated on what the organisation and those responsible for its management can do for survival. To continue the emphasis on service users we stress that program effectiveness be judged primarily from the perspective of users of the program. Efforts to improve management processes do not mean that judgements of effectiveness must be organisationally focused. One of the reasons for stressing this is that, unfortunately, when organisational measures of effectiveness are used, they are often used too narrowly, leading to a confusion of efficiency with effectiveness, and a confusion of administrative performance with program performance. This chapter will outline some of the issues facing small, not-for-profit organisations in determining how they use evaluation, how they integrate planning and evaluation and, particularly, how they can consciously work towards developing more accountable forms of practice.

It is also worth noting that many funding providers and purchasers of service are moving beyond the fairly simple model of 'funding by inputs' (how many service users there are, for example) to a funding formula more dependent on 'outcomes' (what was achieved). This focus on outcomes, however, is framed within a concern about what it costs, in terms of labour, money and time, to achieve the result. This is a real challenge to many small organisations who often lack the expertise, in-house, to account for their programs in this way. This is one of the reasons that this chapter discusses technical concepts such as program logic, and why we have introduced discussion of evaluation types and purpose. In the future, many organisations' survival will depend on their ability to articulate their program rationale and demonstrate their effectiveness—often, unfortunately, by way of criteria that they have not chosen.

EVALUATION AND MONITORING

We use the term 'evaluation' to refer to a process in which needs, efficiency, productivity and effectiveness are measured, and the relationship between them is made clear. In this case, we are talking of program evaluation, rather than, for example, evaluation of individual staff performance, although the interrelationship of these two aspects of evaluation cannot be overstressed.

Evaluation is an 'umbrella' or general term that covers many types of evaluation activity, including summative evaluation and formative evaluation.

It should be noted, however, that strictly speaking the terms 'formative' and 'summative' do not describe different types of evaluation, but different processes undertaken for different purposes. Common usage now, though, often refers to 'formative evaluation', 'summative evaluation' and increasingly, 'design evaluation'.

Summative evaluation, for example, asks:

* What have we *done?*
* How *well* did we do it?
* With what *effect?*
* Was it *worth* doing?

This means that summative evaluation is concerned with effectiveness in the longer term.

Formative evaluation, on the other hand, asks:

* *What* are we doing?

- *How* have we done it?
- *How* can we improve on our performance?

As in the case of summative evaluation, 'How *well* have we done?' could be included, but in the shorter term. This means that formative evaluation is more directed at current practices in the short term.

The importance of distinguishing between these two types of evaluation is in the different timing of the two processes, and the different methods of carrying them out. It is important to note that evaluation can be carried out at any phase in the design and implementation of a program. For example, at the design stage, when shaping a program, a number of options may be evaluated. What often happens in practice, however, is that this design evaluation work is not done as effectively as it should be and at the time when it should be done. When the program's effectiveness is looked at later, the design of the program is analysed as well. In this sense, those who plan evaluations often have a sense that they are doing a form of retrospective planning.

Monitoring

Monitoring generally refers to a process in which specified aspects of practice are routinely recorded and analysed, using a range of methods to identify, for example, trends in program operation. It is an assessment process and does not mean simply keeping statistics. It may also be described as self-evaluation or thought of as a component of formative evaluation. Through monitoring, parts of a program can be viewed systematically. Too often, however, this monitoring is seen merely as data gathering. For example, counting the number of people receiving a service provides data, but the purpose for counting them is the issue. If it is important that more people use a service so that a program demonstrates greater 'reach', then counting the numbers becomes a significant monitoring process. The greatest problem is that the numbers game becomes an end in itself—'we interviewed fifteen people today' should not be a matter of pride unless further questions are asked.

Monitoring is often done at the level of the people delivering the service, or their line manager if it is a larger service. There is an issue, particularly for small organisations, however, about the extent to which these people should be responsible for analysing and interpreting the data, as well as collecting it. At what level should monitoring extend beyond monitoring of individual performance to program monitoring? This raises a crucial point in relation to small, not-for-profit organisations doing evaluation and monitoring. Very often, small organisations lack the expertise to do more than collect data and apply fairly routine trend analysis to these data, and they have to rely on external advisors or consultants to carry out more 'sophisticated' analyses of their program processes and outcomes. The issue is, what is the minimum level of competence that program staff should have in this area?

If evaluation is to be used as a planning tool then this needs to be explicit within the methods adopted by the agency. In other words, it needs to be spelled out as part of the purpose for which the evaluation is intended. One of the most effective ways of doing this is to involve evaluators in the planning process. Where possible, staff should act as evaluators and the existing skills and knowledge within the agency should be the basis upon which the process is built. Many agencies and staff themselves believe they do not know how to evaluate because they have no formal training in the area. This is best overcome by identifying it as a professional development need and bringing in experts, not only to evaluate but to train staff in how to evaluate. The aim is to foster a culture of evaluation within the organisation.

Getting all staff to participate in the evaluation process means everyone becomes an evaluator, particularly of their own work programs. This in turn greatly enhances the relationship of staff to their work and provides them with a stake in the future and development of the organisation. Staff are also given the opportunity to reflect on and articulate their practice and its outcomes.

Monitoring case recording

Mention has been made of case records in earlier chapters and how they can be used in performance appraisal. They can also be used for general program appraisal.

One counselling agency was concerned that its counsellors' records, particularly its clinical records, were in poor shape and did not lend themselves to even a simple form of analysis. The counsellors argued that the pressure of seeing clients made for poor record keeping. By monitoring the performance of this part of the worker's practice, by conducting random audits, the manager was able to demonstrate the worth to staff of collecting particular sorts of information.

This monitoring of recording practice also reinforced with staff the manager's view that good clinical record keeping was not an 'extra', to be done if workers had time, but something that was integral to good practice. The framework used for the records audit is presented below.

This framework clearly demonstrates that, in order to monitor practice in this way, there needs to be a clear set of standards that can be applied when making a judgement about the quality of the process or activity being reviewed. For example, items 4.04, 4.05 and 4.06 all indicate, as do many other items, that some standards had been set in the agency about accountability of individual workers for their records.[1]

Framework for auditing counselling records

Worker _____

Active case _____
Closed case _____

To complete Sections 1 to 3, the following codes should be used:

1 = Information present
2 = Information absent
3 = Some aspects of the information present
4 = Not applicable

1.   **INTAKE PHASE: (Exploration and formulation):**
Presenting problem
1.01 Background to presenting problem   ____
1.02 Client's perception of the problem   ____
1.03 Psychiatric history:
      Previous treatment, contact with other agencies ____
1.04 Psychiatric history:
      Associated problems (e.g. alcohol & drug,
      anger etc.)   ____

Social history
1.05 Family (current and original)   ____
1.06 Relationships, social networks and
      functioning   ____
1.07 Employment history   ____
1.08 Education   ____
1.09 Financial   ____
1.10 Legal   ____
1.11 Health and medical history   ____
Formulation
1.12 Integrated summary   ____
1.13 'Diagnosis': nature, severity etc. of problems   ____
Treatment recommendations
1.14 To be provided by the agency   ____
1.15 To be provided by other agencies   ____
1.16 Nature of interventions   ____
1.17 Time frames, review dates   ____
1.18 *Was this intake documentation completed no
      later than the third contact?*
      1   2   3
      YES   NO   INFO NOT AVAILABLE
1.19 *Is the Case File Cover complete?*
      1   2   3
      YES   NO   NOT KNOWN
2.   **TREATMENT PROGRESS**
2.01 *Notes on process issues*
      (e.g. contact with other agencies, progress
      on goals)   ____
2.02 *Notes on each session*   ____
2.03 *Referral to other agencies*   ____
3.   **TERMINATION**
'Discharge' summary:
3.01 Review of treatment and statement of case
      outcome   ____
3.02 Is this related to initial formulation and goals?   ____
3.03 *Plans for follow-up*   ____
4.   **GENERAL**:
4.01 *Is the content of the record*
      1   2   3
      ADEQUATE   POOR   INADEQUATE

206

4.02 *Are all records written concisely and legibly?*
1	2	3
ADEQUATELY	POORLY	INADEQUATELY

4.03 *Is there a clear structure to the record?*
1	2	3
ADEQUATE	POOR	INADEQUATE

4.04 *Are all records dated?*
1	2
YES	NO

4.05 *Do all records contain the printed name of worker?*
1	2
YES	NO

4.06 *Are all the records signed?*
1	2
YES	NO

Monitoring worker activity

A program in which workers were responsible for placing elderly clients in nursing homes had thought very carefully about the outcomes that the program was trying to achieve, and what workers should be doing to achieve those outcomes. To reflect that this practice represented a standard that should be achieved by all workers, the manager framed a protocol for placement. The manager felt at one point that there were delays in placement, but did not know if these delays were caused by lack of availability of places or by inefficiencies in the way the workers were 'processing' their clients. She monitored practice for a time, by turning the protocol into a useful monitoring or 'research' tool.

This example illustrates the interrelationship between individual performance appraisal and program appraisal. The intention of the monitoring was not to examine the workers' output but the general effectiveness of the placement program. However, inevitably individual workers' performances were identifiable and this raised the question of how that knowledge would be used. This issue needs to be clarified whenever program assessments are made, and staff must know whether the monitoring process involves individual performance appraisal.

The protocol for placement read, in part:

3.1 The social worker will provide the family with a list of up to ten nursing homes that are suitable in terms of geographic area, type of care and quality of care.

3.2 The family will be required to visit, assess the nursing homes and nominate a minimum of six acceptable nursing homes within 7 days of interview.

3.3 If there are extenuating circumstances (for example, carer illness) the social worker will be responsible for finding appropriate care, maintaining contact with the carer and respecting patient and carer wishes as far as possible.

This section, along with the protocol sections on paperwork and follow-up, was translated into the monitoring 'questionnaire' as:

24. Did the family visit, assess and nominate a minimum of six acceptable nursing homes?   Yes/No

25. If the answer to the previous question is 'No', how many nursing homes were nominated? _____

26. What was the reason for not being able to nominate six? _____

27. Did the family have to go outside their preferred region? Yes/No

28. Did this assessment and nomination process take place within 7 days of the initial/major interview?   Yes/No

29. If it took longer than 7 days how many did it take? _____

30. What was the reason(s) for the delay?

Paperwork

31. Was the 'Application for Nursing Home Admission (Code NHS)' form completed?   Yes/No

32. Did a Guardianship Order have to be sought for this client?   Yes/No

Follow up

33. Did the worker follow up with the nursing home to ensure that the placement was satisfactory?   Yes/No

34. If not, why not? _____

35. Did the Aged Care Worker follow up with the family to ensure that the placement was satisfactory?   Yes/No
36. If not, why not? _____

This is a useful illustration of how workers or managers can use material 'at hand' for monitoring or reviewing what is happening in their practice without treating it as something that only 'experts' can do, or treating it as something that intrudes on their day-to-day practice.[2]

Types and levels of evaluation

There are many different approaches to evaluation, and most use their own terminology. We have chosen to talk about three. The first deals with evaluation of different levels of *program* operation. The second looks at various aspects of the *evaluation process* itself, such as pre-implementation. The third, called a 'developmental' approach, focuses on the *service users'* activities.

Program operation

When thinking about evaluation and, to some extent, monitoring, one useful distinction that can be made relates to the different levels of program operation, such as:

- the service itself
- the service support system
- the organisational support system.[3]

These levels relate to various aspects of the *implementation* of a service. Too often, a program is thought not to work because of faulty design of the program, when it is actually ineffective or inefficient implementation that has let the program down. If there are not enough resources to allow staff to do their work properly, for example, not enough vehicles or too low a travel budget to do effective outreach work, then staff may appear to be inefficient in their use of time, when it is the service support system that is ineffective.

Similarly, if the organisation provides poor support to its staff in areas such as processing leave applications, providing supervision and giving administrative support, then competent, motivated staff may leave the organisation, resulting in a lower quality service. This is a failure, then, of the organisational support system, rather than a failure of the service itself.

Frameworks for designing the evaluation

These frameworks provide a way of helping people to focus on the following:

- What is the purpose of doing evaluations?
- Who makes up the audience, typically, for different sorts of evaluation?
- What tasks have to be performed?
- What types of data have to be collected and analysed?[4]

This issue of focus is an important one. Busy people running programs should not have to waste time looking at aspects of their program that need not necessarily be examined, in order to answer the specific questions they may have at the time about their program. Evaluation questions are thrown into sharper relief when they are asked of innovative programs. When testing a new program to see if it is worth putting into operation elsewhere, it is especially important to be clear about what is being evaluated and why. For example, is the new program demonstrating a 'tried and true' way of working, but with a different target group of service users, or is it trying something different in terms of interventions with a client group that a fair bit is known about already? Knowing the answers to questions such as the previous two will help those evaluating the innovation to focus more directly on the specific issues for that particular evaluation.

The following is a useful way of distinguishing between a number of levels, or tiers of evaluation. It was originally developed for evaluation of family programs and has been used by a number of small family agencies.[5]

- *Level One: Pre-implementation.* The purpose of this evaluation is to document the need for a particular program, by detailing the basic characteristics of the program, conducting needs assessments to support establishment of the program and, if necessary, revising the proposed program.
- *Level Two: Accountability.* The purpose of this evaluation is to document the program's utilisation and reach, justify expenditure, increase expenditure and build a constituency. This is done by providing accurate descriptions of program participants and services provided, and by providing accurate cost information per unit of service. This information reflects what is considered necessary for an agency to be minimally accountable to funders, to participants, and to the larger community.

- *Level Three: Program clarification.* The purpose of this type of evaluation is to provide information to program staff to improve the program. The tasks are, typically, to question basic program assumptions, and to clarify and restate, if necessary, the program's mission, goals, objectives and strategies. In this type of examination of a program, a distinction is often made between different sorts of objectives:
  — process objectives, or what staff do
  — outcome objectives, or what effects the program is expected to have in the short term
  — impact objectives, or what are the long-term effects of the program.
- *Level Four: Progress towards objectives.* The purpose here is to document program effectiveness by examining short-term objectives, working out measurable indicators of success, deciding on data analysis procedures and assessing the community's awareness of the program.
- *Level Five: Program impact.* The purpose of this type of evaluation is to produce evidence of differential effectiveness among different sorts of program clients and contexts of service delivery and to suggest models for programs worth developing. This is done by looking at the longer term effects of the program on the service users, and, particularly, by seeing whether these effects persist.

While it is useful to distinguish among the different purposes of evaluation activity, the list above raises one issue that needs to be clarified, and that is the way the levels are named. The evaluation literature tends to use technical language and it is easy to become confused about some of the terms, such as impact and outcome. In some areas of practice, such as in health prevention education, 'impact' is taken to be the immediate effects, and 'outcome' is the longer term effects. This may be because in the health field the importance of dealing with 'impact' is so important in practical terms and longer term effects are often put on hold. This is different from the way that Jacobs, for example, uses the terms in the list of levels above. The particular usage adopted is less important than being clear about the intent in conducting the evaluation, so that the focus can be clear and appropriate.[6]

Developmental approach

A somewhat different approach to determining a focus for evaluation activity is what is sometimes called a 'developmental' model.

It is more obviously service-user based. That is, it deals with what is happening to the service users in their contact with the agency. This contact is sometimes referred to as the service user's 'career' with the agency. The evaluation is aimed at gaining information at different stages in the service users' 'career', such as:

- program referral
- intake
- intervention
- completion
- follow up.

This sort of approach was designed primarily for counselling agencies but can be applied to other types of service.[7] It is a simple formula, but each of the sections above must follow the central principle of evaluation in asking the appropriate questions:

- What are the sequences of action?
- Who is carrying them out?
- With what effect?
- At what cost?
- How can the actual service be improved?

Objectives

In the discussion above on types or levels of evaluation, the question of objectives is raised a number of times. In this section we will clarify some points about objectives.

It is a mistake for evaluations to concern themselves only with assessing whether agencies have met their objectives. The objectives themselves may not have been an accurate statement of how program activity relates to the particular needs that a program is designed to meet and the outcomes it is hoped will be achieved. It is useful in evaluation to examine the objectives as simply another part of the program, but in so doing, to recognise the crucial role that they may have played in program planning, and to use analysis of this planning process as an important source of information about program operation.

Programs need to have clear goals and objectives. 'Clear' does not necessarily mean 'measurable', although it should always be clear why a program operates the way it does, and why its staff act the way they do. Staff activities, and the activities of Boards in prescribing policy that results in those staff activities, are not just random activities. They should be purposeful.

Although the purpose of the program must be recognised, it does not mean that people responsible for a program can always be precise about their objectives. This is because, in the case of some new programs, they may have little information about precisely how a particular intervention affects a particular target group if that group has not been worked with in the same way before. They may not yet be clear about how much of an effect it is possible to achieve through their program, and what sort of effect represents success.

For example, a program working with addictive or compulsive behaviour, involving, for example, drugs, alcohol or gambling, can measure success easily if it uses a simple abstinence model. Providers are successful if users stop. If the program operates from a harm minimisation approach, then limiting the behaviour without necessarily stopping it becomes the goal, as does a reduction in the harm that the behaviour causes. This is much more complex. How much of a problem can remain and still have the intervention considered to be successful?

This example highlights a further problem associated with confusing 'clear' with 'measurable'. The myth that 'objectivity equals number' haunts all human service activities. There is often a presumption that the behaviour or conditions that the program is working with can be measured reliably. One example can be given from problem gambling where judgements are made about the severity of a problem. There is a lot of dispute over how to define 'problem' gambling and 'pathological' gambling. Some of this debate is caused by different ways of understanding the *meaning* of the behaviour, but it can also be an example of the measuring dilemma caused by the very different ways of *measuring* the behaviour and the reliability of these methods.

Effectiveness and efficiency

It has been noted that there is, at times, a tendency to confuse efficiency and effectiveness. Efficiency measures are generally concerned with various forms of expenditure or resourcing and depend on a measure of *effort*, or the amount of resources, that must be used to achieve a desired program outcome. This is complicated, however, by the fact that some efficiencies are specifically about effectiveness, as in the case of cost-effectiveness. It is important to think not just of financial cost but of other resources, such as:

- type of staff
- training and maintenance costs
- time spent with service users
- time and cost of administration of the program
- lost opportunities.

The first four of these are program inputs and are all legitimate targets for analysis if we are looking at the efficiency of a program. The notion of cost of resources should include the concept of opportunity costs, or the cost of giving up other uses of resources to do what the program is doing. Efficiency measures can give us information about the extent to which inputs are converted to outputs. When they do this they are measuring the operational or technical efficiency of a program, and tell us something about the program process. It is almost impossible to talk about 'effort', however, without some consideration of the purpose of that effort, that is, effectiveness.

Often, human service workers see effectiveness and efficiency as two completely separate entities, with efficiency seen as concentrating solely on costs and therefore something negative, while effectiveness is seen as concentrating solely on achieving goals and therefore viewed positively. For these workers the inclusion of effectiveness *in* efficiency is difficult to accept. One way to think about the relationship, which may make it more acceptable, is to recognise that efficiency is equal to effectiveness achieved for a certain amount of effort—hence efficiency in general combines effectiveness and effort.

In our view, the full measure of whether a program is working comes from a consideration of both *efficiency and effectiveness together* (cost-effectiveness), but in saying that we also have to say that operational efficiency is *not* a measure of program value or worth. It is an administrative or management indicator, not necessarily an indicator of program or service performance. It is true that poor operational efficiency is often one of the measures of non-worth, that is, can negatively affect service delivery. We have already shown examples of this throughout the book.

The converse cannot be stated, however, that is, that good operational efficiency will necessarily be a measure of worth. The most efficient organisation may still not be giving the best and most worthwhile service, a fact that is often ignored with all the emphasis on cutting costs and increasing operational 'efficiency'. 'Good' management, in the widest sense of the word, will ensure that all aspects of efficiency are interrelated and that efficiency will not be considered without involving the full range of effectiveness.

There are many different types of efficiencies, just as there are different kinds of effectiveness. The main efficiencies are operational efficiency and cost-effectiveness. It should be recognised that cost-effectiveness is an efficiency measure as it combines inputs (as costs) needed to produce the resulting level of effect. Operational efficiency looks primarily at tangible, short-term results and dollar costs. Cost effectiveness looks closely at all costs and also more closely at all types of results.

Program logic

All programs need to have an explicit 'logic' that links all of the parts of the program together. Basically, program logic begins with a description of the processes by which the program hopes to achieve its objectives or meet the needs of its target group, and goes on to explain why the processes are expected to lead to intended results. The following is a list of suggested components of a program logic. Though people carry out many of these steps in their day-to-day thinking about programs, they are not always aware of their significance. There is value in clarifying them and putting them into a logical framework, that is, a program logic.

- An outcomes hierarchy. This is a cause–effect hierarchy of desired outputs (for example, the number of members of the target group serviced by a program) which lead to immediate impacts (for example, changes in knowledge and skills of the target group), which in turn lead to outcomes (for example, clients live an independent lifestyle, enjoy safer roads).

And for each output, impact and outcome in the hierarchy:

- Success criteria and definitions of terms (for example, what are the desired types of clients? what is meant by an independent lifestyle? what is meant by safer roads?).
- Factors that are *within* the control or influence of the program and are likely to affect the extent to which the outcome is achieved (for example, quality of service delivery, the way in which priorities are set).
- Factors that are *outside* the control or influence of the program and are likely to affect the extent to which the outcome is achieved (for example, the demography of the target group, competing programs, past experiences of program clients).
- Program activities and resources used to control or influence both types of factors (for example, training given to staff to

improve service quality, risk management strategies to respond to factors outside control).

- Performance information required to measure the success of the program in achieving desired outcomes (for example, the percentage of clients who show improved knowledge, information about the way in which the program is being implemented as a prerequisite for testing causal links between program activities and observed results).[8]
- Comparisons required to judge and interpret performance information (for example, comparisons with standards to make judgements, comparisons with control conditions, pre-post comparisons to interpret performance and attribute it to the program).[9]

Source: Funnell, S. (1997) 'Program Logic: An Adaptable Tool for Designing and Evaluating Programs', *Evaluation News and Comment,* Vol. 6, No. 1, July, p. 6.

The program logic needs to be closely linked to the steps in the hierarchy, so that we can answer questions such as:

- What are the key assumptions underlying the program, and how will the program's success be affected if they are not valid?
- What tests or measures might be used to see whether these assumptions are valid?

Program description

The program logic also forms a crucial part of the planning of a program, and forms part of a more complete program description. For either planning or evaluation purposes and, especially important for small organisations, for framing funding applications and considering expansion or change, agencies need to be able to describe their programs comprehensively. The sorts of questions that could be asked to help in defining the program are:

- What is the mandate or authority for the program, including the legislative or policy basis, and are program activities consistent with this?
- What were the catalysts that led to the development of the program, for example, who were the key proponents, what studies/enquiries/political pressures recommended this approach?
- What key needs, gaps in services or problems is the program intended to solve?
- What are the stated objectives of the program?

- What results are expected from the program?
- What reasons are there for believing that the program will be effective in achieving these results?
- What unintentional consequences may we predict might emerge from the program?
- How clear and unambiguous is the definition of the target group at which the program is aimed?
- Have program implementation or other changes in the social/political environment affected the relevance of the original program objectives or introduced new objectives?
- What measures or criteria were identified at the program development and implementation phase as providing appropriate output and outcome information, whether explicit or implicit?
- In the light of experience of other programs or theories of program operation, is there other performance information that is more relevant or which may assist further in understanding the success or otherwise of the program?
- In respect of each performance indicator, were targets (standards, levels of service) set? When? By whom? With what justification?[10]

PLANNING AND EVALUATION

Effective planning and evaluation are necessary, not only to make the organisation more accountable to funding bodies, but also to ensure that the service delivered is the most effective one possible, given the organisation's resources. As we know, most small organisations are set up in response to a perceived problem or to meet a particular need, but this does not mean that this should never be re-examined or that priorities will not change. Very often this re-examination is done through a more or less conscious process of monitoring and evaluation, and we now look at the relationship between planning and evaluation in these organisations.

Relationship between evaluation and planning

It is often argued that doing evaluations within small, not-for-profit organisations is difficult because of resource constraints and the absence of personnel experienced in the area. What is regularly done by agencies, and usually called evaluation, is the collection of basic data required by, and often determined by, funding bodies to justify the existence of the agency in terms of their value for money. The vignette with which we began chapter 1 illustrates the significance of the funding body in evaluation and planning, both of which words were used by the Minister, and which went beyond the mere collection of data and involved qualitative assessment.

Evaluation is a tool that organisations develop and use not only to demonstrate their effectiveness and efficiency but also to provide information about service user needs and quality of service critical to the organisations' effective planning and program design. A cycle of evaluation and planning can be developed, which would use existing personnel and, as much as possible, already existing relationships between staff and consumers to provide an in-built and naturalistic system of evaluation-focused planning.

A disability agency wanted to evaluate the three-year strategic plan it had developed using external consultants. The evaluation objectives were to:

- evaluate the progress of the agency in meeting the objectives set out in the plan
- evaluate the objectives themselves for their clarity, usefulness and feasibility
- document the internal factors which affected the agency's ability to implement its plan
- make recommendations about the process for developing and monitoring the implementation of the next planning process.

The evaluation of the plan was divided into three components covering;

1. the contents of the plan and assessing if objectives had been achieved (service outcomes)
2. assessment of the current planning process (managerial outcome)
3. any other issues arising from the evaluation process that would be useful in the agency's next planning process.

The evaluation highlighted six issues which are not unique to the agency in question but are critical to the relationship between small, not-for-profit organisations and evaluation/planning processes:

- use of evaluation as a planning tool
- role of evaluation as research and the use of findings in planning
- relationship between theories of practice and program design
- problem of planning for the long term in small organisations
- relationship between meeting objectives and meeting needs
- Use of external consultants to assist the organisation, and to ensure transfer of learning from the consultants to the staff.

Principles to be followed in evaluation systems

The planning potential of evaluation can be enhanced if a number of principles are followed. Any evaluative system should:

- be an integral part of human service provision and not either a separate or an additional process
- fit the purpose for which it is intended and not simply gather information that is most easily collected or most readily available
- build on existing knowledge and skills, be simple to use and not require specialists for its implementation, unless the agency has particular reasons for doing so
- actively involve all the program participants, not solely management. It must be demonstrably useful to these participants and not be perceived as a bureaucratic process imposed from the top down
- focus on how to ensure that services fit the needs of their consumers and not vice versa.[11]

The opportunity to think about what they are doing is important for the staff of an agency, in particular, as it helps the agency to focus on the relationship between theories of practice and program design. Often there are problems with theorising practice in small not-for-profit organisations, with different levels of education and training among staff affecting their understanding and identification of theories of practice. Also the agency may not have adequately theorised its purpose. This, linked to a lack of theorising of practice, leads to confusion about approaches used within the organisation and the potential conflicts among them. Different theories, for example about the relative importance given to parents' and children's rights in a family agency, may affect practice profoundly. This may not be fully realised until an evaluation takes place. Going through an evaluation exercise where theoretical conflicts are clearly on the agenda can lead to a lessening of these conflicts and provide a clearer base for future planning.

In order for evaluation activity to reach its potential as a planning tool, the principles outlined above should be applied. The first principle notes the importance of such an evaluation system being in-built, that is, a part of day-to-day practice of an agency rather than something that occurs as an add-on that outsiders are called in to perform. This is particularly important for small organisations whose limited resources restrict their ability to buy in consultants. It also encourages the development of a culture of evaluation within the organisation, with all staff having a role as evaluator and evaluation occurring at every level of service delivery.

Effective use of the knowledge and skills existing within organisations is critical to implementing a successful evaluation/planning system. This principle is closely linked to the principle of active involvement of all service participants in the evaluation process. Often staff do not identify themselves as evaluators but in fact they routinely undertake basic evaluation every day. As well as developing a process that can highlight the evaluation currently hidden but taking place within the organisation, this area could become a priority for staff development and be used as a team-building exercise among staff. It is most efficient to have staff evaluating their practice as it occurs, and making adjustments to their work programs as early as possible.[12]

Implementing evaluation recommendations

An often neglected, or poorly managed, aspect of evaluation is the implementation of findings. After evaluations, agencies are often left with a number of difficulties, such as blaming the evaluation—or the evaluators if they are external to the organisation—for problems which have surfaced during the evaluation but which pre-date the process. This is a not uncommon reaction, and it is understandable, particularly if the problems revealed are threatening and have been denied: 'We didn't have these problems until those people came and stirred up some of the staff'.

Another difficulty is blaming the evaluation for not resolving issues that it could not realistically have been expected to address. There are often hidden agendas, such as the hope that the evaluation will change very entrenched patterns overnight, or magically transform difficult personalities.

External consultants are rarely able to include an implementation phase in their contract and may go on to the next contract with little concern for what happens after they submit their report. Some include an implementation process in the report in the form of recommendations, but often little else. Ideally, implementation should be seen as part of the total evaluation exercise, and should form a post-evaluation phase, just as we have a 'pre-evaluation' or feasibility stage.

Many reports are handed over to the organisation at the termination of the consultancy, and the organisation quite frequently ignores, distorts or 'varies' the report. Staff and others who have made a commitment to the exercise are often disillusioned. One hears the constant complaint that 'nothing was done', or even that the report has been distorted or repressed. This is why, ideally, those commissioning evaluations and those conducting evaluations should come to some agreement before commencing a review process about the use of recommendations and reports and the implementation process. However, if an issue is placed on the agenda of an agency in a new way as a result of an evaluation, even if its recommendations are not acted on, then the exercise will often have been worthwhile.

There can be mixed views about the consultants' involvement in working out what is done with their material, as it is sometimes seen by the organisation as threatening, or as pre-empting the acceptance of the recommendations. It is sometimes seen as too time-consuming and difficult by consultants. Consultants may wish to terminate contact with an agency, once a report is written, in order to continue with other commitments that they have to honour to maintain their consultancy practice.

On the other hand, agencies may see it differently and a frequently heard complaint about consultants is that such disengagement is used as a ploy to avoid responsibility for the report and its recommendations. Much depends on the way the consultants see their role: if they have used the exercise as a learning process for staff, as we believe they should, staff will be able to carry out the implementation after having been committed to the review.

As well as procedural barriers to implementation there are also political issues.

In one agency many of the recommendations of an evaluation related to management aspects and potential

221

changes in the environment outside the organisation. This meant that, after the report was received and accepted, the implementation of the recommendations required an active process to succeed. The consultants' report recommended an implementation process that included the formation of an implementation committee, with a membership including one member of the consultancy team. Although there had been extensive consultation during the evaluation, both within the agency and with many stakeholders in the community, there were still some people both within and outside the agency who wanted to overcome the recommendations and 'fight a rearguard action'. Ensuring that as far as possible the recommendations were carried out was regarded by the consultants as an important part of the total process and a valuable learning experience for them as well.

Problems in implementation

In summary the problems that surface at the point of implementation, which are often made worse when the evaluation is conducted externally, include the following.

- Sometimes evaluation results are seen as being destructive, and are dismissed because they have brought to the surface problems that were in existence and would surface in an even more destructive way without the machinery to handle them. Often the timing is wrong, as evaluations are commonly requested at times of crisis or financial stringency. Criticism is then directed at the process or the recommendations that were necessary to respond to the particular crisis.
- Unreal expectations of the evaluation often bring about criticisms when the results are not the miracle changes that some people expected. Also, there is a danger of an evaluation or a review being used as a 'hatchet job', and this can negate the positive processes that should follow.
- There are often unrealistic expectations of what an evaluation can achieve, particularly in terms of time and resources involved. The 'quick and dirty' evaluation may work in certain circumstances, with certain short-term problems, but is not always effective in the long term and in dealing with the basic changes that may be needed in some organisations. The 'quick and dirty' also rarely deals with processes and therefore does not come to terms with underlying and fundamental problems.

Finally, it does not help in staff development in the ways we have suggested are useful.

• Unscheduled and unexpected changes may negate the possibility of carrying out certain recommendations. One of the problems here is that an organisation may not keep the evaluation recommendations in mind, even though these might in theory have been put on hold. In one organisation there were so many rapid changes just after an evaluation had been completed that the recommendations that could have been carried out were ignored. Those that could have been dealt with at a later stage were not brought forward again when dealing with them was much more feasible.

One of the difficulties is in ensuring that the evaluation process is seen by the agency as part of an ongoing exercise and is not allowed to be lost. It is this type of 'losing' that leads to the rediscovery of earlier processes and recommendations. In small organisations, one person at least should be designated as having responsibility for monitoring a particular set of recommendations in the future, after the 'formal' implementation process is over. This monitoring enables the organisation to have a feeling of success and moving onwards and helps negate the cynicism that often develops about the inactivity following past reviews, evaluations and reports.

Evaluating the evaluation

If the evaluation implementation process is seen as ongoing it should include some analysis of the evaluation process and its success. Also, if recommendations are not carried out, there should be an attempt to give reasons and to see why. It is not necessarily a problem if all recommendations are not carried out, but they do need to be seen to have been taken seriously. Again, if there is a monitoring process, the evaluation itself will be looked at, and in a sense evaluated. Some of the questions that should be asked of an evaluation can be commenced during the process of implementing the recommendations. They may even lead to an agreement that certain recommendations, as accepted, should now be reviewed. If this process takes place it should be done openly and carefully, and include comment on the actual evaluation exercise. In other words, if the evaluation exercises were correctly carried out, the reasons for not accepting the recommendations should be carefully thought through. The following questions could be asked:

- Did the evaluation deal with the terms of reference, and if not, why not?
- Are the recommendations realistic in both resource and time terms? This includes the total organisation, that is, the commitment of the organisation, the staff available, their acceptance of the report, and the time that can be given.
- Do the recommendations arise out of the findings?
- Did the evaluation involve all levels and interests in the organisation and cover a wide range of opinions? Was it biased in the selection of evidence?
- Was the evaluation a learning process and does it lead to a developmental approach that will assist in helping the organisation achieve its goals?

Of course no evaluation would rank 100 per cent on these points for various reasons, perhaps including the fact that the organisation did not allow sufficient time and resources for carrying out the evaluation. In addition, the terms of reference may have been hastily drawn up by the organisation and handed unmodified to the evaluation team. If this is the case, the team should have made clear to the organisation why the terms of reference could not be carried out and how this could be modified in the future.

An examination of the evaluation process does not necessarily indicate that those carrying out the evaluation were at fault, but it does mean that the organisation should look at correcting such faults, so that each evaluation process will be more effective than the last. An examination will also ensure that, after each process, more and more staff will have had experience in the total exercise, that is the pre-evaluation, evaluation and post-evaluation phases. It would ideally ensure a diminishing need for one-off evaluations or reviews as monitoring and evaluation become a routine matter for the organisation, using its own internal skills.

CONCLUSION

Evaluation is now generally recognised as an essential feature of the management of human service organisations, whether they are large or small. Organisations should not always rely on outside 'evaluators' to carry out the evaluation process. There is increasing evidence that more and more staff, even in small organisations, are developing their skills in this important function. It is essential that any use of outside consultants involves a learning process for the staff and Boards of organisations, and that they are used only when a case has been made for why internal evaluators would not be suitable.

Evaluation also has its critics, as is the case with other managerial functions, but many of these criticisms are due to the misuse of evaluations, seen by some critics to be part of the 'new managerialism'. Another basis for criticism is that distortions and oversimplifications take place when measurement is forced upon the unmeasurable.

NOTES

1. This framework was developed as part of a clinical evaluation of the Vietnam Veterans' Counselling Service. See Jackson, A.C., Creamer, M. and Ball, J.R.B. (1994) *Report on the Clinical Evaluation of the Vietnam Veterans' Counselling Service*, Commonwealth Department of Veterans' Affairs, Canberra (chapter 5, 'Clinical Practice: Process and Outcome').

2. For an excellent discussion on the planning and evaluation uses of routinely collected information, see chapter 6 'Designing for Effectiveness-Oriented Practice', in P. Nurius and W. Hudson (1993) *Human Services Practice, Evaluation and Computers*, Brooks/Cole Publishing Company, Calif.

3. This model is derived from Winston, J.A. (1991) '*To See Once . . .'—Alternative Access and Equity Evaluation Frameworks and Techniques*, Office of Multicultural Affairs, Department of Prime Minister and Cabinet, Canberra.

4. See, for example, Owen, J. (1993) *Program Evaluation, Forms and Approaches*, Allen & Unwin, Sydney; Weiss, H. and Jacobs, F. (1988) (eds) *Evaluating Family Programs*, Aldine de Gruyer, New York; Higgins, C.W. (1986) 'Evaluating Wellness Programs', *Health Values*, 10 (6), 44–51.

5. For further detail on this framework, see Jacobs, F. (1988) 'The Five-Tiered Approach to Evaluation: Content and Implementation', in H. Weiss and F. Jacobs (eds) *Evaluating Family Programs*, Aldine de Gruyter, New York.

6. See also, for a detailed discussion on evaluation approaches and issues, chapter 7, 'Evaluation and Accountability' in F. Donovan and A. Jackson (1991) *Managing Human Service Organisations*, Prentice Hall, Sydney.

7. For further details on this sort of approach, see Grasso, A. and

Epstein, I. (1992) 'Toward a Developmental Approach to Program Evaluation', *Administration in Social Work*, Vol. 16, 3/4, 187–203.

8. Although we agree in many respects with this list of program logic components, we need to point out that this issue of the measurement of success is a contentious one. This is primarily because of the point that we raised earlier about difficulties of literal measurement of some effects, and the judgement that needs to be made about whether what is measured is enough of an effect to designate it a 'success'. Other performance information that may be considered could include 'a relationship among 3 or more factors believed to affect results', or 'case summaries or ratings by qualified expert reviewers'.

9. See Wholey, J. (1987) 'Evaluability Assessment: Developing Agreement on Goals, Objectives and Strategies for Improving Performance', in J. Wholey (ed.) *Organisational Excellence*, Lexington Books, Lexington, Mass.; Bickman, L. (1990) *Advances in Program Theory*, New Directions for Program Evaluation, No. 47 (Fall), Jossey-Bass, San Francisco; Rossi, P. and Freeman, H. (1993) *Evaluation: A Systematic Process, 3rd Edition*, Sage, Beverly Hills, Cal.; Patton, M.Q. (1996) *Utilisation-focused Evaluation, 3rd Edition*, Sage, Thousand Oaks, Cal.

10. This has been adapted from Department of Finance and Australian Public Service Board (1986) *Evaluating Government Programs: A Handbook*, Department Finance and APSB, Canberra.

11. This set of principles is from Osborne, S.P. (1992) 'The Quality Dimension. Evaluating Quality of Service and Quality of Life in Human Services', *The British Journal of Social Work*, Vol. 22 (4), 437–53.

12. For more detail on this aspect of evaluation and planning, see Gowdy, E.A. and Freeman, E.M. (1993) 'Program Supervision: Facilitating Staff Participation in Program Analysis, Planning and Change', *Administration in Social Work*, Vol. 17 (3), 59–79.

CONCLUSION

In the introduction we stated that our aim was to provide a balance between theory and practice. In writing the book we realised how difficult this is when the group that we are targeting is so varied. When thinking of our own experiences, both as practitioners and consultants, or when talking to our many colleagues who are interested in our subject, we have been faced with the whole range of different demands and expectations. We are relying on readers to apply and adapt our material as it suits their agencies and their experiences.

There are a number of general issues that surfaced many times and which are worth summarising briefly. The main theme, which is illustrated in many places, is that management has a major influence on the quality of service delivery, and it should not therefore be seen as an either/or situation. It is not concern for management *or* the service user—it is concern for management *for* the service user. This can be a statement of the 'glittering generality' kind but it is still worthwhile to strive for its achievement, though it is admittedly not easy to do.

Another difficulty, when management is being considered, is achieving a balance between feeling, commitment, caring and those processes that are sometimes seen as opposed, that is, analysis and planning. Again, the aim is to balance these two aspects so that the service user benefits. It is incorrect to assume that the first group are always 'good' for the service user and the last usually 'bad'.

These groupings of processes into 'good' and 'bad' illustrate that there is a very important element in the not-for-profit organisation that is often neglected, particularly in the current climate. This element is the significance of values. Values are even more important in the small agency than in the larger organisation. So many of those who join the small group do so for expressive reasons, as mentioned in our discussion of 'smallness', and because they see a value in being less 'bureaucratic'. This results in tensions that need to be acknowledged and addressed.

The final topic that has occupied so much of our thinking and is so relevant to our target group is the role of Boards/committees. This was a subject that we had to omit from our first book, and it was the desire to deal with this issue that was one of the factors in our decision to write this book. Both authors have had experience in working with, or being members of, Boards/committees and have found that the way they function is vital to the success and survival of not-for–profit agencies.

All the topics we have covered are relevant to the present functioning of not-for-profit agencies in terms of both improvement and survival. But they are also of significance for the future. There is a tendency in some organisations to see what is happening in the present as a temporary 'hiccup' which will go away 'if we can only ride it out'. Such a response is scarcely a viable one. Certain trends are here to stay, and certain changes will have to be accommodated. We therefore conclude with some comments on the future, although we realise the dangers in 'crystal ball gazing'.

- Funding will continue to change from the past system of block or core grants to grants for particular programs. This, as mentioned throughout the book, has widespread consequences for the way that agencies function, allied to increased accountability and program costing and budgeting.
- The trend towards privatisation, tendering and contracting will continue for some time, although we think that there will be some swing back to government responsibility in the human services area in the future. It is interesting to see that there have been some cyclical patterns, for example, in the child protection field. The dilemma of monitoring standards for the sake of the service user may force governments to take a more active role.

- The tendering process has created a problem for small agencies and eventually a type of merging or cooperation and sharing will need to be developed. What form this will take is difficult to predict but those agencies that face the challenge will be those that survive. In spite of this, the negative effects of losing the valuable contribution of small, specialised agencies may eventually be recognised.

- The rapidity of the changes that we have noted has been a particular problem for agencies. Not only have Boards and committees had to accept new responsibilities but the staff and volunteers have had to adjust to changes. Only one section in the book has highlighted the problem of change per se, but in effect the book as a whole is about change. It is the speed of change that has made the problem of managing to survive so significant. It is because the changes have made so many demands that small not-for-profit agencies are facing the challenge of learning much that is new, and are having to re-think so much that has been taken for granted. Not only do the agencies facing change have to face an accelerated learning process, but the educational institutions that provide the education and training also have to adjust to change.

- The role of the educational institutions in helping those working in the human services field to adjust to change has not been very evident. Courses and conferences of educators and professional groups still give little space and emphasis to the managerial issues facing practitioners. There seems to be confusion about teaching organisational theory and/or management theory. In addition, there is often a reluctance to include practical examples and techniques. Instead, there is a reliance on managerial competence being 'picked up' in practice. There are also differences of opinion about levels of training. Some educational institutions see 'management' training as being only for managers and more senior students/potential managers, rather than for all those who will be part of the management process at whatever level. By the time someone becomes a manager they should have at least some knowledge of what is 'best management practice'. Most of those working in not-for-profit agencies will have some organisational experience, even if it is only as a victim of poor management practice, and could benefit from some managerial training. This may only mean that they carry out their own tasks more efficiently, but it should also enable them to recognise good managerial practice and to provide some basis of understanding if they should make a transition to a full managerial role. It is not clear whether the educators are not sufficiently aware of the need, or the practitioners themselves do not demand the extra training and assistance that they need. Hopefully this will be adjusted in the near future.

• There is one final consequence of all the managerial changes that is a matter of concern for the future. There is a danger that, in the stress of surviving, the ability to be creative and innovative will be lost. One of the consequences of stress and burnout was the loss of creativity. There has been much talk of the poor morale in a wide variety of organisations as security is lost, patterns change rapidly and 'keep your head down' becomes the defence. Our hope for the future is that it is not too late and that awareness will give strength.

In listing the possible future trends we have been influenced by our own preferences. Throughout the book we have not been occupied so much with what *ought* to happen, but rather what we see as happening at the present time, and how the needs of the service users can be met. We have not thought it appropriate in this book to express our views about some of the consequences of the changes that are taking place, although we are deeply concerned about some of the negative effects of the changes.

These negative effects include aspects that we have implied but not discussed:

• the excessive speed of change, which has not allowed for proper adjustment
• the potential loss of many of the values of the small agency
• the increasing negative impact of the profit motive in the human services area
• the dangers of often inappropriate and excessive privatisation
• the substitution of competitiveness for cooperation.

We have not suggested ways that these negative aspects can be overcome, but in addition to 'survival' many agencies are looking at ways of preserving those qualities that have contributed so much in the past. Hopefully the process is not either/or, that is, either survival or provision of quality programs that stress the importance of the needs of the service users. There is always the possibility of changes that can preserve the best of the current patterns, as well as adapting to the inevitable.

REFERENCES

Alford, J. and O'Neill, D. (1994) (eds) *The Contract State: Public manage-ment and the Kennett Government*, Centre for Applied Social Research, Deakin University, Geelong.

Beilharz, P., Considine, M., and Watts, R. (1992) *Arguing About the Welfare State*, Allen & Unwin, Sydney.

Bickman, L. (1990) *Advances in Program Theory: New Directions for Program Evaluation*, No. 47 (Fall), Jossey-Bass, San Francisco.

Billis, D. (1993) *Sliding Into Change: the Future of the Voluntary Sector in the Mixed Organisation of Welfare*, Working Paper 14, Centre for Voluntary Organisation, London.

Booth, P. (1996) 'Understanding Management Control and Accounting in Voluntary Organisations', *Third Sector Review*, Vol. 2, 19–42.

Boxall, P. (1988) 'The Revolution in Government Accounting', *Australian CPA*, April.

Boyatsis, R. (1982) *The Competent Manager*, Wiley and Sons, New York.

Brody, R. (1993) *Effectively Managing Human Service Organisations*, Sage, London.

Collinson, D. and Hearn, J. (1996) (eds) *Men as Managers, Managers as Men*, Sage, London.

Considine, M. (1988a) 'The Corporate Management Framework as Administrative Science: A Critique', *Australian Journal of Public Admin-istration*, Vol. XLVIII, No. 1, 4–18.

——(1988b) 'The Costs of Increased Control: Corporate Management and Australian Community Organisations', *Australian Social Work*, 41, 3.

Considine, M. and Painter, M. (1977) *Managerialism: The Great Debate*, Melbourne University Press, Melbourne.

Cordingley, Sha (1997) 'Unemployment and Volunteering', *Australian Jour-nal on Volunteering*, Vol. 2, No. 1, 4–8

231

Coulton, C., Friedman, B.A. and Keller, S.M. (1992) *A Minimum Data Set for Hospital Social Work*, Social Work Management Information System Monograph, Society for Social Work Administrators in Health Care, Chicago, Ill.

de Carvalho, D. (1996) *Competitive Care: Understanding the Implications of National Competition Policy and the COAG Agenda for the Community Services Sector*, Discussion Paper No. 11, Australian Social Welfare Commission, Canberra.

Department of Finance and Australian Public Service Board (1986) *Evaluating Government Programs: A Handbook*, Department of Finance and APSB, Canberra.

Donovan, F. (1977) *Voluntary Organisations: A Case Study*, PIT Occasional Paper No. 3, Preston Institute of Technology, Bundoora.

Donovan, F. and Jackson, A.C. (1991) *Managing Human Service Organisations*, Prentice Hall, Sydney.

Drucker, P. (1990) *Managing the Nonprofit Organisation*, HarperCollins, New York.

Ehlers, W.H. (1976) 'Unit III, Planning Lesson 3, Personal Planning', in W.M. Ehlers, M.J. Austin, and J.C. Prothers *Administration for the Human Services*, Harper and Row Publishers, New York.

Ehlers, W., Austin, M. and Prothero, J. (1976) *Administration for the Human Services*, Harper and Row Publishers, New York.

Funnell, S. (1997) 'Program Logic: An Adaptable Tool for Designing and Evaluating Programs', in *Evaluation News and Comment*, Vol. 6, No. 1, July, 5–17.

Gould, M. (1979) 'When Women Create an Organisation: The Ideological Imperatives of Feminism', in D. Dunkerley and G. Salaman (eds) *The International Yearbook of Organisational Studies*, RKP, London.

Gowdy, E.A. and Freeman, E.M. (1993) 'Program Supervision: Facilitating Staff Participation in Program Analysis, Planning and Change', *Administration in Social Work*, Vol. 17, 3, 59–79.

Grasso, A. and Epstein, I. (1992) 'Toward a Developmental Approach to Program Evaluation', *Administration in Social Work*, Vol. 16, 3/4, 187–203.

Hall, M. (1971) *Developing Skills in Proposal Writing, 2nd Edition*, Continuing Education Publications, Portland, Oregon.

Handy, C. (1988) *Understanding Voluntary Organisations*, Penguin, London.

Harris, M. (1991) *Exploring the Role of Voluntary Management Committees: A New Approach*, Working Paper No. 10, Centre for Voluntary Organisation, London School of Economics, London.

Higgins, C.W. (1986) 'Evaluating Wellness Programs', *Health Values*, 10, 6, 44–51.

Hunt, J. and Wallace, J. (1997) 'A Competency-based Approach to Assessing Managerial Performance in the Australian Context', *Asia Pacific Journal of Human Resources*, 35, 2, 52–66.

Industry Commission (1996) *Competitive Tendering and Contracting in the Public Sector*, Report No. 48, AGPS, Canberra.

Jackson, A.C., Creamer, M. and Ball, J.R.B. (1994) *Report on the Clinical Evaluation of the Vietnam Veterans' Counselling Service*, Commonwealth Department of Veterans' Affairs, Canberra.

Jackson, A.C. and Tangney, S. (1997) 'A Service Mapping Approach to the Analysis of Service Use for People with Acquired Brain Injury', in G. Auslander (ed.) *International Perspectives on Social Work in Health Care*, The Haworth Press, New York.

Jackowski, E. and Stevens, B. (1988) 'Integrated Information Systems Concepts: An Information Resource Management Approach', in J. Rabin and M. Steinhauer (eds) *Handbook on Human Services Administration*, Marcel Decker, New York.

Jacobs, F. (1988) 'The Five-Tiered Approach to Evaluation: Content and Implementation', in H. Weiss and F. Jacobs (eds) *Evaluating Family Programs*, Aldine de Gruyter, New York.

Kilmister, T. (1993) *Boards at Work: A New Perspective on Not-For-Profit Boards*, NFP Press, Wellington.

Knapp, M. (1990) *Time is Money: The Cost of Volunteering in Britain Today*, Volunteer Centre UK, London.

Kramer, R.M. (1994) 'Voluntary Agencies and the Contract Culture: "Dream or Nightmare?"', *Social Service Review*, March.

Lendrum, T. (1995) *The Strategic Partnering Handbook*, McGraw-Hill Book Co., Sydney.

McSweeney, P. and Alexander, D. (1996) *Managing Volunteers Effectively*, Arena, Aldershot.

Milkovich, G.T. and Boudreau, J.W. (1988) *Personnel/Human Resource Management*, Business Publications Inc., Plano, TX.

Miller, D. (1995) 'Models of Management for Occupational Morbidity and Burnout' in L. Bennett, D. Miller and M. Ross (eds) *Health Workers and AIDS: Research, Intervention and Current Issues in Burnout and Response*, Harwood Academic Publishers, Switzerland, 175–190.

Murray, M. (1991) *Beyond the Myths and Magic of Mentoring*, Jossey-Bass Publishers, San Fracisco.

Nishimoto, R., Weil, M., and Theil, K.S. (1991) 'A Service Tracking and Referral Form to Monitor the Receipt of Services in a Case Management Program', *Administration in Social Work*, 15, 3, 33–47.

Nurius, P. and Hudson, W. (1993) *Human Services Practice, Evaluation and Computers*, Brooks/Cole Publishing Company, Calif.

Osborne, S.P. (1992) 'The Quality Dimension: Evaluating Quality of Service and Quality of Life in Human Services', in *British Journal of Social Work*, Vol. 22, 4, 437–53.

Owen, J. (1993) *Program Evaluation, Forms and Approaches*, Allen & Unwin, Sydney.

Paterson, J. (1988) 'A Managerialist Strikes Back', *Australian Journal of Public Administration*, Vol. XLVII, No. 4.

Patton, M.Q. (1996) *Utilisation-focused Evaluation, 3rd Edition*, Sage, Thousand Oaks, Cal.

The People Together Project (1998) Turning People into Commodities:

Report of the Public Hearings on Competitive Tendering in Human Services, People Together Project, Melbourne.

Popovich, I. (1995) *Managing Consultants*, Century/Random House, London.

Renton, N.E. (1994) *Guide for Meetings and Organisations, Sixth Edition*, The Law Book Company Ltd, Sydney.

Rossi, P. and Freeman, H. (1993) *Evaluation: A Systematic Process, 3rd Edition*, Sage, Beverly Hills, Cal.

Sandwith, P. (1993), 'A Hierarchy of Management Training Requirements: The Competency Domain Model', *Public Personnel Management*, 22, 1, 43–62.

Schoech, D., Schkade, L. and Mayers, R. (1981) 'Strategies for Information System Development', *Administration in Social Work*, 5, 3/4, 11–26.

Simon, H. (1976) *Administrative Behaviour, 3rd Edition*, Free Press, New York, pp. 192–97.

Sterling, T. (1981) 'Humanising Computerised Information Systems', in M. Gruber (ed.) *Management Systems in the Human Services*, Temple University Press, Philadelphia.

Vinter, R. and Kish, R. (1984) *Budgeting for Non-profit Organisations*, The Free Press, New York.

Volunteering Victoria Inc. (1997) *Standards for Involving Volunteers in Not for Profit Organisations*, Melbourne.

——(1997) *Information Sheet: Definition and Principles of Formal Volunteering*, Melbourne.

Wallace, J. and Hunt, J. (1996) 'An Analysis of Managerial Competencies Across Hierarchical Levels and Industry Sectors', *Journal of the Australian and New Zealand Academy of Management*, 2, 1, 36–47.

Weeks, W. (1994) *Women Working Together*, Longman Cheshire, Melbourne.

Weiss, H. and Jacobs, F. (1988) (eds) *Evaluating Family Programs*, Aldine de Gruyter, New York.

Wholey, J. (1987) 'Evaluability Assessment: Developing Agreement on Goals, Objectives and Strategies for Improving Performance', in J. Wholey (ed.) *Organisational Excellence*, Lexington Books, Lexington, Mass.

Winston, J.A. (1991) 'To See Once . . .', *Alternative Access and Equity Evaluation Frameworks and Techniques*, Office of Multicultural Affairs, Department of Prime Minister and Cabinet, Canberra.

Yu, Jane (1997) 'Pre-schools Lash Out Over Unfair Checklist', *Diamond Valley News*, 17 September.

Zanetic, S. and Jeffrey, C. (1997) 'Understanding the Other Half of the Workforce', *HR Monthly*, May.

INDEX

235